STRATEGIC ISSUES IN MARKETING

Strategic Issues in Marketing

by

GORDON WILLS

in association with colleagues especially

Martin Christopher, Roy Hayhurst,
Sherril Kennedy, Leonard Magrill,
David Walters and John Cantlay.

A HALSTED PRESS BOOK

JOHN WILEY & SONS
New York—Toronto

First published by
International Textbook Company Limited
Kingswood House, Heath & Reach, Leighton Buzzard,
Beds LU7 0AZ and 450 Edgware Rd., London W2 1EG

© Gordon Wills 1974

First published 1974

Published in the U.S.A. and Canada by Halsted Press, a Division of
John Wiley & Sons, Inc., New York.

Library of Congress Cataloging in Publication Data

Wills, Gordon.
  Strategic issues in marketing.
  1. Marketing—Addresses, essays, lectures.
2. Marketing—Europe—Addresses, essays, lectures.
I. Title.
HF5415.W54737 1974   658.8   74–14910
ISBN 0–470–94958–9

Printed in Great Britain

Contents

Adaptive Patterns of Marketing Education—how can conventional education programmes for marketing executives be developed and improved to take account of the strategic considerations indicated as vital in chapters 1–11? A new structure is proposed with syllabus details, but the need to also inculcate entreprenneurial spirit in the student is not overlooked. How can the trainer himself be trained effectively?

Survey of UK Marketing Organizations

Delphi Study of Distribution Trends

Preface

The past two decades have seen the widespread dissemination of marketing ideas into leading European and North American companies. Most major companies today can boast an identifiable Chief Marketing Executive who is responsible for planning and coordinating the company's total approach to its customers. Most such Chief Marketing Executives have within their departments experienced staffs, several of whom have formal education and training in marketing studies. It is to these organizations and people that *Strategic Issues in Marketing* is directed, together with the growing body of advanced marketing students in universities, business schools and polytechnics, who are undergoing formal education with a view to working in such organizations. Such an audience is already familiar with the fundamental concepts, and with the prevailing technology, of marketing. Hence, I have taken this knowledge for granted. Rather, I look forward over the next five to ten years at the strategic issues which will impinge upon effective management in marketing.

The issues explored here have not been chosen at random. Since the late 1960s colleagues and I in marketing studies, at Bradford and Alberta Universities, at the University of Prince Edward Island, and more recently at Cranfield School of Management, have undertaken a series of probes to identify with some reasonable certainty what the key strategic issues will be. In particular, we conducted a survey, with British Institute of Management support, of the pattern of marketing activities in British industry. This study was then followed up with a Delphi exploration of likely marketing 'futures' with senior European executives. The issues discussed here come into focus as a result of our analysis of the gap between extant company practices and perceived future tasks.

Some of the key strategic areas are readily obvious to most observers, such as the extension of the concept of the 'home market' to embrace the enlarged European Economic Community. But seldom has there been any *in-depth analysis* of such issues which can afford a valid operational, yet intellectual, understanding for marketing action. This led to a deliberate series of studies over a period of four years which has provided the basis for this book.

This volume looks first at the necessary patterns of marketing organization which companies must move towards in the next decade to meet the challenge of changing markets and the ever-changing technology base from which most products/systems emerge. The knowledge that has emerged in organizational development is applied to the problem, and an adaptive design structure is proposed. As an important facet of the organizational dilemma, the contribution of output budgeting and its concommittant missions' approach is explored. It is, in fact, a logical extension of brand and venture management and technological forecasting. The treatment highlights the role of information in reducing uncertainty and risk in marketing and leads logically to an examination of the future structure of total marketing information systems.

If marketing in Western Europe is a readily apparent challenge, the problems and opportunities which Eastern Europe affords are less well perceived. The success of West Germany's Ostpolitik and the US détente with China and the USSR, have begun to open up a whole new area for marketing initiatives. Yet it is only too apparent that the marketeer must tread warily. An understanding of the true nature of socialist marketing is fundamental to any success in such markets. The successful planning of communications effort is also of paramount importance in the years ahead; and what is true of communications is also true of product design, and logistics. In each area, company organization must be organic in its response to changing tasks and the marketing professional must be able to cope with the problems posed. He must also seek to examine the diffusion of marketing ideas into service industries such as banking, social services and insurance, local government and research institutes: transferring knowledge and professional capability to those sectors at a time when their role in society is changing rapidly. Hence it is logical to focus in the concluding chapter of this book on the need for adaptive patterns of marketing education. How can we be certain that our business schools will not breed marketing dinosaurs? How can we ensure that the marketing education of today will educate men able to meet and master the challenges of the next decade?

*   *   *   *   *   *   *

A book of this nature inevitably owes a great deal to many people, colleagues at my universities and to discussants on programmes with which I have been involved. To all these I am deeply grateful. In particular, some colleagues have collaborated with me in the preparation of earlier drafts or versions of a number of the chapters. In two instances I played no significant role in preparing the chapters—Martin Christopher prepared the chapter on 'Marketing Logistics' and I offered only technical and editorial guidance to David Walters in his Delphi study of the likely structure of 'Distribution and

Retailing in the Eighties.' I have tried to be scrupulously exact where others have helped me and the contents page records such assistance.

Several of the chapters have been published before as internal discussion papers, as articles in learned journals or as monographs. They appear here in updated and amended form with permission of those publishers whose agreement is gratefully acknowledged.

Within my own offices, I am especially pleased to acknowledge the assistance of my secretary Dora, and the secretarial pool at the University of Prince Edward Island who did much of the typing whilst I was finalizing the text during the UPEI Summer School of 1973.

CHAPTER 1

Organizational Development in Marketing

The successful marketeer of the sixties became familiar with the concepts of profit-gap analysis, profit planning and new product development as three interlinked stages in ensuring that requisite corporate profitability was attained. Profit goal-seeking activity, as opposed to sales volume goal-seeking activity, is the distinguishing feature of modern marketing philosophy. Passage through these three stages, however, has increasingly been shown to encounter a series of organizational problems which few attempts have so far been made to overcome. The purpose here is to explore the relevant concepts which organizational development in the marketing area must embrace during the seventies if these problems are to be faced and countered.

In association with former colleagues (most especially James Mann, Charles Margerison and Roy Hayhurst), we have identified a series of steps in a process we have dubbed 'organizational forecasting'. This is the process which seeks to identify the type of organization structure likely to be most effective in filling the organization gap, which we anticipate will emerge in the future as the marketing tasks confronting the organization evolve or are totally transformed (*see* Fig. 1.1). The steps in this process are as follows:

STEP 1—Identify the future marketing tasks for the company organization structure over the relevant planning horizon (say three or four years).

STEP 2—Observe and measure the company's organizational *status quo* today.

STEP 3—Prepare an inventory of organizational theoretic knowledge that is germane to the company's situation and environment.

STEP 4—Develop and describe the organizational pattern in the light of Step 3 knowledge which is most likely to achieve the tasks identified as Step 1. (These are the normative organizational structures.)

STEP 5—Examine the possibilities and then implement the best alternative approach to moving from the *status quo* towards the patterns

1

identified in Step 4. (This phase is dubbed the *normex reconciliation—* normative extrapolative—and is the key focus for much of what is now widely described as OD or organizational development. Here we prefer to call it organizational transfer since it encompasses greater dynamics to the process than conventional OD.)

These five steps go beyond conventional OD precisely because they introduce a time dimension to the planning activity and seek to identify and build organizations which will cope simultaneously with present, intermediate future, and long-term future marketing tasks.

Our thinking in this direction has been the outcome of the first major investigation of British marketing organization structures ever undertaken in the United Kingdom. Supported financially by the British Institute of Management, the University of Bradford Management Centre have undertaken three representative studies since 1966—first, solely amongst Yorkshire businesses,[1,2] then amongst three sectors of the textile industry,[3-6] and finally with all British companies with gross turnover in excess of £$\frac{3}{4}$m in 1967 (the latest year for which Board of Trade statistics were available when fieldwork began in 1969).[7-11]

Here, we are particularly concerned to describe the organizational patterns which our investigations have indicated may well be normative to marketing's future tasks and to examine the transfer problems implicit in them in the light of evidence of the *status quo* in British marketing. We focus our attention on the requirement to routinize the operational marketing task and to achieve a fusion of the marketing development task with research and development planning. The dichotomy we shall propose in organizational structures will create its own tribological problems to which we shall seek to propose a viable solution. In this chapter we do not cover some vitally important dimensions for transfer which are fully described in *Organizational design for marketing futures.*[7] These other dimensions are the customer service function; effective marketing intelligence;[9,10] the stimulation of a total approach to marketing logistics and PDM;[12] increasing attention to educational development and training;[13] a total approach to marketing communications;[14] and the ethical and aesthetic dimensions of marketing activities.

THE ROUTINIZATION OF OPERATIONAL MARKETING ACTIVITIES

Routinization is something that the traditional marketeer resists; he dubs it bureaucracy which he normally associates with the financial area of the business. The routines with which marketing has hitherto been familiar are to a considerable degree perceived as wasted; a frequently cited example is the sales visit or contact report which is laboriously prepared and filed carefully away. No cogent use is made of many such documents which are in any event perceived as something of a distraction by the aggressive man in the field. The annual planning exercise is sometimes seen in a similar light. Although the act of planning is enjoyable enough, the implementation of plans is less easily accomplished and considerably less agreeable. The temptation to oversell a line which is obviously in substantial demand, to a level which disrupts the planned activity, is hard to resist. The sheer work involved in boosting a flagging line to reach target is sometimes difficult to muster.

The application of work-study procedures and the implementation of new travel cycles which disrupt existing habit patterns and go against personal convenience are often eschewed. Such resistance is justified by senior marketing executives in an organization in the cause of encouraging initiative by allowing a maximum of discretion to the individual within the marketing function. Flair and the need for creativity in the advertising or public relations sector of the business is denied by none; equally so in the new product conception and development process for a company. But the encouragement of flair and creativity can become an excuse for an almost total lack of analytical rigour in the development of such activities. It is not sufficient to have even the most brilliantly creative promotional campaign without that campaign moving in on the designated target market and without the routinization of media planning and selection procedures. In the public relations field neither the indiscriminate lobbying of journalists, television contributors and producers, nor the incessant bombardment of news desks with press releases, can be a substitute for the cogently thought out strategy which is implicit in media planning and selection above the line.

The distribution area also suffers from a similar lack of routine analysis. Service levels are a classic example of the way in which externally oriented marketing enthusiasm can substantially reduce corporate profitability when levels of 90 % or more at 24 hours are insisted upon by marketing executives. A more selective approach and a thorough cost/benefit analysis are mundane, yet vital marketing routines for all businesses.

Marketing's problem, in identifying those areas where a routinized approach is necessary and can make a valuable contribution to effective future operations, surely lies in the nature of the marketing animal we have bred in the past decade. Much of this breeding has been incestuous—taking salesmen and technical staff from their professional field and calling upon them to change their nature, to change from being essentially creative men who live by their wits and inventiveness rather than by their capacity to grapple with analytical routine. Those with the inclination to go it alone, to make their own personal sale or develop their own personally improved technique or system, are seldom suited to the detailed planning and control procedures which must underpin the complex and sophisticated pattern of marketing activities in our large and medium-sized enterprises. The man with the technical background is probably better equipped intellectually for the task in that he will have strong scientific training in analytical methodology which will stand him in a better marketing stead. Inevitably, though, the great majority of marketing men today are former salesmen whose experimental background will often militate against effective marketing performance.

The marketing man of the sixties can be caricatured as a corporate extrovert seeking opportunities rather than solving problems and glorying in the chase after profitable sales volume. Inevitably, he fell down on an important part of his task and was a constant source of anxiety to colleagues elsewhere in the business—in the production and financial sectors in particular. He often exacerbated their problems of production scheduling and/or cash-flow analysis. In truth, the marketing task of the seventies demands an organization which attends to the tribological problems of the marketing animal of the sixties, the marketing interface with production and finance as well as the company interface with the customer. The assignment, the organizational need, will be hard to fulfil. Marketing's traditional authority in the firm is externally derived as the generator of the revenue flows for the business from people, customers which only the marketeers meet. To create a sense of inner directedness, an introverted corporate responsibility within such an environment, demands bold skilled management and imaginative initiatives.

An analogy can perhaps usefully be drawn with the separation, even the divorce, of production management and research and development within many enterprises in the twenties and thirties. Historically, these two activities in the business were linked or joined together in one single departmental activity. The divergent nature of the tasks which were implicit in producing products to sell this week, month or year, and those implicit in a programme of pure basic or applied developmental research to ensure the company's future growth and success, ultimately forced an organizational separation. In some businesses, engineering development departments or units are present to ease the transition from R & D to the routine of production and delivery schedules, but at root an organizational separation has generally emerged. Are not the two elements in marketing's task diverging in such a way as to justify, even to demand, the organizational separation of 'operational marketing' and 'marketing development'? It is our contention that the seventies demand such a separation in the marketing area and that much of the corporate planning backlash against marketing has arisen because of marketing's failure to discern this need and to adapt the institutional structure by which the marketing task is traditionally accomplished.

In Fig. 1.1 we have identified what seem to be the critical tasks for operational marketing activity in the future. There is little to be seen which is new in conception; what we wish to emphasize is that a shift in balance is required,

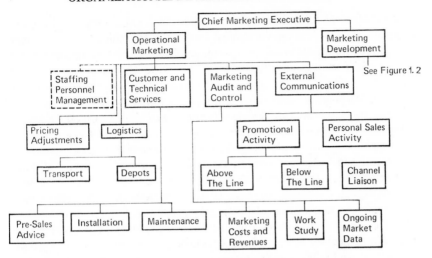

FIG. 1.1 *Operational marketing's organizational tasks.*

in favour of the routinization process, to such an extent that the marketing man of the sixties must be excused if he proclaims our proposal a charter for the bureaucrats. The powerful focus for operational effectiveness must be the department charged with the world of auditing and controlling the marketing activity as it unfolds during the current planning period. This is, of course, a much wider concept than the conventional budgetary control process with its analyses of variances of performance against target. It involves control on several additional dimensions within the marketing sphere to cover marketing costs in the sales promotion and distribution sectors as well as revenue flows. It encompasses the application in the short term of work study and measurement procedures within the office and without, and even more importantly, the variance between own and competitive performance. One of the major criticisms which can be advanced against the previous separation of budgetary control in the finance department and competitive market performance in a marketing department (in those firms where both tasks were in fact being undertaken) is that the total perspective on performance was not obtained. A marketing audit and control department or unit will be in the position to exercise this overall assessment and to bring about any adjustments to plans which *either* failure to meet own plans *or* external competitive shortfall makes necessary. The rapid response to gross market movement or individual competitive activity must be built right into the operational marketing activity. This inevitably involves the use of trade sales and stock audit procedures, user panels and the like as well as the analysis of internal company sales records.

Logistics is a routinized sector where the implications of total cost approaches to distribution will make a major impact. Suffice it here to observe that, in the marketing structures of the next decade, rapprochement between the physical handling and distribution activity, and channel strategy, must take place; and that within this sector routinization has a very substantial role indeed to play. Service level cost implications have already been described; transportation problems of vehicle scheduling and the like are all susceptible to logically more valid analytical solutions than we have traditionally been accustomed to implement in marketing. Despite such a growing concern with routinized logistics, however, the task of channel liaison can probably most sensibly remain linked with the personal sales activity sphere when a business is selling via intermediaries as well as directly. It is this sphere which already has the face-to-face contact.

Two other departments of operational marketing merit comments here. Promotional activity has linked, as a task, with personal sales activity under the general umbrella of external, persuasive communications. For two or more decades lip service has been paid to the concept that personal sales activity and above-the-line promotions are substitutable in part, or even in whole, one for the other. Institutional structures have conspired, by placing a senior sales executive and a senior advertising man in direct contact with the chief marketing executive (CME), to prevent any critical or serious exploration of possible trade-offs between these two major alternative media for persuasive external communications. The task for the marketing activity in this field is clearly to identify and deploy the optimal media of communication in the optimum mix. The historically dominant and discrete status of sales and above-the-line advertising demands mitigation in the seventies and beyond, and this is a further problematic functional element in our current concepts of marketing organization. If such an external communications orientation can be developed strategically, at the routinized level of operational activity such coordination of implementation must be present.

A further element of such coordination must also emerge. It is the integrated consideration of above- and below-the-line promotional effort in a total approach to the use of impersonal media of persuasive communication. As Martin Christopher has demonstrated, such coordinated consideration seldom takes place. Within the operational marketing sphere, such coordination must be firmly integrated within the media planning and selection routines of the business.[15]

The final area for concern must be the operational selection and management of marketing staff in a markedly more professional manner. The contributions of occupational psychologists to the identification of skills and attitudes which are correlated with sales success are better known than the very, very small amount of work done to date on staffing policies in the logistics and communications fields. A considerable body of knowledge exists which enhances our understanding of those characteristics likely to yield success in new product development fields. The task of implementing this knowledge in terms of recruitment testing and the like lagged severely in the marketing climate of the sixties. This is explicable in terms of the style of approach which marketing had inherited from the sales-oriented era of British business, both before World War II and after the Korean War. Not only can extant knowledge be routinely administered; the emergent knowledge of the seventies should be more rapidly routinized than previously.

In parallel with the routinization of selection procedures, however, must come a coherent effort to improve operational marketing management in general. The application of profit centre approaches and management by objectives has long characterized operational marketing, most noticeably through the use of product and brand management systems of organization. Marketing is even notorious in many firms for the organic, flexible nature of its managerial approach; too casual and disrespectful are frequent descriptions by traditionalists, either of the Theory X schools of thought or from more mechanistic or bureaucratic functions in the business. If routinization of operational marketing activity means anything, it means a noticeable but not an irrevocable shift away from the casual, organic, flexible approach in the management of current operations and the relegation of much but not all of that flair, hunch, brilliance and creativity which can only thrive in the organic, flexible structure to that sector of the business concerned with marketing development.

It is to marketing development and its interface with R & D in the technical sector that we shall now turn our attention. As we do, however, it behoves us to make one comment concerning the observations we have just made on routinization of operational marketing activity and on the following observations on the problems of marketing's organizational transfer to meet the tasks of the next decade. We have hypothesized the firms which we discuss in general terms to be relatively dependent on the development of new technology and that they are concerned with the fields of basic research. We realize that not all firms will be so based or concerned. Hence these observations will seldom, if ever, be a neat fit for any particular firm, and we have not sought to make them so. Rather, we hope that the flow of ideas and their conceptualization will trigger thoughts in the mind of the reader which stimulate him to do the organizational transfer problems from his contemporary corporate base with his contemporary and anticipated resources, both human and physical.

Neither are we suggesting that because certain tasks have been identified here as 'marketing' tasks, they should be the exclusive preserve of the CME with full corporate responsibility. All the empirical evidence collected shows that would be a naïve conception. We have dashed and dotted certain boxes as obviously not marketing's preserve; we could have dotted more since many tasks will be shared.

Finally, we are not suggesting that each task in every company should have a full-time employee to perform it. Many businesses will be able to combine some of these tasks in the recruitment job specification in one man. That is fine so long as the awareness and critical importance of these future tasks are perceived.

THE FUSION OF MARKETING DEVELOPMENT AND TECHNICAL RESEARCH AND DEVELOPMENT

It would be erroneous to suggest that routinization is solely a dimension of the operational marketing task. The activity of marketing development within the company requires a considerable degree of routinization as well. The formalized generation of new ideas and their gestation into products or services are each susceptible to routine without stultification. The procedures for screening and comparatively evaluating a vast reservoir of new ideas, product concepts and scenarios are routines. The standardized panoply of marketing research techniques for new product testing or for simulation of alternative competitive strategies are further instances. And in each of these sectors the routinization process can be seen actively at work. Hence, in the sector of business activity concerned with marketing development we shall be less concerned with the issue of routinization than with a shift in the balance of the developmental activities of marketing. We see the prime requirement to be a fusion of marketing development activity with the technical work undertaken in what we generally know as R & D.

This will not be the only dimension of our developmental concern, but it is the one we see as most critical. Other vitally important shifts in emphasis have already been trailed in our earlier consideration of operational marketing—the need for a total external communications approach at the strategic level and a concentration on strategy in the channel/logistics and funding areas of the business.

The lynch-pin of the fusion is the process of technological forecasting (TF), allied in many instances to the emergent technology of social forecasting. A recent investigation amongst British industry[16] has indicated that TF has to date gained only a marginal foothold within the total planning process of the business, even in the most progressive concerns. Even in these companies, the scope of its implementation is sporadic and partial with only the simplest and most imaginative techniques, such as the Delphi forecast method, in use. The requirement to master technology or be mastered by it must, however, ensure a continued development of TF activity at both corporate and national levels. We say this despite the early steps to dismantle the Ministry of Technology's strategic activities which the Heath Government undertook in 1970 when the Ministry of Technology merged with the Board of Trade to form the Ministry for Industry and Trade.

TF, perforce, brings technical planning and the marketing development activity together, the one to plan a technical capability and the other to assess the market availability for any such capacity when it may reach fruition. The divorce of these two processes, the tendency to bring the marketeer in only as an afterthought once any given technological capability has emerged, has been a costly phenomenon for British companies for decades and virtually catastrophic for the British economy.[17,18] We have only to look at Japanese technology in the fifties and sixties to see clearly what can be achieved by the intelligent fusion of marketing and technical development. The marketing development function of the seventies has to combat, simultaneously, both technological and marketing myopia, and TF is the arena in which that combat is forced and, hopefully, resolved. Our enthusiasm for TF should not be thought to advance the case that it is a panacea for development problems. It is, rather, an aid to minimize the difficulties and to clarify the objectives of corporate techno/market strategy. Nor can the marketing development expert be expected to prepare technological forecasts. He will not have the technical expertise. What the marketing activity can contribute, and where the marketing task lies, is the probabilistic assessment of the time dimension of market availability. It is worth noting, if fairly apparent, that a technical development programme which brings a new project to fruition a year or so too late for the market is often a severe handicap in competitive terms. A less apparent danger is the premature commitment of R & D resources and the incurrence of marketing investment as well before the flow of market-derived revenue can sensibly justify it. A completed product development which is a year or so ahead of market availability is capital fruitlessly tied up, and the implications of a too-early completion of technology must be simultaneously considered with the costs of delay. This type of cost is frequently encountered in the component technologies which go to make up an aggregated delivered technological capability. The slack time which the conscious building-in of delays into development programmes can generate is normally seen as a method of allocating resources to other more critical tasks. Such a concept is implicit in most of the CPA and PERT techniques of network analysis and indeed in Normative Relevance Tree Analysis in TF. Slack time may, however, be something we seek to generate quite specifically as a way of slowing down the movement forward of component capabilities ahead of the critical need for their completion, especially if sizeable financial or human resource commitments are involved.

Fig. 1.2 indicates the preference we have for hypothesizing that the task of TF should be partly encompassed within the overall activity of techno/market assessment under the aegis of the marketing development activity. Two separate sectors would prepare the detailed technological and market forecasts which would provide the assessable information. This assessment function would be separated conceptually from the more traditional new product/market planning and development task of the firm, although there would undoubtedly be considerable cross-communication between the two areas, especially if they were operated within the company by different groups. It will be commonplace, for example, for market-derived new product ideas to be fed into the techno/market assessment activity via the new product/market planning route.

Within the new product/marketing planning and development task, the formal routinized techniques for the development of new ideas will be appropriate, as alluded to earlier on. In particular, the specific consideration of each of the product/market sectors identified in Ansoff's now famous matrix for growth must be encompassed.[19] These are typically as shown in Fig. 1.3 with each of eight possible positions demanding change and development in one form or another. It is obvious that some make greater demands on TF, and others on the market forecasting arms of the techno/market assessment task.[20]

We have already mentioned in our discussion of operational marketing that the promotional elements of marketing activity are likely to require a substantial restructuring during the decade ahead. It must be within marketing development that plans for this are laid. A useful dichotomy may well be between the deployment of human resources in face-to-face contact and the use of impersonal methods of persuasive communication both above and below the line. The strategic alternatives must be evaluated, and the total and marginal benefits of resource allocation in given directions assessed, as well as maintained under continuous review. Such a fundamental examination of strategy must also be undertaken within the field of channels of distribution and modes for the physical movement of goods and raw materials; an area of vast potential development.

Marketing's interplay with the financial area of the business in the strategic analysis of growth opportunities in its turn must undergo some considerable development. Two major fields of interaction are apparent—the development of a pricing strategy and the appraisal of new projects as they come forward. This latter task will of course be undertaken in alliance with the technical evaluation of new product concepts and the various stages of market assessment already described. For today's marketeers to make any really coherent contribution in this sector of the company's marketing development, however, will require an extensive programme of education and training in the field of

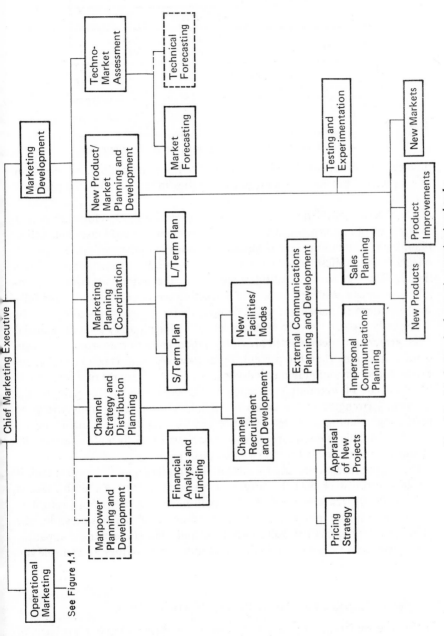

FIG. 1.2 *Marketing development's organizational tasks.*

Technology Base			
	Existing	Improved	New
Existing	No Change	Product Improvement	Product Development
Extended	Market Extension		
New	Market Development		Diversification

FIG. 1.3   *Product/market planning and development dimensions.*

finance. The objectives of such training will not be to make finance experts out of marketeers but rather intelligent colleagues in the coordinated planning process.

The fulcrum of all these separate tasks in marketing development is that major area of concern which we have left for comment until last—marketing planning coordination. This is marketing's answer to the corporate planning backlash as manifest in so many business organizations at the turn of this decade. Through such an institutionalized task, the senior marketing development officer can ensure that his chief marketing executive is participating fully in the pattern of planning for the company's future whilst avoiding a technologically myopic view. In addition, equally difficult areas such as financial management are encompassed providing a more efficient grass-roots approach towards planning than the present top-downwards-push which characterizes extant corporate planning methodology. A typical advantage of a grass-roots development of marketing planning is the greater attention paid to the marketing strengths of the company. Symbiotic marketing and synergistic marketing, building perhaps on an extensive branding investment or on existing channels of distribution, tend to be more carefully and systematically attended to than under top-downwards-push planning.

Once again, we would enter a caveat. The marketing development task is not to overthrow or oust the corporate planning activity of the business. It is to cogently reassert marketing's involvement, as a sensibly reformed corporate animal, in the total planning process of the business. By the intelligent development of well coordinated and compatible plans, compatible that is with technological capability and funding possibilities, such a role can surely be re-established.

THE PRESENT/FUTURE DICHOTOMY IN ORGANIZATIONAL DESIGN

It may be said that we are merely creating a new unfamiliar problem of integration in order to overcome a lesser problem—that of persuading the marketing executives to spend somewhat more time thinking about the future in the course of an already integrated activity. In a small or small–medium firm we must partially or substantially accept such an argument and also concede that separation of the task in terms of specific individuals may well not be economically feasible. Having made such a concession, we adhere firmly to the view that the two tasks demand formalized, separable treatment in the medium or large organization if they are to be effectively executed. Not only the future will benefit; the present pattern of operational activity will benefit also from its specific professionalization.

We already see the dichotomy between R & D and production, and we see it emerging within the financial area of the business between straightforward budgetary control methods and the funding and financial appraisal tasks which are increasingly important.

We suggest that the venture-group concept, so effectively employed now in many major corporations for new product development work, be conceptually extended to cover a much wider gamut of the marketing activity. Hence, we propose that a continual movement of executive personnel in the marketing sector from the marketing development task to operational marketing, and then back to development, should be attempted. Obviously not all staff will be involved in this systematic movement. Specialists in forecasting activity and the like will remain in the development sector indefinitely, but plans will be operationally implemented by those executives who develop them. Such is the present pattern of activity; but the sabbatical concept of removing the operational executive from the operational sector for a full plan period to develop his next operational plan is not generally practised.

Such a rotation of key staff has two major advantages. First, the planning is undertaken by men who have an intimate knowledge of the market in which operations will take place. Secondly, the implementation of plans will be in the hands of those who have devised them and had the opportunity to ensure that they are well laid. The cycle of planning and human rotation would be as indicated in Fig. 1.4 for two executive teams, A and B.

We have no illusions that all these tasks will be the sole concern of the chief marketing executive. No man could coordinate them all alone. Many will

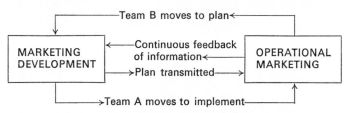

FIG. 1.4 *Planning human resource marketing system.*

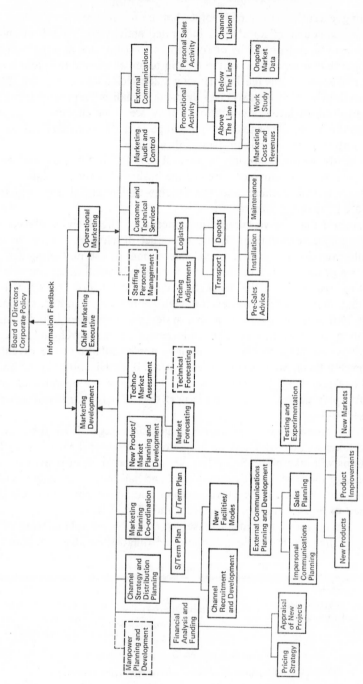

FIG. 1.5 *The future/present pattern of marketing tasks.*

be shared responsibilities with the other areas of activity in the firm. But they must be areas of marketing concern with some element of responsibility resting with the chief marketing executive of the future.

CONCLUSION

We have not given full discussion to all the dimensions we perceive for profitable organizational transfer to the futures which lie in wait for industrial marketing, but sincerely trust that what we have accomplished on the basis of a macro-analysis of British marketing today can act as a fillip to the necessary micro-analysis which each and every firm should undertake as an integral part of its planning.

We believe that organizational planning is something of considerably greater complexity than conventional Organizational Development (OD) approaches suggest. Furthermore, that it is something the chief marketing executive must initiate, using OD personnel in a staff capacity. Whilst implicitly saying, therefore, that the chief marketing executive must shoulder yet one more responsibility, in doing so he will be able to avoid many of the short-term organizational dilemmas which currently occupy much of his time.

REFERENCES

1. Mann, J., 'Nominal and effective status of chief marketing executives in Yorkshire industry', reprinted in Wills, G. (ed.), *Exploration in marketing thought*. Crosby Lockwood for University of Bradford Press, 1971.
2. Baker, M., Braam, T. and Kemp, A., *Permeation of the marketing concept in Yorkshire manufacturing industry,* University of Bradford Project Series, University of Bradford Press, 1967.
3. Saddik, S. M. A., *Marketing in the wool-textile, textile machinery and clothing industries,* Ph.D thesis, University of Bradford, 1969.
4. Saddik, S. M. A. and Wills, G., 'Product strategy and management in the British textile industry', *Journal of Management Studies,* 8(1), 1971.
5. Saddik, S. M. A., 'Manufacturer toleration of channels of distribution', in Wills, G. (ed.), *Exploration in marketing thought,* Chap. 7. Crosby Lockwood for University of Bradford Press, 1971.
6. Saddik, S. M. A., 'Marketing orientation and organizational design', *British Journal of Marketing,* 2, pp. 273–86; 1968.
7. Hayhurst, R. and Wills, G., *Organizational design for marketing futures.* Thomas Nelson, 1971. This book is the full report of the study financed by the British Institute of Management.
8. Hayhurst, R., 'Marketing organization in British industry', Occasional paper 148, British Institute of Management, 1970.
9. Wills, G., 'Marketing research in British Industry', Working paper, British Institute of Management, 1971.

10. Wills, G. and Hayhurst, R., 'The pattern of marketing research in the UK and its future development', Paper presented to the 14th conference of the Market Research Society, 1971.
11. Margerison, C. and Wills, G., *Seminar manual: marketing organizational development*, University of Bradford, 1971.
12. Christopher, M. and Wills, G. (eds), *Marketing logistics and distribution planning*. George Allen & Unwin, 1971.
13. Christopher, M., Magrill, L. and Wills, G., 'Educational development for marketing logistics', *International Journal of Physical Distribution*, 1 (1971), pp. 79–82.
14. Wills, G., 'Marketing's educational challenge in the 70s', *Advertising Quarterly*, Autumn, 1971.
15. Christopher, M., *Marketing below-the-line*. Thomas Nelson, 1971. The studies on which this was based were funded by Horniblow, Cox–Freeman. A further three-year study funded by a score of business firms at Cranfield School of Management on the joint consideration of above- and below-the-line promotion and measurement of their effectiveness. Results are due by 1975 (*see* chapter 8).
16. Currill, D., *The role of technological forecasting in the integrative planning of technological development—a study of 6 UK companies*. M.Sc. dissertation submitted to the University of Bradford.
17. Wills, G., *Technological forecasting: the art and its management*. Penguin Books, 1971.
18. Wills, G., Ashton, D. J. L. and Taylor, B. (eds), *Technological forecasting and corporate strategy*. Crosby Lockwood for University of Bradford Press, 1969.
19. Ansoff, I. *Corporate strategy,* Penguin Books, 1969.
20. Taylor, B. and Wills, G. (eds), *Long range planning for marketing and diversification*. Crosby Lockwood for University of Bradford Press, 1971.

CHAPTER 2

Output Budgeting in Marketing

WHAT IS OUTPUT BUDGETING?

> The basic idea of an output budget is to relate all cost items to hard functional objectives by constructing a broad framework within which it is clear what resources are being devoted towards what end and with what results.[1]

Traditional accounting methods have tended to concentrate on 'who' does the spending, for example, departments or functional areas within the firm, rather than on the 'ends' to which these expenditures are directed. This orientation has hitherto been dictated by the requirement of the firm for each of these functional areas to meet specific objectives, usually in terms of profit contribution or minimum cost operation. A view that is increasingly being accepted, however, is that the true objectives of the firm cannot be stated in terms of functional performance criteria, but rather in terms of 'corporate missions' that cut across these functional areas. Thus a brewery, for example, might define the purpose of some of its activities in the following manner:

(a) We are in the business of *thirst-satisfaction*.
(b) Because our public houses are more than places to drink, they are in fact social centres; we are in the *entertainment* business.
(c) It is also apparent from trends that we must be in the *catering* business.
(d) Utilization of our by-products can be a profitable venture, for example, possible uses for spent hops suggests that we could be in the *fertilizer* business.

This company has thereby defined four broadly based missions each of which, if adopted, would have a set of associated goals. The achievement of these goals will involve inputs from all the conventionally accepted functional areas of the firm: marketing, production, R & D, information, personnel, etc. Fig. 2.1 describes the superimposition on a traditional organization of the mission approach we have identified.

The setting of budgets using mission orientation requires the adoption of a radically different method from current accounting practice. What is required in its place is the determination of the necessary level of input from each area to achieve mission goals. Thus, what impact is required from marketing to

17

achieve the stated goals of the thirst-satisfaction mission? What input from production, from R & D and so on? Having determined these, in itself a problem which requires an evaluation of alternate strategies, it is then possible to arrive at functional budgets by summing for each function the inputs that each mission requires from that function. Thus in Fig. 2.2, the functional budgets are determined by summing vertically all the financial demands that are made upon a functional area in the fulfilment of the corporate mission.

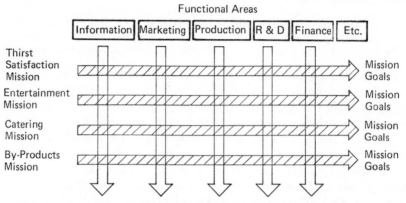

FIG. 2.1   *The corporate missions and goals of a brewery.*

The important difference in this approach, and the feature that distinguishes it from traditional accounting, is that functions are not allocated a budget which is historically or arbitrarily defined and then exhorted to perform as effectively as they can within that budget. Rather the functional budget is the result of a careful statement of mission goals and an analysis of the requirements placed on functions in order that such goals might be fulfilled. If, therefore, in Fig. 2.2, Function 4 was the corporate information system, then its budget would be £140,000.

In the same way that mission costs are clearly identified, it is necessary to have an indication of the benefits that each mission is producing. Benefits may be measured in terms of how well the mission goals are met by that particular corporate structure; the point being that alternate structures may achieve greater, or at least equivalent, benefits but with different costs. Output budgeting clearly presents the decision-maker with a means of evaluating alternatives in terms of cost-effectiveness and requires that he makes such comparisons.

Applications of this approach to planning and budgeting are increasingly reported. The earliest were in the United States Department of Defense, where some method of evaluating complex systems and defence objectives was required.[2] It has been adopted by UK government departments. The Home Office, for example, is implementing this system of accounting into police forces, and the impact that this is having on the evaluation of programme effectiveness is startling. For example, before the introduction of this method, the cost of police dogs was taken to be only the cost of feeding and housing the dogs. Now, the cost of police dogs includes 'all' relevant costs, such as the wages of the trainers and handlers and the running costs of the dog vans. In one police force, the cost of police dogs was put at £1,600 by conventional accounting methods. A year later, with the new method of accounting, the cost in programme terms was shown to be £37,900.[3]

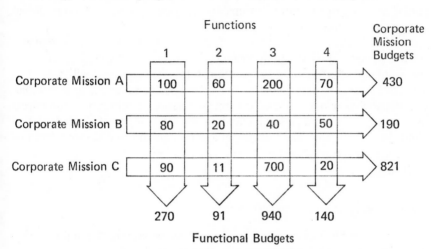

FIG. 2.2   *Deriving functional budgets* (£000).

Within the business sector, too, output budgeting methods are finding a growing acceptance. One of the earliest adopters was the International Minerals and Chemical Corporation (IMC) where they adopted almost wholesale and with great success the planning, programming and budgeting system (PPBS) developed by McNamara at the Department of Defense.[4] Since then the adoption of the principles of output budgeting and their incorporation into corporate planning procedures has rapidly increased.[5]

BRAND MANAGEMENT VENTURES AND LOGISTICS AS PRECURSORS

We have for a considerable time had certain patterns of organization within marketing companies which have manifest a similar underlying philosophy although, unfortunately, without a great degree of success. The brand management concept could be said to be a forerunner of the cross-company organization implied by output budgeting.[6] In this case the brand manager was concerned with the development, launch and continued health of a product or group of products. Such concern obviously necessitated some degree of involvement in several functional areas of the company other than marketing. Nevertheless, there was no attempt at relating brand(s) to corporate missions, nor were the costs and benefits of the cross-company involvement specifically assessed.

Similarly, the current movement to organization for product development along *venture management* lines is an attempt to break down functional and departmental boundaries.[7] However, whilst it does constitute a highly fruitful pattern of organization to achieve specific mission goals, unless it is accompanied by a linking of venture groups to corporate missions and to functional budgets, it is unlikely to achieve its full potential payoff.

Another parallel movement in industry is the development of *logistics* strategies based upon the total costing of their company-wide impact. Thus the planning of a depot system, using total cost analysis, will take into account its likely impact on all sections of the business; for example, production capability, materials handling, transportation requirements, the effects on the level of customer service and so on. This approach is designed to highlight the true costs and benefits of a particular course of action[8] and this has a significant relationship to the company-wide orientation of output budgeting.

THE CORPORATE INFORMATION MISSION

We have already indicated our preference for regarding the information-gathering activities of the company as an integrated function.

It follows that information-gathering, like any other business activity, must be planned. Furthermore the information-gathering process must be viewed in total, not discretely; not just as research into markets, economic situation reporting, special projects to obtain information from accounting, or production analysis. Smith and Levitz[9] define commercial intelligence as:

> the result of a continuous process which takes data of a commercial nature and creates intelligence which is directly useful to the manager in planning and operating the business.

This orientation is summarized in Fig. 2.3. For example, information on and from suppliers can and should be obtained from the purchasing department, while R & D should, as a matter of course, channel information on new techniques through to a central focus. The specific concern of the marketing function is to deploy the information available to optimize its pursuit of corporate mission goals. The origins of such marketing information stretch from raw materials to post-consumption. The entire continuum of information

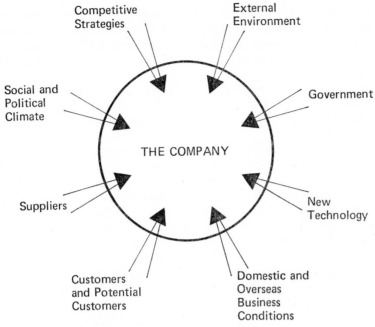

FIG. 2.3 *The corporate information environment.*

requests—search—collation—presentation—assimilation, is in fact one process, not a series of discrete or partially interrelated processes. The company accordingly needs a total information function capable of coordinating the flow of information from and to all functions within the company.

Such an integrated concept of information gives rise to an information system such as we propose in Fig. 2.4. The essential features of the system are:

—Centralization of the information flow.
—Separation of marketing research into developmental and operational sectors.[10]
—Inclusion of the long-range planning information requirements.
—Emphasis on greater use of internal information.
—Overall cost-reduction possibilities.

It involves centralizing the information processing operation and planning the use of expensive resources, talented analysts and computer time.

The system we have described thus proposes the inclusion of the marketing research activity within a larger organization which embraces information outputs from, and inputs to, all other functions within the firm. The information system has as its basic function the provision of information from which decision-makers will formulate policy, determine strategies and make operational decisions. In the context of the marketing research activities we presently know, this may be analogously described as follows. Let us distinguish between three broad categories of customary marketing research:

—Basic *curiosity-oriented research:* wide-ranging examination in depth or breadth of areas of current interest to the researcher.
—*Action research:* directed specifically at overcoming or illuminating a specific problem.
—*Mission-oriented research:* more loosely structured programmes designed to produce data pertinent to the attainment of mission goals.

Market researchers will usually have had experience of all three forms at some stage in their career, but probably the most common experience is with action research. It is our general contention, however, that emphasis on solving problems, rather than on the identification and exploitation of market opportunities, has tended to constrict the usefulness of marketing research and to ensure its virtual exclusion from the higher levels of decision-making in the corporate structure. This divorce of marketing research from the real business of marketing is a widespread phenomenon, as a study of over 500 major UK companies has clearly demonstrated.[11] There is an urgent need to relate the organization of marketing information to the identified missions of the company. From this point of view, therefore, it is probably the latter category of research that is more likely to provide the effective basis for this integration we believe essential.

The definition of corporate missions logically leads to an identification of a series of related information activities. A recent activity example was as follows:

> An identified mission of the ABC company was to seek an 'established position' in the UK frozen foods market over the next ten years. The marketing research mission which followed from this statement has been defined as: 'the provision of information upon which judgements may be made concerning possible technological and societal futures relating to our activities in this market'.

Here the operational activities of marketing research are now clearly linked to the policy-making process. Further than this, however, the requirements of the information activity will involve inputs from several distinct areas of the company—from the economic analysis group, from the personnel concerned with technological forecasting (perhaps the R & D group), from the marketing department(s) concerned, from the company library and from the marketing research department itself. Sources external to the company will also need to be utilized. Once the full requirements of such a programme of research are realized, and an attempt to cost them in company-wide terms is made, it becomes apparent that it will probably involve the company in greater 'total costs' than was initially realized.

This is the first step in the output budgeting approach to marketing research expenditures—the exploration of the likely pattern of involvement of individual areas inside the company, and without, in such an information activity.

The second stage is to consider how these stated information goals may

FIG. 2.4 *Structure of the information system.*

be met by 'alternative means'. For example, one alternative may be to sub-contract the complete research activity to an outside agency. Another may be to bring together a group, drawn from all the company areas involved, specifically charged to deal with the need. Whatever the number of feasible alternatives, they should be considered and evaluated. The evaluation takes the form of examining their capability to meet the specified goal and the impact on corporate resources that end would make—in other words a cost/benefit appraisal of the alternate research programmes. Assuming that a given 'benefit', that is goal achievement, must be reached, then the objective is to compare research programmes that meet this level of benefit in terms of the cost that each entails. This, it is emphasized, must be a total costing; thus, for example, if a research programme involves groups and a com-missioned survey, then the total cost is calculated by allocating costs and summarizing them.

Problems do arise because of the difficulties of assigning costs to each input to the research programme. Often these costs have to be forecast, thus adding further uncertainty to the situation—the number of man-hours to be expended by the company librarian on any specific programme, for example. In other cases it will be possible to make highly accurate estimates of costs; for example, the purchase of trade panel or media data. However, when alternate research programmes are being compared, as long as similar assumptions are maintained, then it will often be the 'relative' costs involved rather than the 'absolute' costs that will be important.

PRODUCT/MARKET MISSIONS

We must now turn our attention to the products and services which the company will utilize in reaching the corporate mission goals we have so far identified (*see* Fig. 2.5) and to the functional activities in which both marketing executives and information scientists will engage (*see* Fig. 2.6).

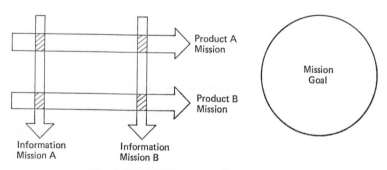

Fig. 2.5 *The corporate marketing system.*

Marketing has long been characterized as a system, with information flows from the competitive environment, trade, customer and consumer/users as system feedback. Fig. 2.5 describes this process in output-budgeting terms and assumes that the company is pursuing its mission goal via two products, A and B. Fig. 2.6 sets out in selective yet extensive detail the nature of marketing and information activities at the interstices of Fig. 2.5.

Fig. 2.6 has drawn upon Neil Borden's original formulation of the marketing mix,[12] although modified and extended considerably. We have seen fit, conceptually, to integrate personal and impersonal persuasion activities in the marketing function into a total communications activity, and to incorporate contemporary concepts of physical distribution management and channel management into the marketing function. Finally, we have provided for a continuous treatment of 'marketing development' as a functional activity. These component activities of the marketing function are matched against component activities of the information function where that function interacts with each.

It will be apparent after careful study of Fig. 2.6 that the 'marketing facts' component of the marketing mix identified by Neil Borden has disappeared as a component from the listing of marketing activities. It does, of course, remain vital but resides within the total corporate information function. It will also be appreciated that the paradigm provided overlooks the mission goals of channel members which may either hinder or further the company's own product market missions, or simultaneously do both. Multiple dealerships, for example, frequently make the dealer a more attractive contact as a supplier, but may well reduce the possibilities of sale for a particular product our company has in mind for its market. Equally, confusion can arise at the distribution level as a result of 'leap-frogging' promotional activities by manufacturers over the heads of channel members direct to customers. Appropriate sub-analyses can, however, be assigned to take care of such issues within channels.

SETTING THE MISSION INFORMATION BUDGET

We have already indicated in Fig. 2.2 that the total budget for marketing information within the company should be the sum of each mission's budget. We must now explore the nature of budget determination within each mission. Our starting point is that marketing information is required to reduce mission uncertainty to acceptable levels for the marketing executives concerned. We therefore propose an integrated deployment of Bayesian and risk analysis. Fig. 2.7 demonstrates the reconciliation of the marketing executive's attitudes towards information budget expenditure and taking risks with company resources.

MARKETING FUNCTION *in toto*		INFORMATION FUNCTION (*Marketing dimension only*)	
Theme component	*Component elements* (e.g.)	*Competitive intelligence* (e.g.)	*Competitive performance* (e.g.)
I. PRODUCT, SERVICE offered	Range	Trade inventory. Salesmen's feedback. Monitoring media etc.	Order analysis, product tests and user feedback.
	Quality/service levels. Design.	Comparative laboratory tests. Salesmen's feedback. Monitoring media, etc.	Product tests and user feedback.
	Branding/trade marks (*e.g.* positioning own labels).	Monitoring and analysis. Salesmen's feedback. Trade feedback.	Brand shares. Brand legalities. Sales data.
	Replacement policies.	Life-cycle analysis. Salesmen's feedback. Trade feedback. Monitoring media, etc.	Life-cycle analysis. Product tests and mix tests, etc.
II. PRICE LEVELS and financial services	Price field.	Monitoring price lists. Trade inventory.	Price expectational research.
	Specific prices.	Monitoring price lists. Trade inventory.	Price tests.
	Discounts and margins.	Monitoring price lists. Trade inventory.	Comparative analysis and control. Trade feedback.
	Credit facilities, etc.	Monitoring media.	Trade feedback. Bad debt analysis.
III. COMMUNICATIONS	Level of spend overall. Trade/customer split. Personal *v.* impersonal split.	Expenditure analysis. (*e.g.* MEAL)	Dynamic difference analysis, etc. Experimentation. Evaluation (*e.g.* DAGMAR)

FIG. 2.6—*continuing*

III. COMMUNICATIONS —continued	Image.	Trade feedback. Salesmen's feedback.	Image research.
	Timing.	Time-series analysis (*e.g.* MEAL)	Experimentation.
	Development of creative platform	Monitoring (*e.g.* MEAL)	Concept testing.
(i) Personal selling	Level of spend.	Monitoring call frequency.	Experimentation. Evaluation.
	Resource deployment in the field, *e.g.* sales territories and routeing.	Salesmen's feedback.	Potential analysis. Call response function.
	Sales proposition.	Monitoring. Trade feedback.	Proposition testing.
(ii) Packaging	Level of spend.	Monitoring. Trade inventory.	Experimentation. Evaluation.
	Unitization. Design. Physical dimensions.	Monitoring. Trade inventory. Salesmen's feedback.	Pack testing with trade and users.
(iii) Impersonal above-the-line	Level of spend	Expenditure analysis (*e.g.* MEAL)	Experimentation. Evaluation.
	Media mix, schedule and buy	Monitoring etc.	Recall, reading/ noting. JICTARS/ JICNARS. Market coverage.
	Copy platform	Monitoring, etc.	Copy testing.
(iv) Impersonal below-the-line	Level of spend	Salesmen's feedback. Trade feedback. Monitoring, etc.	Experimentation. Evaluation.
	Promotion mix. Schedule and buy. Trade *v.* customers.	Monitoring.	Reading/noting. Market coverage.
	Merchandising/ display.	Trade inventory. Salesmen's feedback.	Observation studies.

Fig. 2.6—*continuing*

MARKETING FUNCTION *in toto*		INFORMATION FUNCTION (*Marketing dimension only*)	
Theme component	*Component elements* (e.g.)	*Competitive intelligence* (e.g.)	*Competitive performance* (e.g.)
(iv) Impersonal below-the-line —*continued*	Copy platform.	Monitoring, etc.	Copy testing.
IV. LOGISTICS AND CHANNELS	Channel selection.	Vendor appraisal. Channel audit (*e.g.* Nielsen)	Sterling and unit distribution achieved in-stock (%)
	Selection of transport mode.	Monitoring, etc.	Total delivered-cost.
	Facility location.	Monitoring, etc.	Incidence of sales points. Stock-holding costs, etc.
	Service levels and despatch	Monitoring, etc.	Total cost for service levels required.
V. PURCHASE AGENCIES	Buyer identifica-tion. Trade, retail, surrogate and end-user.	Behavioural analysis to identify nature of buying process, any surrogate activity, etc.	Sales volumes achieved in buyer categories.
VI. MARKETING DEVELOPMENT	Experimental mix. Develop-ment.	Monitoring. Sales-men's feedback. Trade feedback.	Experimentation, *e.g.* Pressure tests; town tests.
	New-product planning and development.	Monitoring, etc.	Concept testing. Product testing.
	New-product launch.	Monitoring. Sales-men's feedback. Trade feedback.	Pilot/test marketing.
	Education and training.	Monitoring, etc.	Monitoring, etc.

FIG. 2.6 *Selective description of matched activity components in the corporate marketing system.*

Our approach goes some way towards explaining a frequently perceived paradox in decision theoretic approaches to the expected value of perfect information (EVPI) for the marketing executive. All too frequently the EVPI is very considerably greater than any expenditure the company or the individual concerned would even contemplate committing. We suggest that the difference, or gap, is an estimate of the level of market experience and risk preference of the individual concerned (some might term it bravado).

Derivation of risk/expenditure trade-off curve for the marketing executive
One of the basic precepts of cost-effective information usage in marketing is that it is not justifiable to spend more on information than the value of the

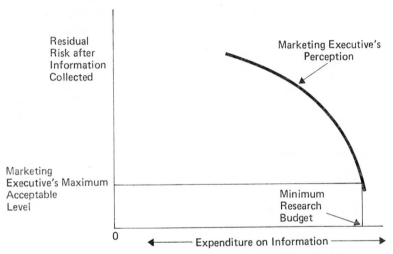

FIG. 2.7   *Perceived risk/information expenditure trade-off analysis.*

maximum expected loss that could occur in the *absence* of that information. The exact value of this maximum figure is given by the EVPI, which is simply the highest product of the monetary value of possible outcomes and the likelihood of those outcomes actually occurring. To simplify, if the absolute worst that could happen is that the project under consideration could be a total failure involving a loss of £10,000, and if the prior expectation of this loss was 5%, then there would be little point in spending much more than £500 (that is, £10,000 × 5/100) to obtain *perfect* information.

We have developed a technique which provides a means of determining the risk/expenditure trade-off curve. Knowing the characteristic of this curve enables the minimum budget consonant with a maximum level of residual risk to be set. It also enables the manager to appreciate and to quantify the extent to which he is exchanging his personal judgement for purchased information; that is, the difference between the EVPI and the actual expenditure that he is prepared to make.

The value of the information budget that emerges is of course a budget for the information needs of a *mission*. What is now required is a consideration of how this mission budget may be assigned to products and markets within the mission.

ALLOCATING THE MISSION INFORMATION BUDGET

The determination of the total information budget for any mission is the important first step to its allocation amongst the information function's germane activity components. The simplest method of allocation involves the ordinal value ranking of all information activity components and, starting from that deemed most important, the allocation of budget to as many components as possible whilst funds remain. This method is demonstrated in Fig. 2.8. It involves making assumptions about the optimum level of spend for each information component—for example, how statistically significant does any information set need to be. Although such assumptions can be competently made in many circumstances, a more rigorous approach may sometimes be required. The most effective allocation can be made by heuristic search procedures.

Information activity component	Ordinal value ranking for single product	Most likely reasonable 'total' expenditure (£)	Budget at £35,000
Internal sales analysis (level 1)	1	18,000	√
Market share data	2	6,000	√
Image research	6	41,000	
Price testing	4	12,000	
Concept testing	5	15,000	
Product testing	3	8,000	√
Internal sales analysis (level 2)	7	4,000	

FIG. 2.8   *Ordinal ranking method for allocation of a mission information budget for single product.*

Fig. 2.8 indicates that within a developed budget constraint of £35,000, only internal sales analysis at level 1, market share data and product testing would be undertaken. There is, however, considerable likelihood that one or more of these components will offer substantial synergy effects with information procurement from other mission fields. Hence, a more complex analysis will be required of a type illustrated in Fig. 2.9. Let us take a fairly typical example.

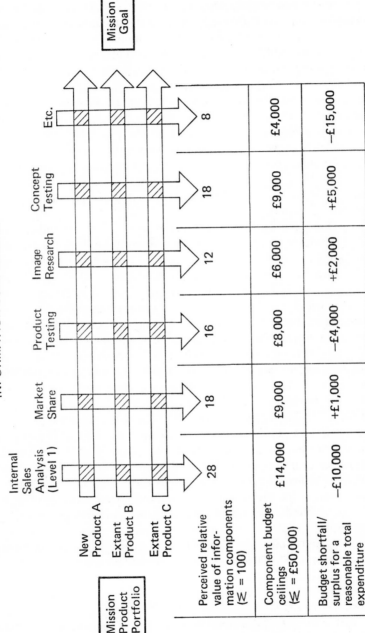

FIG. 2.9 *Cardinal ranking method for allocation of a mission information budget for a mission product portfolio.*

The typical corporate mission, if examined in cross-section, will normally deploy a mix of new and old products at differing stages in their life-cycles, which together provide the vehicles for achieving the mission goal. Thus, for example, a profile of a mission might reveal one new product and two existing products. Almost certainly these individual products will differ in their information requirements, yet there will quite likely be considerable opportunities for information sharing, for achieving joint economies of information—in other words information synergy. For example, whilst a regular check on attitudes towards the new brand will have its highest pay-off there, it is possible for attitude checks on the two existing brands to be carried out at the same time. The incremental cost of this additional information will be slight yet the improvement in knowledge of all the brand positions attitude-wise will be of some magnitude. The same rationale can be applied in almost every area of information collection undertaken within the mission (and perhaps even without).

If research budgets are set for the mission product portfolio, other than for individual products within a mission product portfolio, then the problem of cost allocation between products does not arise. Instead the problem becomes one of determining the expenditure to be made on alternate sources of information. Thus in Fig. 2.9 we have identified several information activity components within a single mission. The marketing executive has indicated his perceived relative value of each information component. This can simply be done by employing Fig. 2.6 as a checklist of information components and ascribing weights rising to 100 to each information component. The numerical distance between the highest and next highest is taken as our measure of cardinal ranking. The cardinal rank order is then used as the basis for allocation of the already determined global budget. This analysis, for a hypothetical £50,000, appears as the next line in the analysis. Finally, the budget shortfall or surplus against a reasonable total research expenditure for the information component is made. It will be seen that the cardinal ranking allocates insufficient of the total budget for a 'reasonable' internal sales analysis at level 1 to be made. Nor is there a sufficient allocation for product testing or the 'etcetera' information components. On the other hand we have saved funds allocated to market share data, image research and concept testing.

The managerial choice now is whether to proceed to make savings on these latter three items of £8,000 and simply to deploy the budget at £42,000, or to make a second allocation. If so, in which direction?

A heuristic search routine

As was earlier indicated, the preferred method is a heuristic search routine. It is posited on the development, for each information component, of its cost-effectiveness function. A series of such relationships are postulated in Fig. 2.10. If we examine them visually in the context of Fig. 2.9 it will be readily seen that a small extra allocation to internal sales analysis (level 1) promises a major advance in effectiveness whilst the £1,000 surplus for market share data can be retained, and so on. A computer can, of course, be programmed to undertake a heuristic search to produce that configuration of

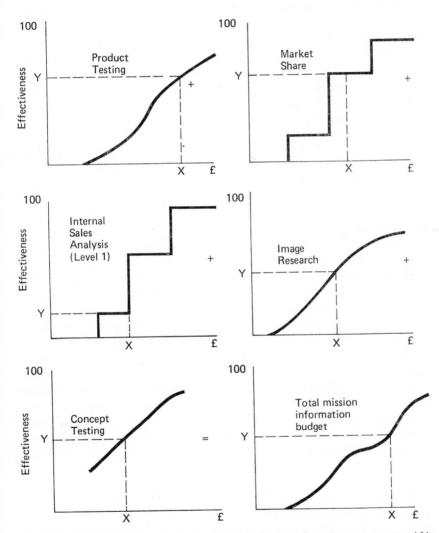

FIG. 2.10 *Hypothetical cost/effectiveness functions for five information components within a mission product portfolio.*

allocation of the £50,000 budget which maximizes total cost-effectiveness. It is this process which we have termed 'zetetic programming'.

It has been discussed elsewhere[13] how a 'value-function' for information (components) may be postulated and related to the total cost of providing that information. Expenditures on marketing information were considered in terms of their marginal addition to the total value of research—the point of optimal cost-effectiveness being reached where the marginal cost of providing that information equalled the marginal value that it gave the firm. A major operational problem is that marketing researchers are not noted for their attempts to place a value on the research they undertake; and certainly it would be, as we have seen, misleading to equate the cost of the research with its perceived value. It could be more or less. Rather the value of information components must be measured in the harder terms of how they contribute to stated information missions. Thus if we are considering a test market prior to making a national go/no-go decision for a new product, the crucial determinant of the test market's value is: what is the size of the possible loss it can help us avoid?[14] On the other hand, assessing the value of a technological forecast can only be seen in terms of its general contribution to the identification of opportunities and threats over the time horizon of the corporate mission.[15]

Derived value against time

One frequently occurring evaluation problem is the question: do we buy research or do we do our own? This buy-or-make decision crops up regularly in all areas of the business operation and its resolution on the research front can be achieved by a similar approach to its resolution in these other areas. The question is basically what is the opportunity cost of doing our own research?—that is, what resources will it tie up within the company and will it be as effective as external research in meeting the mission goal(s)? If it seems, when taking a total view, that it will probably cost more to perform internally and/or its effectiveness will be inferior, then the answer is clear-cut. A similar analysis can fruitfully be applied to the maintenance of a company library or a current-awareness service—here the pertinent question is: what is it costing us for the luxury of a 'real-time' service as against the cost of purchasing the information from external sources when needed, albeit with a longer lead-time for retrieval? We are already looking into how much more a university library service, giving almost immediate access to information is valued by its users, than one giving a reduced level of service through a smaller book-stock. The question here is: does this increase in perceived value by the users warrant the additional cost? The fundamental query we are posing goes well beyond the operational researcher's concept of a service level; it demands a measurable indication of derived value against time.

CONCLUSION

This chapter has sought to demonstrate an integrated pattern for corporate marketing activity. The interstices of the marketing and information functions of the business have been identified and a mission approach suggested for global research budget setting. The budget allocation problem as between various information activity components has been discussed and ordinal ranking, cardinal ranking and zetetic programming proposed as three increasingly sophisticated levels for its resolution.

We have emphasized our firm belief that, although the valuation of the service that the information function provides will always remain a hazardous affair, attempts to wrestle with it are long overdue. The very act of wrestling, we feel certain, will of itself bring considerable benefits in the identification of information priorities and the examination of the cost-effectiveness of various specific levels of expenditure.

REFERENCES

1. Williams, A., *Output budgeting and the contribution of micro-economics to officers in government*. CAS Occasional Paper No. 4. HMSO, 1967.
2. Fisher, G. H., *Some comments on programme budgeting in the Department of Defense*. The RAND Corporation RM-4279-RC (September 1964).
3. HMSO, *Economic Progress Report No. 8*, October 1970.
4. Smalter, D. J. and Ruggles, R. L., 'Six business lessons from the Pentagon', *Harvard Business Review,* **44**(2), March/April 1966.
5. Dougharty, L. A., 'Developing corporate strategy through planning, programming and budgeting', *Long Range Planning,* **2**(3), March 1970.
6. Medcalf, G., *Marketing and the brand manager*. Pergamon Press, 1969.
7. Peterson, R., 'New venture management in a large corporation', *Harvard Business Review,* **45**(3), May/June 1967.
8. Christopher, M. G., *Total distribution: a framework for analysis, costing and control*. Gower Press, 1971.
9. Smith, H. M. and Levitz, W., 'Commercial intelligence and the computer', *Computer Operations,* October 1968.
10. This dichotomy was first proposed in Hayhurst, R. and Wills, G., *Organizational design for marketing futures* (Part 4). George Allen & Unwin, 1972.
11. Wills, G., 'Marketing research in British industry', *Proceedings from the 14th Annual Conference of The Market Research Society,* March 1971.
12. Borden, N., 'The concept of the marketing mix', in Schwarz, G., *Science in marketing*. Wiley, 1965.
13. Christopher, M. G. and Wills, G., 'Cost/benefit analysis of company information needs', *UNESCO Bulletin for Libraries,* **XXIV**(1), January 1970.
14. Wills, G., 'Cost/benefit analysis of a test market', in *Exploration in marketing thought* (Chap. 11). Crosby Lockwood for University of Bradford Press, 1971.
15. Wills, G., *Technological forecasting: the art and its managerial implications*. Penguin Books, 1972.

CHAPTER 3

The Future Structure of Marketing Information Systems

This chapter is based on a series of enquiries conducted since 1966. Despite the growing membership of the two United Kingdom professional bodies which concern themselves particularly with marketing research, its practice in British industry today is in a poor condition by almost any standard one cares to identify. It is poor, not because of any lack of professionalism in the way the studies are conducted, but because of two failures: first, the failure to regard research as anything other than a fragmentary operation; secondly the failure, after many years, to secure the correct role for marketing intelligence within corporate structures. We have quite simply failed to accomplish the implementation of conceptually valid approaches which have been widely known since the early fifties. The distance which all but a handful of British-based companies stand from the ideas which are conceptually exciting today is virtually unmeasurable.

Taking stock has proved difficult and the task has not altogether been completed to our entire satisfaction. However our strategy has been to conduct extensive fieldwork with all British companies which had an annual sales turnover of £¾ million or more in 1967 (the latest year when we commenced work for which the Board of Trade statistics were available). The evidence which we collected from 553 companies in that study constitutes the main body of this report. It was collected within a survey framework which embraced the totality of corporate marketing operations, and the complete picture is reported upon elsewhere.[1,2] In addition, the classic BIM Pilot Study conducted in 1960, with 86 companies,[3] was replicated in 1969 to unearth any indication of movement and progress during the past decade.[4] (Survey response levels and universe details are provided in Appendix 1.)

We shall outline our findings and conclusions in three sections—The Firms Who Do; The Firms Who Do Not; and The Comparative Statics of 1960–1970–1980.

THE FIRMS WHO DO

Three-quarters of all firms we interviewed reported that they do carry out marketing research activities. Fig. 3.1A indicates that the proportion was highest in consumer-goods companies at 80%, and lowest within the services sector. Even there, however, fully 50% reported some activity. Propensity to undertake some marketing research work can be seen as highly correlated both with sales turnover and with total number of people employed in the business. The most backward industry sector can be seen as retailing, closely followed by construction. Textiles and printing also make a relatively poor showing.

If most firms with a turnover above £¾ million claim to undertake marketing research from time to time, they most certainly do not have the aid of a full-time marketing research executive or officer.

Fig. 3.1B indicates that only 28% of companies had a full-time executive devoting his undivided attention to marketing research issues. Consumer-goods manufacturers put in no more statistically worthy a record than their industrial peers. Size undoubtedly tended to be correlated with such a full-time appointment having been made but even in the £25–£49·9m turnover group, barely 50% of all firms had such a person in post.

Of the 162 firms which have a full-time research executive in our sample, the majority report that the post was established more than three years prior to our fieldwork, that is, pre-1966. However, 43% of all appointments had been made in the last three years.

Fig. 3.2 sets out the sequence of appointments. At the rate of new additions currently being made, some twenty new full-time posts per annum amongst our sample, it will be 1991 before all the firms we sampled have just a single full-timer on their staffs.

Such full-time jobs as do exist currently are generally styled market research manager (32%) or officer (19%). Three-quarters of all such employees had written down job descriptions and reported to the marketing director or

	(%)
Less than one year (that is, 1968/9)	13
1966–8	30
1964–6	20
1959–64	23
Pre-1959	14

FIG. 3.2   *How long companies have had someone responsible for marketing research on a full-time basis* (N = 162).

	A. Do you carry out any MR activity?	B. Does anyone have full-time responsibility for MR?
	No. of firms	% Yes	% Yes
TOTAL ALL FIRMS	553	74	28
Nature of business activity			
Consumer goods	189	80	32
Industrial goods	278	75	30
Distributors	40	60	8
Service industries	28	50	11
Others	18	56	33
Sales turnover in 1967			
£¾m–£0·999m	57	47	0
£1m–£4·9m	257	71	20
£5m–£9·9m	96	79	36
£10m–£24·9m	66	86	43
£25m–£49·9m	27	100	55
£50m and over	19	100	89
Not established	31	61	27
Number of employees			
Less than 250	93	55	3
250–499	113	66	17
500–999	138	75	28
1,000–2,999	120	84	38
3,000–4,999	33	88	45
5,000 and over	41	95	71
Not established	15	60	31
Industry sector (*where base* > 9)			
Food	10	70	30
Chemicals and allied industries	61	93	41
Metal manufacture	22	68	40
Non-electrical engineering	91	79	37
Electrical engineering	33	87	21
Vehicles	19	65	30
Metal goods	36	83	28
Textiles	51	60	16
Bricks, pottery, glass, cement, etc.	27	66	26
Timber, furniture etc.	15	60	7
Paper, printing and publishing	31	78	45
Construction	17	53	12
Wholesale distribution	36	61	22
Retail distribution	26	52	8

FIG. 3.1 *Marketing research activities.*

marketing manager. Although many firms took no view about formal reporting patterns for our man, 56% of all companies surveyed indicated that their chief marketing executive, however designated, exercised full responsibility for marketing research activities; the remainder either felt it should appropriately be shared with other senior executives or that it was not a germane activity for the company's senior marketing man.

It is also relevant at this juncture to interject an additional piece of information concerning the conduct of marketing research within the 553 firms which emerged in the context of an overall evaluation of the use of external agencies for a wide range of marketing services. Some 47% of all companies reported that they did use external contractors 'partly or occasionally', and 7% used them exclusively. Hence, just one-fifth of all companies relied entirely on their internal marketing research facilities (74% − [47% + 7%]).

Expenditure on marketing research

The total UK market value of marketing research services is a problem which has taxed the minds of many of us from time to time. We were able to collect from our 553 respondent companies some indication of the level of their expenditure during their preceding financial year—normally ending December 31st, 1968, but also April 5th, 1969 and on other significant dates. Fig. 3.3 indicates the level of spending by firms overall and within the conventional consumer/industrial dichotomy. The groupings are deliberately broad because in hardly any instance was a clear idea of exact expenditure available. This point is further reflected in the very low percentage of companies able to provide any estimate at all.

The figures which are presented, however, indicate the first major difference between consumer and industrial sectors. Very few industrial sector companies (12%) reported spending above £10,000 per annum on marketing research,

Total spending	All firms carrying out any MR (%) (N = 408)	Consumer goods (%) (N = 151)	Industrial goods (%) (N = 209)
Less than £10,000	33	17	35
£10,000–£19,999	10	13	7
£20,000–£29,999	4	5	4
£30,000–£39,999	2	5	0
£40,000–£49,999	1	1	0
£50,000–£99,999	3	5	1
£100,000 and above	2	3	0
Not established	45	51	47

FIG. 3.3   *The total cost of marketing research activities in the last financial year.*

compared with 32% of consumer-goods companies. No companies in the below-£1m sales turnover group spent £10,000, but only half the firms in the largest sales turnover category (£50m and above) spent £20,000 or over during the year under review.

The total expenditure within the companies in our sample which undertook marketing research and reported their expenditure was £5m or a company mean somewhat better than £20,000. If we assume that all companies which undertook research but made no report of expenditure were identical to those which did report, we could certainly begin to put an upper ceiling on the value of marketing research services. This indicates an estimated total expenditure amongst our 408 companies of (408/225) × £5m, say £9m. This is also our total estimate of all marketing research expenditure amongst the 553 firms in our sample, since no other reported any activity in this field.

The market value estimate is completed by multiplying £9m by the proportion of the total universe of turnover which our sample of 553 constitutes in its total population—approximately one-quarter. Our best estimated ceiling of expenditure for 1968/9 is accordingly some £36m.

An additional basis for computation of the expenditure ceiling is available in the replication of the BIM 1960 study which Alan Slater documented in 1969.

Fifty-seven companies, which together had an annual turnover of £3,612,500,000 in 1968 amongst their universe total of £36,000m for the same year, spent a total of £3,210,000 on marketing research during that year. Slater's ceiling estimate is accordingly of the order of £32m for total value of marketing research services in 1968/9. Slater further furnishes evidence that, of his companies' expenditure, £1,896,000 was for externally contracted work as opposed to £1,314,000 carried out internally.

That these estimates are ceilings is evident because a considerable proportion of total value of UK sales is produced by companies with an annual turnover below £¾m. We have a range of indications in this study already reported that increasing size and sales turnover are correlated with increasing marketing research expenditures. It is therefore perhaps more helpful to ignore all companies with turnover below £¾m per annum and to identify our 553 companies as proportionate simply of the universe from which they were selected; that is, some one-third of all relevant turnover giving a total estimate of market value for our services of £24m–£28m. This leaves as our only outstanding assumption that our non-respondent companies in our total universe were no different from the 553 who replied. We did do a 5% telephone check on them; they did not seem or sound different—we must leave it to you to adjudge. Certainly our market seems bigger than the £12m–£15m often talked about, and it is probably split in the ratio of 40% internal work; 60% externally sub-contracted.

The profile of marketing research activities

Fig. 3.4 sets out the pattern of involvement by the 408 companies conducting some marketing research in various areas of evaluation and analysis. With the exceptions of retail audits, measurement of special-offer effectiveness, copy research and test marketing, a majority of firms undertake each of the activities indicated. The most noticeable sub-contracted elements are in the field of advertising research, new products and market analyses. Companies are particularly prone to undertake, exclusively within their own organization, matters affecting sales activities.

The simultaneous use of internal and external facilities is noticeably greater in all activities than exclusive sub-contracting, save within the

	Not carried out	*Carried out internally*	*Carried out externally*	*Carried out both internally and externally*
Studies of acceptability and potential of new products	15	48	6	24
Studies of present products *v.* competition	13	56	7	17
Packaging research	41	23	6	11
Research on competitors' products	21	53	4	9
Product testing, blind products tests	34	33	6	11
Assessment of market potential	13	52	6	16
Determination of market characteristics	18	45	8	16
Market share analysis	13	53	11	16
Studies of market changes	30	37	9	12
Sales analysis	6	79	1	9
Establishment of sales quotas	24	65	—	3
Establishment of sales territories	21	67	1	3
Studies of effectiveness of salesmen remuneration	39	43	2	8
Analysis of effectiveness of channels of distribution	40	39	2	7
Distribution cost studies	35	46	2	5
Test marketing	51	22	2	11
Retail audits	65	6	9	5
Measuring effectiveness of special offers	61	15	2	5
Copy research	58	9	12	7
Media studies	49	12	17	9

FIG. 3.4   *Percentage of companies which carried out the listed market research activities during* 1968 ($N = 408$).

advertising field. Even here internal checks are present. Fig. 3.4 simply shows some involvement in the areas indicated. Fig. 3.5 gives a measure of the extent to which the total marketing research budget is allocated in various fields of interest. It will be seen that Fig. 3.5 affords but fragmentary evidence. Once again, inadequate records made the identification of proportional allocation often quite impossible. We can do little more here than derive a

Proportion of MR budget (%)	PERCENTAGE OF FIRMS (N = 408) SPENDING ON			
	Product research	Total market	Sales and distribution	Advertising and promotion
0–9	2	2	7	—
10–19	8	4	5	12
20–29	9	10	7	5
30–39	4	5	3	1
40–49	5	6	3	1
50–59	8	8	3	1
60–69	2	4	1	1
70–79	3	2	—	1
80–89	2	2	—	3
90–100	2	2	1	11
Percentage of firms reporting:	45	45	30	36

FIG. 3.5 *Proportion of total market research expenditure on specific areas of marketing activity.*

few hypotheses for future analysis—most obviously perhaps that, given the present state of affairs in British companies, a greater slice of any available budget goes on product and total market research than on sales distribution or promotional research.

A somewhat clearer picture emerges in Fig. 3.6, however, in reply to our enquiry as to the allocation of budgets between various techniques. The two most-used techniques are *ad hoc* surveys and qualitative investigations. More firms also allocate a greater proportion of their budget to *ad hoc* studies than to techniques which can afford a sustained flow of marketing information.

This particular observation is deliberately noted here; it is symbolic of the general situation which we have reviewed. Its other salient features are few full-time marketing research executives with very poorly organized budgetary approaches. The overall perspective is dismal. *Ad hoc* marketing information is no basis for effective marketing performance in the seventies or eighties.

Our final information on techniques employed is explicable in terms of our

Proportion of MR budget (%)	PERCENTAGE OF FIRMS (N = 408) SPENDING ON					
	Qualitative research	Trade/ retail audits	Customer panels	Customer surveys	Ad hoc surveys	Experimentation
0–9	4	3	5	3	4	6
10–19	7	2	5	4	8	7
20–29	6	5	2	5	10	4
30–39	4	2	2	4	4	2
40–49	1	1	—	3	2	1
50–59	1	4	1	3	3	—
60–69	2	1	—	1	2	—
70–79	1	1	1	1	2	—
80–89	1	—	—	—	2	—
90–100	—	—	—	2	5	—
Percentage of firms reporting:	27	19	16	26	42	20

FIG. 3.6   *Techniques used in terms of expenditure on each as a proportion of the total research expenditure.*

continuing interest since 1966 in marketing experimentation and especially in test marketing.[5]

Fig. 3.7 indicates the pattern of usage of that particular technique and demonstrates some important differences in the pattern of its deployment. The relatively high level of usage in consumer-goods industries is less remarkable than the flattening-out of its incidence for around 40% of all companies in all turnover categories of £5m and above. The inter-industry comparisons are also worthy of note and the surprisingly high incidence of tests for industrial goods.

THE FIRMS WHO DO NOT

One-quarter of all companies with annual turnover of £¾m or more do not carry out any marketing research. Nearly three-quarters of all companies with at least that turnover floor have no full-time marketing research executive in their employ. We might well wonder how they survive; especially the not-inconsiderable numbers of very large companies indeed who fall short on these two issues (*see* Fig. 3.1).

There are two readily obvious explanations. The first, one which is likely to be valid on a reasonably broad basis, is that the cost/benefit of carrying out market research is insufficiently attractive. This will certainly be true of a

	No. of firms	% Yes
TOTAL FOR ALL FIRMS	553	30
Nature of business activity		
Consumer goods	189	50
Industrial goods	278	21
Distributors	40	23
Service industries	28	14
Others	18	39
Sales turnover in 1967		
£¾m–£999,999	57	14
£1m–£4·9m	257	25
£5m–£9·9m	96	37
£10–£24·9m	66	41
£25m–£49·9m	27	41
£50m and over	19	47
Not established	31	26
Industry sector (where base > 9)		
Food	10	70
Chemicals and allied industries	61	43
Metal manufacture	22	32
Non-electrical engineering	91	26
Electrical engineering	33	33
Vehicles	19	31
Metal goods	36	14
Textiles	51	25
Bricks, pottery, glass, cement, etc.	27	33
Timber, furniture, etc.	15	20
Paper, printing and publishing	31	23
Construction	17	18
Wholesale distribution	36	33
Retail distribution	26	19

FIG. 3.7 *Number of firms to have tested new products by marketing them in a restricted geographical area.*

considerable number of the smaller companies in our sample, and even more so amongst those we have excluded with turnovers below £¾m per annum.

The second obvious explanation is ignorance of the benefit likely to accrue from such an activity as the MR profession affords. (Certainly in our work as marketing educators we meet many members of medium-sized and surprisingly large companies in this category. An interesting cross-analysis with background information on our 553 companies' chief marketing executives shows that 83 % of those who have attended educational courses in marketing use marketing research as against 50 % who have not.) Ignorance of what we

Attitude statement	ATTITUDE OF CME IN COMPANIES WHO DO NOT (N = 145)					
	Strongly agree	Agree	Undecided	Disagree	Strongly disagree	Not established
The marketing man's job is simply to sell what the works produce	1 (1)	15 (6)	3 (1)	36 (29)	34 (61)	11 (2)
Our main task is to increase sales volume; profits will follow naturally	4 (2)	22 (12)	8 (2)	42 (43)	19 (39)	5 (32)
A well-made product will sell itself	3 (0)	14 (8)	4 (1)	60 (61)	13 (28)	6 (2)
Diversification policies should build on existing company resources	5 (5)	52 (60)	16 (12)	14 (18)	3 (2)	10 (3)
Provided we are selling a planned level of production we should not be too concerned with trends in the total market	0 (0)	6 (4)	5 (2)	64 (51)	14 (42)	10 (1)
Further increases in profitability will be attained mainly by more efficient production	7 (3)	40 (27)	8 (6)	30 (46)	6 (14)	9 (4)
In our type of business we know the market too well to need marketing research	2 (0)	22 (4)	16 (4)	42 (54)	10 (36)	8 (2)

N.B. The percentages in parentheses throughout are the comparable attitudes of CMEs in companies that do carry out some marketing research (N = 408).

Fig. 3.8 *Attitude statements.*

have to offer is a function of at least two elements: the recipient's predisposition to learn and our effectiveness at stimulating any learning. Lack of predisposition to learn is normally associated with a good profit record without bothering; and hence we may need to bide our time in certain cases. But there must also be a great task of ignorance reduction still ahead of us. For that task, we felt it would be useful to report the attitudes of the chief marketing executives amongst the firms who do not do marketing research as well as inviting you to read Figs. 3.1–3.7 in the opposite light to that which our earlier remarks have emphasized.

We administered a battery of attitude statements to our respondents, whose views are described in Fig. 3.8. In parentheses below each score are the comparable attitudes of users of marketing research. Fig. 3.9 looks further at the attitudes of firms who do not use marketing research in a cross-analysis against definitions of marketing.

Summary of definition given	PERCENTAGE OF FIRMS WHO	
	Do not do MR ($N = 145$)	Do some MR ($N = 408$)
Satisfaction of customer needs profitably	9	22
Satisfaction of customer needs	10	15
Selling	23	9
List of functions (all or most)	8	9
The total business operation	9	8
Market research	5	5
Advertising and promotion	10	4
The coordinative element in the firm	1	5
The four Rs—right goods, place, time and price	2	4
Textbook quotes (for example, Institute of Marketing)	0	4
Not answered	23	15

FIG. 3.9   *What firms understand by the term marketing.*

We do not wish to over-interpret these two sets of information. It seems to us, however, that both the attitude measurements and the definition assessment of our non-researching companies indicate a less than total orientation towards what we normally accept as 'good marketing'. On almost all important dimensions the doers of research diverge in their attitudes from the non-doers—not dramatically, but significantly. Perhaps most starkly in the definitional assessment analysis, we find marketing viewed more as 'selling' by the non-doers than as anything else. For the doers, a good marketing definition wins the highest score.

The lesson to be learnt from these statistics is reasonably clear—MR professionals must further the cause of marketing in order to further the cause of marketing research.

THE COMPARATIVE STATICS OF 1960–1970–1980

If things frankly look none too rosy in the totality of British industry, they were less rosy in 1960 when the BIM Information Note reported on eighty-six companies. As we indicated earlier, Alan Slater returned to those eighty-six companies during 1969 to ask them what developments and changes had occurred during the decade. He found fifty-seven of them willing and able to respond; twelve unwilling and seventeen unable as a result of liquidations and takeovers. One-third of all responding companies reported that their marketing research organization either had been recently re-organized or was currently undergoing that process. (Sample details are included in Appendix 1.)

By 1969, only eight out of the fifty-seven companies were without a marketing research department. Four had abandoned departments which they previously operated (three in favour of an autonomous company; all of which were advertising agencies). The other four had never run such a department and had no intention of establishing one. This overall situation indicates a distinct movement from the start of the decade when twenty-two out of the fifty-seven had no such department. The fourteen additional departments amongst fifty-seven companies, a 25% increase, compares with twenty-three additional departments, or a 50% increase, in the fifties for this particular group of companies. The increase in the sixties was equi-proportional in industrial and consumer goods companies who responded.

Growth of marketing research expenditures
Fig. 3.10 shows the reported expenditure on marketing research in 1968 or 1969. The total expenditures are given and also the amount of that total which was spent 'outside'; that is, paid to marketing research organizations. The companies without marketing research departments reported that they did not spend any money on marketing research by outside firms.

Fig. 3.10 should only be taken as a guide to the amount spent on marketing research. It is worthy of note, however, that the 1969 figures for the average expenditure on marketing research per company are over twice the amount of the 1960 figures in the majority of cases. The exception is the average amount of marketing research expenditure by industrial goods manufacturers which has only risen from £20,600 in 1960 to £26,800 in 1969. The proportion of total expenditure spent 'outside' is higher in all cases in 1969 than it was in 1960.

Turnover (£m)	TOTAL		INDUSTRIAL GOODS MANUFACTURERS		CONSUMER GOODS MANUFACTURERS		DISTRIBUTION		ADVERTISING AGENCIES	
	Total	*Outside*	*Total*	*Outside*	*Total*	*Outside*	*Total*	*Outside*	*Total*	*Outside*
ALL FIRMS	3,210·3	1,896·2	723·3	198·2	1,861·5	1,264·2	280·0	206·3	345·5	227·5
Under 1	—	—	—	—	—	—	—	—	—	—
1–4·9	238·5	137·5	—	—	—	—	—	—	238·5	137·5
5–9·9	132·0	109·6	25·0	19·6	—	—	—	—	107·0	90·0
10–24·9	249·3	130·6	77·8	38·4	171·5	92·2	—	—	—	—
25–49·9	403·0	85·0	163·0	33·0	240·0	52·0	—	—	—	—
50–99·9	1,010·0	755·0	160·0	35·0	850·0	720·0	—	—	—	—
100–249·9	58·5	4·0	58·5	4·0	—	—	—	—	—	—
Over 250	1,100·0	669·3	220·0	63·0	600·0	400·0	280·0	206·3	—	—
Not stated	19·0	5·2	19·0	5·2	—	—	—	—	—	—
Number of firms with research departments	49		27		10		3		9	
Average expenditure per company in £000's										
1969	65·5	38·7	26·8	7·3	186·1	126·4	93·4	68·7	37·2	25·2
1960	34·6	12·9	20·6	4·6	66·0	30·4	—	—	17·9	4·4

FIG. 3.10 *Amounts spent on marketing research (£000) in Slater's 86 Company Group.*

	Increase in total expenditure (£000's)	Percentage increase in total on 1960 as a base	Increase in 'outside' expenditure (£000's)	Percentage increase in 'outside' on 1960 as a base
All firms	30·9	89	25·8	200
Industrial goods manufacturers	6·2	30	2·7	59
Consumer goods manufacturers	120·1	182	96·0	316
Distribution	—	—	—	—
Advertising agents	19·3	108	20·8	160

FIG. 3.11   Comparative average expenditures on marketing research 1960 and 1969.

The comparative average expenditures in Marketing Research in 1960 and 1969 are shown in Fig. 3.11. No account has been taken of inflationary effects. The expenditures shown are in money terms. Median expenditures within each turnover group are shown in Fig. 3.12.

Turnover (£m)	Industrial goods manufacturers	Consumer goods manufacturers	Distribution	Advertising agents
Under 1	—	—	—	—
1–4·9	—	—	—	30·0
5–9·9	25·0	—	—	53·5
10–24·9	10·0	25·0	—	—
25–49·9	25·5	120·3	—	—
50–99·9	18·5	425·0	—	—
100–249·9	29·2	—	—	—
Over 250	110·0	600·0	100·0 ·	—
Not stated	9·5	—	—	—

FIG. 3.12   *Median marketing research budgets* (£000) 1968/9.

Fig. 3.13 indicates the average marketing research expenditure as a percentage of turnover. Once again an increase in use of marketing research with size is partially apparent within consumer goods firms, but not within the industrial goods companies. We are speaking of only ten and twenty-seven firms respectively, however.

Fig. 3.14, however, seems to suggest a clearer distinction between industrial and consumer goods marketing research work in the pattern of sub-contract activities. The ratio of thirty inside staff work/seventy sub-contracted in consumer goods is totally reversed in the industrial goods sector.

The marketing research department's work pattern
The fifty-seven companies reported, as in 1960, on the range of studies they undertook in 1969. It showed very little change over the decade.

The work most frequently done (more than 60% of the companies reporting) was in connection with:

Acceptability of new products
Present products versus competition
Research on competitors' products
Development of market potentials
Determination of market
   characteristics
'Share of the market' analysis

Study of market changes
Sales analysis
Media studies
Short-range forecasting
Long-range forecasting
Studies in business trends
Profit analysis

Turnover (£m)	TOTAL	Industrial goods manufacturers	Consumer goods manufacturers	Distribution	Advertising agents
All firms	0·035	0·014	0·099	0·049	0·021
1–4·9	1·363	—	—		1·363
5–9·9	0·587	0·334	0·196		0·714
10–24·9	0·012	0·064	0·320		
25–49·9	0·119	0·062	0·567		
50–99·9	0·168	0·036	—		
100–249·9	0·167	0·167	—		
Over 250	0·052	0·029	0·168	0·025	—

Fig. 3.13   Average marketing research expenditures as a percentage of turnover.
(Turnover group midpoints were taken with the exception of over £250m where £375m was used.)

	TOTAL		Industrial goods manufacturers		Consumer goods manufacturers		Distribution		Advertising agents	
		(%)		(%)		(%)		(%)		(%)
All firms	3,210·3	100	723·3	100	1,861·5	100	280·0	100	345·5	100
Sub-contract	1,896·2	59	198·2	27	1,264·2	68	206·3	74	227·5	66
Own staff	1,274·1	40	499·1	69	583·3	31	73·7	26	118·0	34
Other	40·0	1	26·0	4	14·0	1	—	—	—	—

Fig. 3.14   Inside and sub-contracted allocations of marketing research expenditure (£000).

The above list is very similar to the 1960 findings; media studies and profit analysis have reached over 60 % but product testing has fallen away. The work done on export marketing research was very low but 7 % of the companies reporting stated that they had subsidiary companies undertaking specific research in the export marketing field. There is very little difference between the amount of work done by the consumer and industrial firms; but replies from the distributive sector are lower than the others.

Patterns of communication by the marketing research manager have seen a shift within the fifty-seven companies, away from the use of committees for new products and marketing planning. In 1960, 53 % of companies used that method but by 1969 it held in just 38 %. Planned schedules and informal discussions as a more clearly identified member of the marketing group have gradually replaced committees. Changed methods of communication seem to have occasioned little improvement in the extent to which recommendations in reports are acted upon. 'Occasionally/sometimes' is still the majority verdict on the use made of professional MR advice.

Finally, it is worth while to note that the fifty-seven companies followed up, which are responsible for some 10 % of all UK turnover in manufacturing industry, had marketing research departments with an average size of thirteen people, structured as:

	% ($N = 626$)
Managerial	14
Executive	28
Clerical	33
Fieldworkers (full-time)	19
Others	6

Thirteen per department is a drop from 1960, when the comparable number was seventeen. One-third of staffs today are university graduates. Salaries in 1968/9 were as indicated in Fig. 3.15 and show only modest rises since 1960.

Fig. 3.15 will be read with a mixture of disbelief and amazement. The problems we faced were a low response overall and complications in the

	Mean (£)	Highest (£)	Lowest (£)
All firms ($N = 626$)	1,325	3,500	625
Industrial goods ($N = 216$)	1,692	2,640	1,102
Consumer goods ($N = 202$)	793	2,120	625
Distribution ($N = 31$)	1,645	3,500	1,000
Advertising agents ($N = 177$)	1,317	2,000	1,173

Fig. 3.15 *Annual staff salaries in marketing research departments* 1968/9.

consumer goods field occasioned by three fairly substantial full-time field-force groups. Clearly, some of the managerial employees have declined to identify their salaries in the highest category on the questionnaires their secretaries were due to return to us.

What trends can we detect for the 1970s and 1980s?

From a comparison of the 1960 data with the 1969 survey a number of trends can be indicated for those companies reporting, which may reflect the general pattern throughout Britain.

There is evidence that the organizational structure of marketing research within the companies is being re-organized from marketing research within a central department only, towards central and divisional departments, especially among industrial goods manufacturers. This is partially due to the rapid development of corporate planning over the last ten years which has given rise to a demand for centralized marketing research particularly for forecasting and new product planning. This has given rise to a difference between demand on marketing research by the central department and by the divisional departments, which has led to a re-organization of marketing research to include special departments at the divisional level.

The demands for marketing research services come from a number of sources: the corporate planning function; the marketing planning function and the marketing departments. There have also been significant increases in the percentage of companies reporting undertaking studies into establishment of sales territories, effectiveness of channels of distribution, distribution costs and plant and warehouse locations—all of which reflect that research into distribution and services will increase in the future.

In 1969 the average money expenditure on marketing research per company is over twice the amount spent in 1960; one notable exception, however, being the average total amount of marketing research expenditure by industrial goods manufacturers, which only rose slightly. The proportion spent on commissioned work from 'outside' is higher in all cases. Expenditure on marketing research is rising rapidly, particularly for consumer goods manufacturers.

The average number of staff employed per company in marketing research dropped from seventeen in 1960 to thirteen in 1969; but the mean salary has risen slightly from £1,008 to £1,325 per employee.

All other conclusions of the 1960 survey still stand, the two most notable ones being the comparatively small number of companies engaged in export marketing research and the large percentage of research reports which are not acted upon by management.

How can we summarize the MR position at present? Poorly paid; little understood and acted upon; not even present in visible, institutional form in the vast majority of medium/large companies in British industry. We are highly professional to the point of sophisticated vanity, concentrating on the esoteric and ultra-sophisticated at the expense of entering the real mass-market for our services—if there is a mass-market there at all. Certainly marketing research has a slow, very slow, rate of diffusion. We are still, to use Everett Rogers's analogy, selling to the early majority. The rump of that early majority is not yet sold effectively let alone the late majority and the laggards. In the seventies, given the right marketing approach towards the sale of MR services the mass market lies within our grasp, a market worth £100m a year or more in conventional terms. We need a Japanese approach in the next decade as well as the traditional British unprofitable invest-ment at the frontiers of knowledge. 'Our customers can have any colour marketing research so long as it is black'.

Such a market breakthrough will, in our view, go hand in hand with the coming of age *within industry* of the marketing approach.

Though the marketing concept is now, intellectually, something of a bore, it is still news and hope for the future in many companies. Its intelligent operationalization will bring greater demands for marketing research services.

Equally important for marketing research will be the growing demands for our services in the larger companies which will increasingly dominate the economic scene. Growth in size and use of marketing research are highly correlated in our majority findings. Corporate planners, a group whose presence also appears to be correlated with size, have an increasingly voracious appetite for market facts and figures, as do good technological forecasters and financial analysts.

None of these remarks are intended to deny the existence of exciting, professionally advanced segments within the market for our services by 1980. To conclude, we will briefly examine the shape of one of the most widely tipped phenomena—the marketing intelligence system.

Marketing intelligence for 1980

We have seen that marketing research techniques have hitherto been largely used for the *ad hoc*, static analysis of marketing problems. Although in the field of fast-moving consumer goods such as groceries and pharmaceuticals such techniques as the retail audit and the consumer panel have given more potential for dynamism, these sectors have been uncharacteristic of the great majority of organizations. Marketing research has not, generally speaking, been employed to monitor the marketing environment on a continuing basis. However, an important shift in orientation within previously largely *ad hoc* users of marketing research, and the conversion of new organizations and service industries to the use of such techniques, has led to a considerable change in organizational requirements. This movement, involving a transformation of tasks, demands a reconsideration of organizational design in the seventies. We can identify a need for marketing data both in the planning and coordinating role in the area of marketing development, and a need for short-term market measurement data to guide operational marketing activities. The total process can usefully be conceptualized in an overall view of the marketing process within society and the role for a marketing intelligence system within it.

The total systems approach to marketing information is posited on a thorough analysis of intelligence requirements for the individual organization. Any normative statement of information needs must necessarily be arbitrary, but there can be no doubt that if it is to be increasingly effective as a starting point for systems design then the senior intelligence officer must necessarily be privy to the formulation of future directions for development by the business. Too frequently in the past decade the information function has failed to meet corporate intelligence needs due to insufficient warning of an impending demand such as that occasioned by a policy of market extension overseas or product line extension in the domestic market.

We have no wish to enter a plea that the information function in the business should necessarily have the answer to all marketing demands made upon it for the most unlikely information. Adequate cost/benefit analysis can show the service level at which information can be expected to be held. This does, however, require a careful analysis of the cost of bringing in information from without the corporate system and the implications to the company profit situation of any delays. It also demands a rigorous examination of the value of information to the business organization. Our work during the past five years on test marketing and experimental method in British industry already referred to, has shown us that a logical use is not always made of empirical research findings and that action is taken prior to the arrival of data which has been commissioned at considerable expense.[6] It is a field of activity which will demand great effort at refinement in the seventies if the problem of arriving at sensible intelligence budgets is to be grappled and coped with. Alan Slater has suggested a simplified model of the information and decision flows in a typical corporate marketing intelligence system[7] (Fig. 3.16).

One of the most significant transformations of information organization implicit in the systems approach is the conceptual integration of internally derived data and both styles of the externally derived—either specifically commissioned investigation reports or general data available to all in a competitive framework. The concept of a central information unit or data bank is then implicitly grafted onto the integrated data processing system of

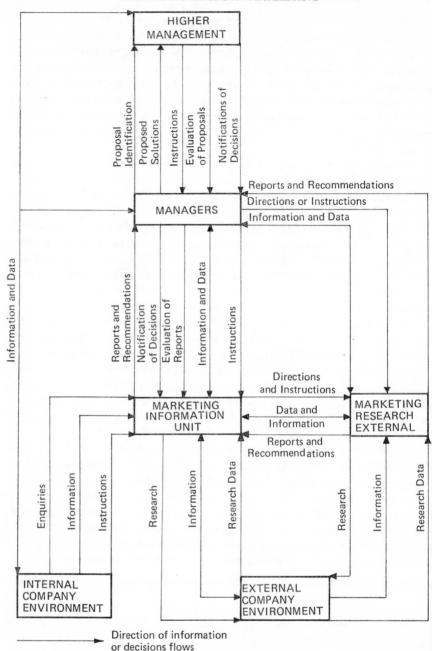

FIG. 3.16 *Model of information and decision flows for a marketing intelligence system*
(*after A. Slater*).

the fifties and sixties which carries out conventional analyses of customer accounts and sales, giving budget variances and the like.

The opportunity for interrogation of the information unit or data bank also arises and constitutes one of the most important additional strengths of marketing in the corporate power structure as it moves across the seventies. The models, the construction of which the creation of a data bank facilitates, will enable extensive simulation of marketing alternatives in planning future strategies as well as the accomplishment of sensitive response to short-term vicissitudes in the operational marketing sector of affairs. The response function of the market is, after all, the great unknown in business. The simulation potential will increasingly afford the opportunity to reduce the gross level of uncertainty under which any business operates although we would be the last to suggest it will remove the need for creative judgement in the context of simulation outputs.

The advantages of the central computerized holding of marketing information seem to us to outweigh the benefits which can be obtained by each division or product level of marketing activity maintaining its own monitoring procedures.

Hence, our postulated organizational framework isolates the marketing intelligence system from every main-line activity and proffers a staff service with a strong line liaison activity in operations. In particular, the liaison staff need to be men or women who comprehend the full scope of the marketing activity and see the research and data facility they provide as the servant of the line activity. This staffing requirement demands a new breed of marketing intelligence professional. Within the data bank core of the intelligence system activity, the specialist statisticians, mathematicians and computer experts are to be found.

The starting point for this type of structure is, of course, the operational and the development executives within the organization. It is their requirements which the intelligence system must meet and they, both through their chief marketing executive and through their own senior colleagues, must ensure that the intelligence objectives are clearly established and reviewed. Granted these premises, the cogency with which marketing activities can be directed in the decade before us will be grandly enhanced. Unless our marketing profession can truly see itself as the servant of marketing managements, however, our futures are likely to continue to be unsatisfactory and frustrating to ourselves and to fall short of meeting the national interest.

REFERENCES

1. BIM, *Marketing organization in British industry*. Information Summary No. 148, April 1970.

2. Hayhurst, R. and Wills, G., *Organizational design for marketing futures*. Allen & Unwin, 1971. This is the full report and includes a review of the future shape of marketing organizations which can be anticipated as necessary to accomplish the emerging tasks for marketing managers in British industry.
3. BIM, *Survey of marketing research in Great Britain*. Information Summary No. 97, 1962.
4. The direct comparison of results is reported in Slater, A., *A survey of marketing research in Great Britain*, University of Bradford Management Centre, 1970.
5. Papers have been presented in recent years to the 12th Annual Conference of the Market Research Society, *Test marketing in practice*, 1969; and to the 22nd Conference of ESOMAR/WAPOR, *Broadscale projection method from test marketing data*, Hayhurst, R. and Wills, G.
6. We have explored that issue in a number of other places, most particularly 'Cost–benefit analysis of a test market', reprinted in Seibert, J. and Wills, G., *Marketing research* (Penguin Books, 1970).
7. Slater, A., *The organizational structure for marketing information*. M.Sc. dissertation submitted to the University of Bradford, September 1970.

CHAPTER 4

Marketing Logistics

The developing science of marketing has gradually been extending the frontiers of its concern. The previous emphasis on marketing as a means of creating customers, identifying and anticipating market needs and building a franchise with the market-place, has proved to be too narrow in focus. The pursuance of marketing strategies and the definition of marketing goals without consideration for their impact elsewhere in the corporate system is a recipe for sub-optimization—in other words the effect of ignoring interfaces between marketing and other functional areas in the company is to produce disturbances elsewhere in the system such that total company performance is impaired. Nowhere is this tendency more noticeable than in the interface between marketing and distribution.

An alternative, integrative approach to the management and supply of markets based upon the recognition of the role of distribution in the company's marketing effort and by the development of a total systems approach to the company's activities, is *marketing logistics*.

DISTRIBUTION SERVICE—A KEY ELEMENT IN THE MARKETING MIX

The old cliché 'the right product in the right place at the right time' still has more than a ring of truth. Yet in fact this simple statement implies a degree of integration in our activities that few companies can claim. The conventional emphasis on the management of the marketing mix has tended to include distribution solely from a mechanistic point of view: 'if you can get the product there, we can sell it'. This view disregards the time and place utility that adds value to the product in the customer's eyes—an added value that comes only from distribution.

This added value is in essence *distribution service*. Distribution service is the key ingredient in devising logistics strategies; the rationale behind this viewpoint is two-fold.

1. The level of distribution service determines the degree of time and place utility contained in a company's product offering, the added value that is given by availability and the knowledge of a replenishment capability by

the company; this service offering may be perceived and reacted to in a variety of ways. To the motorist service may be perceived in terms of the nationwide availability of spare parts, to the car dealer it may be perceived in terms of how speedily his spare part stocks are replenished with a subsequent effect on his own inventory levels.

2. The level of distribution service will be a major determinant of total corporate costs. The higher the level of service the greater the number of deliveries and so on. In many companies with distribution perhaps accounting for 20% or more of all costs, the pressure is to reduce distribution costs with the concomitant problems of reconciling a high level of customer service with the lowest possible distribution costs.

The management problem can now be clearly seen. Do we view distribution as being an inevitable source of profit erosion and thus make distribution cost reduction the first priority? Or do we more sensibly see distribution as one further means of influencing demand for a product, of equal importance as the product's promotion, package and so on—in other words as a possible source of revenue generation? If we subscribe to the latter view new horizons open up. For example, perhaps by spending more on distribution we may so improve service that the increase in sales revenue more than balances the extra costs involved. Viewed in this light spending on distribution service is an investment with measurable pay-offs.

Distribution service can be provided in a number of ways, but primarily through delivery service and 'back-up' service.

Delivery service itself has two aspects. In the first instance it implies a concern with the length of the order cycle lead-time, in other words the elapsed period between a customer placing an order and his taking receipt of that order. Within this lead-time we may distinguish three separate activities:

1. Order transmission—the time taken for an order to reach the vendor.
2. Order preparation—the time taken by the vendor to prepare an order for dispatch.
3. Transport—the time elapsing between dispatch of the order and receipt by the customer.

The customer, over time, will build up some expectation about the order cycle lead-time and in addition he will be concerned with the second aspect of delivery service—consistency of lead-times. Consistency, or lack of it, can be a key determinant in the choice of supplier by a customer. There is evidence to suggest that a customer may be willing to accept longer lead-times, within reason, if they can be maintained with a high degree of consistency. Hence the importance of consistent lead-times.

The second element of distribution service is back-up service. Primarily this is the service that is provided by holding stocks of the items offered for sale. In the absence of this stockholding then either the customer must maintain his own stocks or he must accept a stock-out situation. Either alternative will involve the customer in additional cost, and by helping him avoid this cost the supplier is providing a tangible service.

Pervading both these aspects of distribution service is the attempt to meet customer requirements. Whether these requirements be for deliveries at specific times or for orders to be delivered on pallets, by attempting to meet them as nearly as possible we are improving our service offering.

SERVICE IS THE ABSORPTION OF OUR CUSTOMERS' COSTS

It will be apparent that the provision of distribution service will involve the distributing company in possibly quite large expenditures. In fact it can be demonstrated that once the level of service increases beyond the 70/80% mark, the associated costs increase far more than proportionately ('service level' reflecting the percentage of orders that can be met from stock within a given period). Fig. 4.1 demonstrates the typical exponential service cost function.

The implications of this cost function for the distributing company are worth some attention. In the first place, many companies are simply unaware of what level of service they are operating at—let alone have any laid-down service policy. Even if the company does have a declared service policy it is

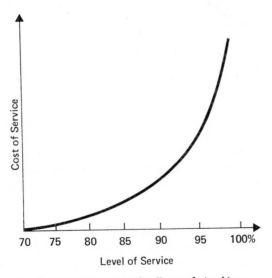

FIG. 4.1   *The service level/cost relationship.*

often the case that service levels have been arbitrarily set. The effect of offering a 97% level of service instead of a 95% level may have only a slight effect on customer demand, yet it will have a considerable effect on distribution costs—for normally distributed demand this 2% increase in the level of service would lead to a 14% increase in inventory investment alone!

This disturbing feature of distribution costs is at the hub of cost-effective service management. To re-emphasize a point made earlier: *management must be certain that the marketing advantage of an increase in service more than outweighs the additional costs.* However, what little empirical research

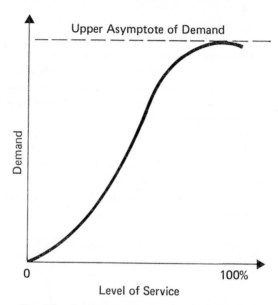

Fig. 4.2   *Customer response to distribution service.*

there is has tended to suggest an S-shaped response curve to distribution service—that is, at the very high levels of service the customer just cannot distinguish between small increments in the level of service.[1]

The requirement for marketing management is that it must recognize the cost implications of a service strategy. Indeed it is possible to go further and to suggest that by offering distribution service we are in fact absorbing a cost that would otherwise have been borne by the customer. For example, if we deliver twice a week instead of once a week, we are relieving our customers of a certain responsibility for holding stock—the more frequent our deliveries, the less stock he needs to hold. Similarly if the customer knows that when he places an order with us we will rarely be out of stock on that item, then again his stockholding can be lower. Because it costs money to hold stock—perhaps as much as 20% of its value a year—we are absorbing this customer cost by our service offering.

Marketing and sales managers, therefore, who insist on offering maximum service to all customers, whatever their profitability and wherever their location, are quite probably doing the company a disservice. By carefully reviewing customer service policy, perhaps even introducing differential service levels for different products or for different customers, marketing can enhance its contribution to corporate profitability.

Such an approach calls for realignment and a reappraisal of the conventional role of marketing in the company. As long as the marketing department is judged for performance in terms of sales and market shares, there will be a tendency to push distribution service costs into someone else's cost centre. Indeed if distribution costs are not a consideration in the marketing budget this tendency is perfectly understandable.

To overcome the problems caused by this compartmentalization of the corporate effort a new, integrative approach to marketing and distribution has appeared—this new orientation is the 'logistics concept'.

LOGISTICS IS AN INTEGRATIVE ACTIVITY

The emphasis behind the logistics concept is on systems. It suggests that the 'movement' activity in a company is so wide-reaching and pervasive in its impacts that it should be considered as a total system. Thus instead of marketing, production, distribution, purchasing, etc. all working away oblivious of the others and attempting to optimize their own activity, the logistics concept suggests that it may be necessary for some, or all, of these areas to operate sub-optimally in order that the whole system may be more effective. So, for example, the marketing manager must be prepared if necessary to accept a lower level of service than he would really like; or the production manager must be prepared to schedule shorter runs with more changes, if the overall effectiveness of the system is to be maximized.

To move this concept from the realms of theory to those of practice involves a consideration of the areas of concern to logistics management. There are five key decision areas that together constitute the 'logistics mix'.

Facility decisions
Inventory decisions
Communications decisions
Unitization decisions
Transport decisions

Together these five areas constitute the total costs of distribution within a company. Further, however, it is frequently the case that a decision taken in one area will have an effect on the other four areas. Thus a decision to close a depot (a facility decision) will affect the transport costs, the inventory allocation and perhaps data processing costs—this is the idea of a 'cost trade-off'. Managing the logistics function involves a continuous search for such trade-offs, the intention being to secure a reduction in total costs by changing the cost structure in one area.

The important feature of this logistics mix concept is that 'transport' is seen as being just one element amongst five. Conventionally in many companies transport *is* distribution; yet viewed in this total sense it may be that it accounts for only a small proportion of total logistics costs.

Logistics can provide an integrative force in the company's activities in three major ways:

1. Logistics brings sub-systems together.
2. Logistics mirrors the marketing missions of the firm.
3. Logistics improves the efficiency of materials and information flows.

Bringing sub-systems together
One of the major problems of conventional approaches to distribution is that responsibility for it is spread over many discrete functional areas. It has already been suggested that a too-heavy emphasis on compartmentalization in the company leads to sub-optimal situations overall. In one company responsibility for stock levels throughout the system was in the hands of the production department; yet at the same time the purchasing manager was pursuing policies which conflicted with production policy, the distribution manager operated an inflexible delivery system and the marketing manager was driven to despair with the erratic service levels that resulted. All this came from a failure to take a systems approach to the logistics function within the company.

The acceptance of the integrative, systems-based approach that characterizes

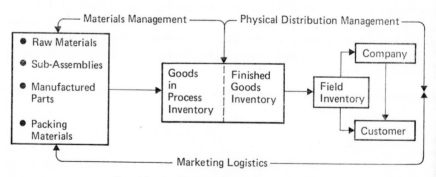

FIG. 4.3 *Logistics management: a paradigm.*

the logistics concept implies a recognition that there is an interrelationship between the parts of the whole of such a nature that action affecting one part must affect all others. Any action taken must therefore be considered in the light of its effects on all parts of the business and on the overriding objectives of the company. Thus the company can be viewed as a number of interlinked sub-systems which must somehow be united if overall effectiveness is to be maximized. The distribution planner under this new orientation must be concerned with the flow of materials through the whole business process, from raw material through to the finished goods arriving at the customer's premises.

Fig. 4.3 brings together those aspects of the company's operations involving flows, either of materials or information, which are the core concern of an integrated approach to logistics management.

Thus, while physical distribution management is concerned only with those flows from the end of the production line to the consumer, the integrated approach of logistics encompasses the total flow of materials and related information into, through, and out of the corporate system.

The missions approach to distribution
Recently a good deal of attention has been paid to the organizational and accounting concept of 'output budgeting'. Essentially this concept suggests that whereas traditional organizational and accounting structures are designed along functional lines, it is more appropriate to organize and control along 'mission' lines. That is, an acknowledgement is made that business is not about using up inputs but about creating outputs and therefore it is logical that our thinking should be in terms of outputs first and inputs second.

A distribution mission is a set of goals to be achieved by the system within a specific product/market context, the initial aim of the distribution planner being to specify closely the exact nature of the distribution mission(s) in which the company is involved. Such a statement of mission could be expressed in terms of the nature of the market to be served, by which products and within what constraints of service and cost. A mission by its very nature cuts across traditional company lines. The successful achievement of the mission goals involves inputs from a large number of functional areas and activity centres within the firm.

As may be gathered from Fig. 4.4, in order to achieve successfully the mission objectives, inputs of various kinds are required from the functional areas and activity centres within the company. Conventionally, however, all internal accounting has been on these functional lines, each department having a budget and a target. The various contributions (inputs) each function

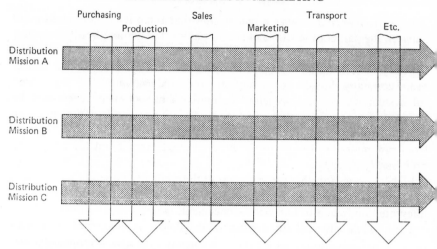

FIG. 4.4 *Distribution missions that cut across functional boundaries.*

was making to the mission (outputs) of the company are now clearly identified and costed.

The very nature of integrated logistics management requires that we now reverse the lines of accounting within the firm by examining the horizontal cost and revenue structures rather than concentrating on the vertical, functional structures. Fortunately in recent years a method of accounting has been developed which enables us to do just this—output budgeting.

	Activity Centre 1	Activity Centre 2	Activity Centre 3	Activity Centre 4	Total Mission Cost
Mission A	100	90	20	80	290
Mission B	50	70	200	20	340
Mission C	70	30	50	70	220
Required Activity Centre Inputs	220	190	270	170	850

FIG. 4.5 *The output budget.*

Fig. 4.5 illustrates how three distribution missions may make a differential impact on activity centre/functional area costs, and in doing so, provide a logical basis for budgeting within the company. As a budgeting method, output budgeting is the reverse of traditional techniques—a functional budget is determined now by the demands of the missions it serves.

Thus in Fig. 4.5 the initial analysis is horizontal by mission and the required inputs from each activity centre are determined—the functional budgets are determined as a result of this analysis by summing vertically.

More effective materials and information flow
One of the biggest, and seemingly most intractable, of the problems facing management today is the integration of related information and materials flows. It is all the more disturbing that it is only rarely recognized as a problem by management. Perhaps the reason for this failure to recognize the problem lies in the fact that the information flow within the logistics system is not always seen as being an essential component of the system, but rather it is seen as being quite separate. Thus the information system design may not parallel the logistics system design. To give an example of how this lack of integration can lead to a loss of efficiency in the total system, let us consider the following example.

The MGC company was concerned with the size of its 'accounts receivable.' In total its average collection period was sixty days which represented sales of £850,000. The terms which the company offered its customers were thirty days net. Initially the management of MGC interpreted these figures to mean that they had a major problem of slow payment. In fact when the situation was examined in greater detail it was found that on average fifteen of the sixty days were created solely by inefficiencies in MGC's own order processing and invoicing system. In other words it was taking fifteen days from the despatch of the goods from the warehouse to the customer actually receiving the invoice. Because of the involved accounting system used by the company, the conveyance of information about the despatch of an order took over a week to reach the attention of the accounts clerk. Further delays were then experienced before it was actioned. Finally there was the delay caused by transmitting the invoices through the post.

Because of the problem of part-orders it was not possible to invoice with the goods. The solution to the problem was found in the construction of a multi-copy order note which enabled an invoice to be prepared and to be sent directly on receipt of the confirmation of despatch from the warehouse—a confirmation which was now received with a maximum delay of one day. In all the fifteen days internal lead-time was reduced to an average of four.

The cost savings of this type of simple integration can be considerable. In the example of the MGC company a reduction in the collection period was made of 18% from sixty days to forty-nine days. This is equivalent to a freeing of cash of £125,000 (that is £850,000 × 18%). If we reckon that the cost of capital to this company is at least 15 % then this represents a minimum annual saving of £18,750.

There are many other similar possibilities for the integration of materials and related information flows. The despatch note can be used to trigger an invoice, which itself can be used as an automatic inventory control device. Information is the basic raw material of any logistics system, without it the system can only respond inefficiently and in a random, uncoordinated way. A major problem in the design of coordinated logistics/information systems is the problem of what is sometimes called 'reverse communications'. Whilst materials generally flow in one direction, the initiating information pulse is in the reverse direction—the order from a customer that initiates a despatch from the warehouse, the inventory status report that results in shipments from the plant to the warehouse, and so on. Here again leads and lags in the information system can lead to real costs being incurred. For example, if inventory recording is only carried out at discrete intervals—say once a week—then the average inventory on hand would be considerably greater than it need be. And with inventory costing up to 20 % per annum of its value just to hold, this simple lag in the system can be a major source of profit leakage.

There are many other examples of the inefficiencies that occur through a failure to integrate information and materials flows in the distribution system, but these suffice to demonstrate the need for a total logistics approach if for no other reason than that considerable cost savings can be achieved. However a more compelling reason is that 'reverse communications' is the very essence of distribution service. The provision of a responsive communications system is a major marketing weapon and one which is becoming of increasing importance as markets become more service conscious.

LOGISTICS IS A TOP-LEVEL CORPORATE CONCERN

The very nature of the total approach to distribution, requiring as it does a systems view of the corporate activity, implies the need for an integrated organizational structure. More than this, however, the ability of the firm to benefit from trade-offs between functional areas hinges to a large extent on the degree of top management commitment to the logistics concept. Without the wholehearted support of top management there can be no chance of introducing integrative policies which will probably involve individual sectional interests accepting less than optimal tactics. It is so much easier for, say, the purchasing manager to formulate his own set of goals based on his view of the business rather than on a total non-sectional basis.

It is interesting to note that those companies who have successfully introduced totally integrated logistics systems, Ford Motor Co. and Massey-
Ferguson are examples, generally started with a board-level appointment
charged with integrating the logistics activity. It was then possible to achieve
integration of policies at lower management levels.

The exact organizational structure that will be needed to facilitate the
introduction and operation of integrated logistics policies will obviously vary
from company to company. Different products and different markets will
have different requirements. Nevertheless one may generalize the basic
organizational requirements for logistics management. Fig. 4.6 suggests that
within the company's operating system decisions concerning logistics are
made at three levels: strategic, tactical and operational. The strategic decisions
are the decisions of a corporate nature: 'What markets do we wish to serve'
and so on. At the tactical level the decision-maker is concerned, for example,
with choosing between alternative systems for implementing the strategic
policy. Operational decisions, as the name suggests, involve day-to-day
situations and problem-solving—inventory levels, routing and so on. The

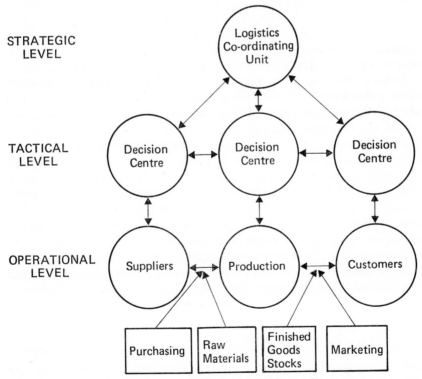

FIG. 4.6   *The hierarchy of distribution decisions and systems.*

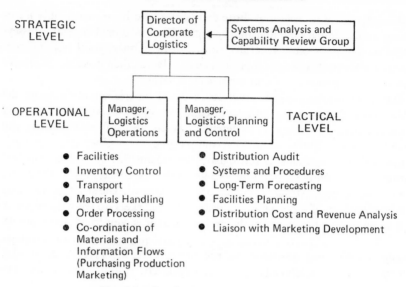

FIG. 4.7   *Coordinating the logistics function.*

fact that these levels are interdependent and that at each level decisions taken in one area will have impacts on others, implies that a means of coordination must be devised which is reflected in the company organization structure.

As far as the specific allocation of responsibility is concerned, then, one viable proposition is to distinguish organizationally between operations and planning/control tasks. Essentially the planning and control section is concerned with the future, whilst the operations section is concerned with today. The coordination of these two areas is achieved through a director of corporate logistics, or some such appointment, whose responsibility it is to translate corporate policy into logistics requirements. To aid in the evaluation and examination of the global impact of logistics strategies on the company and its marketing channel, the director can call upon the services of a systems analysis and capability review group. Fig. 4.7 suggests one way in which this operational/planning split might be achieved.

Slowly organizational patterns along these lines are beginning to emerge in some advanced companies in North America and Western Europe, and while individual structures may differ in detail from this generalized structure, it seems to hold considerable promise for widespread adoption.

SCENARIOS FOR THE FUTURE

The marketing and managerial impacts of the logistics concept are only now becoming fully realized. A number of innovations in this area are quite likely on the horizon; four of these possible developments are discussed here: the concept of a 'service package', the new profession of 'logistics management', the spread of the 'distribution service firm' and computerized coordination of materials and information flows.

The 'service package'

It has already been suggested that the provision of logistics service can have a major impact on sales. A logical development of this fact is the attempt to engineer cost/effective customer service by the construction of a 'service package'. Essentially all that this implies is that the firm adopts a total approach to its service offering. The company must identify all those interfaces where customer contact can be enhanced by service in any form and must consider all the costs and benefits accruing from such service offerings. Thus delivery service and consistency, returned goods policy, terms of trade, reverse communications and all the other manifestations of logistics service are considered together. More than this, however, the service package is consciously recognized as a marketing tool like any other, and it is used explicitly to develop sales. Similarly it is subjected to the same cost-effective scrutiny as any other marketing expenditure, for example, advertising.

The logistics manager

Already it is becoming apparent that a new breed of professional is appearing on the corporate logistics scene—the logistics manager. The logistics manager bears only slight resemblance to the traditional traffic manager or distribution manager—these positions still remain to supervise highly specialized tasks. The new logistics manager is as likely to be a corporate planner as he is to be a transport manager. His skills are in the planning of total systems, in the quantification of costs and benefits, and in the evaluation of logistics strategies. He will therefore be knowledgeable about facilities planning, inventory allocation, communications systems, transport mode decisions and unitization possibilities.

It is likely that the logistics manager of the future will have had formal training in marketing logistics management at graduate level. He will be recognized as a professional in his field exactly equivalent to the accountant or the marketing manager.

The distribution service firm

For many companies the operation of their own logistics system may not necessarily be cost-effective. Currently a number of North American companies are experimenting with a new approach. Essentially this new approach involves the 'leasing' of a distribution system from a company that specializes in the provision of distribution services. Such a company will offer its clients

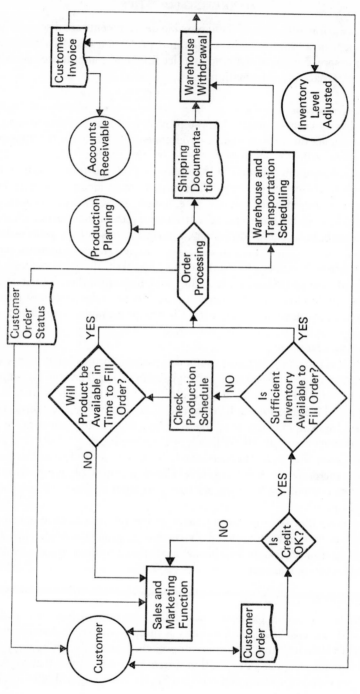

Fig. 4.8 *Computerized order processing (after B. J. La Londe).*

a complete logistics system comprising order processing, invoicing, inventory control, warehousing and transportation. Communication with the client company is via an on-line time-shared computerized information system.

For many companies with particular product/market characteristics it makes considerable sense to lease a service that would be beyond their financial capability to own. In the UK a number of companies, particularly in the public warehousing field, are beginning to move in this direction—becoming in fact 'distribution service' companies.

Computerized coordination of materials and information flows
As the movement towards total systems integration gathers pace the introduction of computerized coordination of all logistics flows will become essential. In many companies on-line inventory control is now an established activity. In such systems the computer maintains a continuous profile of inventory and automatically updates the situation as orders flow through the system. Similarly stock replenishment orders can be issued by the computer and re-order levels adjusted in the light of changed patterns of demand.

By means of teletype terminals the manager is able to interrogate the system at any time in a 'conversational' manner and receive accurate, up-to-date status reports on any aspect of the logistics system.

Fig. 4.8 gives one commentator's suggestion for a computerized order processing system that provides a continuous check on inventory investment.

The computerization of the total logistics system obviously poses considerable problems of implementation. However, a number of companies are now operating fully computerized systems, and because of the considerable savings in lead-times and the reduction in inventory levels that these systems provide, the benefits clearly outweigh the costs.

In this chapter an attempt has been made to describe the impact on the company's marketing effort of the total distribution concept. As more and more companies become aware of the tremendous promise of marketing logistics and as its profit improvement potential becomes apparent, it will become more and more an established part of the management scene. Whilst the number of European and even North American companies that have adopted the total logistics concept is still relatively small there can be no doubt of the growing interest that is being shown in the principles and practice of total distribution.

REFERENCE

1. Lewandowski, 'S-curves', *Industrial Marketing Management,* 1(2), pp. 132, 134, 377, 1971.

CHAPTER 5

Marketing and Distribution in Europe

Efficient, or seemingly efficient, distribution of goods and services is something most of us take for granted most of the time in western advanced economic systems. Yet, as catastrophes and wars have repeatedly shown, a distribution system is a sophisticated and often fragile institutional phenomenon. In the face of such fragility and sophistication we tend to over-compensate; we tend to generate excess capacity to meet almost any demand. Our understanding of channels of distribution and the complex relationships within them is accordingly adolescent rather than mature. During the coming decade, as the economies of the nine EEC countries seek to adapt to their rapidly changing environments, there seems little room for doubt that greater maturity will be necessary and that it will emerge. Here we seek to discuss two conceptual constructs as the basis for understanding movement from adolescence to early maturity. First, we explore the *total systems approach*; then we shall take a look at the use of the *comparative analytical method*.

THE TOTAL SYSTEMS APPROACH: THE CHANNEL

A channel of distribution comprises all the institutions involved in moving goods or services from producer to end-user or consumer. Identifying the optimum operating basis for such a set of institutions can only be accomplished by a combination of economic and behavioural analyses. Economic analysis illuminates, *inter alia*, the merits and demerits of sorting goods and breaking out quantities at various junctures; behavioural analysis illuminates, *inter alia*, the effectiveness of any particular channel member.

We can perhaps begin by making a simultaneous evaluation of the principles of postponement and speculation in a channel enunciated by Bucklin.[1] The principle of postponement suggests that efficient marketing channels will refrain from differentiation until the latest possible time and that changes in inventory location will likewise be postponed as long as possible. The actual postponement, of course, reduces risk by shifting it elsewhere. But risk cannot be eliminated merely by shifting it within the channel. Its obverse, the principle of speculation, posits that the movement of goods to forward inventories should be made at the earliest possible movement in the flow of exchange to reduce overall channel costs. The principle explains economies of scale in manufacture and reduces the disproportionately large costs of repetitive orders, their sorting and transportation. Finally, of course, by shifting risk to groupings of institutions which are better informed about their own next levels, it can reduce uncertainty. These two principles act as limits one on the other.

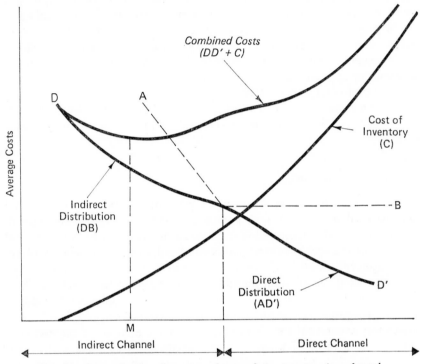

FIG. 5.1   *Determination of presence of a speculative inventory in a channel.*

To determine whether *an indirect channel with inventory holding* should logically appear, these two elements must be quantified. A speculative inventory will appear in the channel at each point where its costs are less than the net savings both to buyer and seller from postponement. Analysis is based on such cost functions relative to time. Fig. 5.1 describes the average cost functions for delivery of one unit of a commodity to a customer by indirect (DB) and direct (AD') channels, and the average inventory cost incurred in achieving such delivery (C), both functions in terms of delivery time. The combined cost curve (DD' + C) determines the channel mode which is optimum at the point of minimum average combined cost (M). Such theoretical analysis does, of course, ignore any customer service constraints we might seek to impose on the solution; these appear as a pattern of trade-offs which we shall explore more fully when we turn to examine total physical distribution system design.

The output of any marketing decision to use indirect channel members will be a normative specification for recruitment by salesmen. Existing marketing conditions, that is, competitive strengths already, may well prevent the enlistment of the most desired channel members. The converse problem occurs when more than one channel member is available as a potential agent for the product or service in question. The effectiveness of a channel member can be evaluated in terms of probable levels of performance of key tasks to which weights have been assigned. (Terry and Watson[2] have suggested a decision-tree approach to the problem.)

Attention to factor interactions must be paid, however, and this of course requires an extension of the pattern of analysis beyond straight total scores to an understanding of the effectiveness of various combinations of factor scores.

THE TOTAL SYSTEMS APPROACH: LOGISTICS

So far we have looked at illustrative aspects of the channel decision and emphasized that a total systems approach is important. Let us now turn to examine the total marketing logistics system as perceived by producer and intermediate channel members; that is, all the physical movements involved.

Management's traditional stance has been to analyse the separate exchange acts involved in distribution logistics and to exert pressure within each to reduce costs. This type of thinking has been especially applied in the fields of warehouse location studies and transportation. Only in the past decade has a satisfactory theoretical treatment emerged for the analysis of the exchange flows involved in distribution. It is now increasingly accepted that a total systems approach to the entire exchange flow, which seeks to minimize *total* costs within any set of management constraints deemed appropriate, is more effective. It cannot be too strongly emphasized that few firms attempt this pattern of total cost analysis: rather they treat the reduction of costs as a major goal at each level of flow regardless of its ramifications elsewhere within the system. Within the total system context, different activity centres are willing to trade off their own cost-minimization possibilities against superior gains at other levels. Fig. 5.2 indicates the nature of some of the cost functions encountered in ten discrete sectors as reported by Le Kashman and Stolle.[3]

These are combined to represent the total system cost function; it is where *this* attains its minimum that optimum warehouse capacity will be indicated. It can be clearly seen how optimal positions vary in the discrete cost areas.

A whole variety of trade-offs are potentially worth examination: shipping by air entails a high level of freight cost but will often occasion savings on packaging, insurance charges and inventory costs both in transit and held against demand for a given service level. These can sometimes make it the *least-total-cost* alternative. It is vital not to become mesmerized by the prospect of minimized total costs, however. Costs must only be reduced to

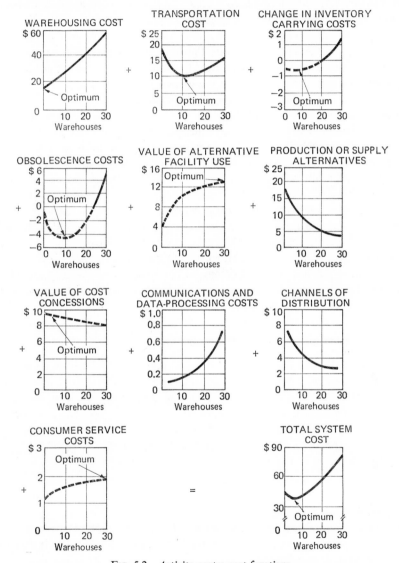

FIG. 5.2   *Activity centre cost functions.*

the level which is compatible with the profit objectives of the business; that is, within the constraints of customer service which management deems most appropriate. Logistics cost and service levels of performance, in terms of consistency of delivery, have a non-proportional relationship. Many firms offering 96% reliability of a twenty-four hour service will be involved in nearly *double* the cost of one affording forty-eight-hour service with a 90% consistency. Virtually immediate delivery can be afforded at greater cost by the proliferation of storage facilities at the sites of all customers. Whilst it can readily be recognized that there will be occasions when such high levels of service are appropriate, it behoves the marketing manager to avoid over-servicing his customers; that is, offering levels of service which are not justified in terms of overall profitability to the business.

A case can be logically argued for differential levels of service to customers in accordance with their importance to the business, and the level of service they can be potentially afforded by competitors. Sophisticated system design can encompass such differential requirements for different classes of customers. Bowersox and others have shown the way.[4] They proceed from an audit of the present distribution status of the organization in terms of product market profiles, competitors, and existing facilities to the determination of constraints and to model construction. The operational models most appropriate are simulations, and a range of static and comparative static formulations have been developed. Dynamic simulation is, however, the most powerful integrative technique. It relies on the sequential testing of the system model in terms of both data sets and flows or demands. Improved system arrangements are identified. The approach also incorporates feedback mechanisms to approximate to stability of the system.

DYNAMICS OF EUROPEAN DISTRIBUTION SYSTEMS

The great unknown for which distributors across Europe today must plan, however, is the period of EEC integration for nine nations. What can usefully be said of the likely future developments of distribution systems in the ten years to come? Perhaps the best analytical framework has been provided by Bruno Tietz of the Institute of Commerce at Saarbrücken University.[5] His model is reproduced as Fig. 5.3. Tietz identifies some seven general trends affecting retailing institutions, that is, offerers of retail goods:

(a) As far as size is concerned a further increase in large shop units may be expected. That will be true for shops with specialized assortment as well as for those not specialized.

(b) Many small businesses will be squeezed out of the market, medium-sized businesses—also in the food sector—will grow in absolute figures but lose relative significance.

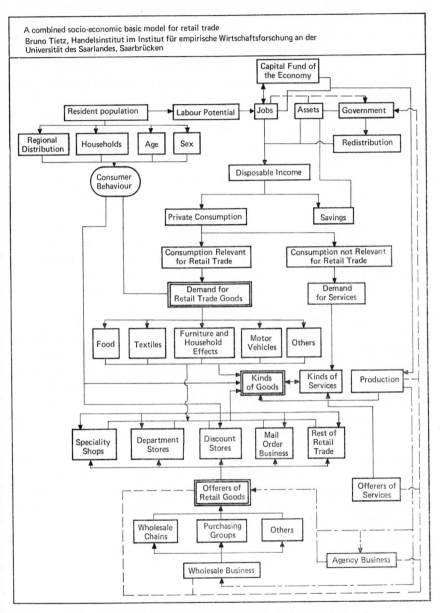

A combined socio-economic basic model for retail trade
Bruno Tietz, Handelsinstitut im Institut für empirische Wirtschaftsforschung an der
Universität des Saarlandes, Saarbrücken

FIG. 5.3   *A combined socio-economic basic model for retail trade.*

(c) There is a general trend in favour of a widening of the assortment in existing article groups; this is due to the differentiation of taste relating to existing items and to the emergence of new goods. In addition to this, there is a trend towards the regrouping of assortments combined with the elimination of existing specialization barriers.

(d) Speciality shops will combine their assortment with other establishments and thus create new assortments again and again. The general mixed-merchandise store, selling food, textiles and hardware, is expected to prosper at the expense of the special shops dealing with such lines.

(e) The relative share of low-price shops, especially with multi-line assortments, will rise considerably.

(f) Trends with regard to retail trade locations can be summarized as follows:

improvement of present locations by extending selling space and providing adequate space for movement and parking of individual motor traffic; creation of new retail trade locations in and outside the cities; to satisfy the increasing purchasing power, the city centres will keep their importance; for part of existing purchasing power, in order to ease traffic in the centre, new retail locations will emerge.

The last possibilities for extension of city centres will be used up during the decades to come: passenger and goods stations will be built over. Projects of this kind have been designed for Hamburg–Altona, Wedel (Holstein) and for the goods station of Wuppertal–Steinbeck. The Wuppertal project earmarks 250,000 m^2 for a residential area providing room for 3,000 flats and shops but the cost would be extremely high.

(g) In Western Europe the share of food items sold in self-service stores will have risen to two-thirds of total turnover by 1980. Turnover of non-food items in self-service stores is also expected to increase.

A host of other generalized issues can be examined. However, it is perhaps more useful to turn to examine two specific case histories of restricted scope, but of substantial depth. In the next section we look at two particular research studies conducted at the University of Bradford in the Management Centre and the School of European Studies.

CASE STUDY ONE

Out-of-town shopping: the German experience
In general terms, the structural changes being experienced by the West German retail trade today are similar to those going forward in other advanced economies. The trend towards the larger retail unit with consequent efficiency benefits; the rapid decline, particularly in the food trades, of the

smaller shop; and the resulting situation of higher turnover from a lower absolute number of shops, can hardly be described as features peculiar to the German retail scene. It is when we turn our attention to the question of out-of-town shopping that we find an area where Germany has a dominant position in Europe. Whereas continental retailing has traditionally taken ideas from the United States and Great Britain and modified these to suit its own requirements, this situation has been to some extent reversed by the advent of out-of-town shopping. As we shall see, some German out-of-town developments are conceptual novelties and could well prove to be more indicative than contemporary North American preoccupations, of the direction that European retailing will take in the future.

We must be clear about the meaning of the term 'out-of-town' before discussing the various business forms engaged in this type of operation. For our purposes, 'out-of-town' is to be understood as any location other than central shopping areas: accordingly this could be: off-centre, suburban or green belt. We will, therefore, use the terms 'out-of-town' and 'in-town' to distinguish between these two types of location.

The two basic business forms engaged in out-of-town shopping in Germany are the Verbrauchermarkt and the Einkaufszentrum; but, as these two terms have a variety of interpretations, further examination is necessary.

Hypermarket is perhaps the term most commonly used to translate Verbrauchermarkt but this alone is insufficient. There has been much discussion as to what exactly constitutes a Verbrauchermarkt[6] and agreement seems to have been reached on at least one point—that a Verbrauchermarkt has a minimum sales area of 1,000 m^2. This in itself tells us very little about the institution, since 1,000 m^2 is not an uncommon size for a *super*market. Three important distinctions have been made concerning units operating under the general term Verbrauchermarkt and these are as follows:[7]

—*Discount-Supermarkt* (discount supermarket): sales area of between 400 and 1,000 m^2, across-the-board discounting, merchandise being heavily weighted in favour of foodstuffs, non-foods being peripheral.

—*Verbrauchermarkt* (hypermarket): sales area of between 1,000 and 6,000 m^2. Using the self-service principle, a wide range of 'problem-free' articles, including foodstuffs, are sold; the service element being minimized. Locations are normally out-of-town, parking facilities being provided.

—*Selbstbedienungs-Warenhaus* (self-service department store): this is what might be termed the second generation hypermarket. Sales area must be at least 2,500 m^2, some say 5,000 m^2, and the store offers a range of goods similar to that offered in a city department store; the main difference being maximum use of the self-service principle. Customers are also offered other services such as restaurants, banks, kindergarten facilities, petrol stations, etc., in addition to ample car parks, generally calculated as three times the size of net selling area. Locations are out-of-town.

It should now be clear that to talk simply in terms of hypermarkets is misleading. Only the hypermarket and self-service department store, as defined above, can be termed out-of-town developments, and even here we

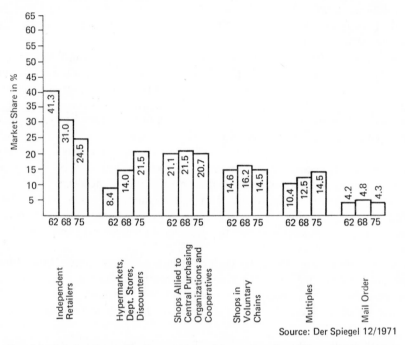

Source: Der Spiegel 12/1971

FIG. 5.4   *Market share of businesses engaged in retailing for* 1962 *and* 1968, *with a projection for* 1975.

can see a functional division. The discount supermarket sometimes operates in out-of-town locations but is also found in-town.

Obviously statistical problems are going to be met when trying to assess the hypermarket in the general context of German retailing and Figs. 5.4 and 5.5 are to be taken as an indication of trends. Fig. 5.4 shows the percentage market share of the various business forms engaged in retailing for the years 1962 and 1968, together with a projection for 1975. The greatest growth is quite clearly in the section entitled 'hypermarkets, department stores and discount shops'. Fig. 5.5 shows the respective growth of department stores plus variety chains and hypermarkets in the same years. The most dynamic growth has been and will continue to be in the hypermarket sector.

Another out-of-town retail development, quite distinct from the concept of the hypermarket, is the regional shopping centre, or Einkaufszentrum. Whereas a hypermarket scheme is generally operated by one retailer with or without concession agreements, the shopping centre is owned and developed by one company, usually responsible for public relations, advertising and general administration work, and premises are leased to a number of retailers.

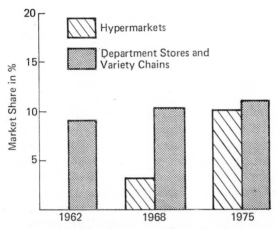

FIG. 5.5　*Growth of department stores, variety chains and hypermarkets in 1962 and 1968, with a projection for 1975. Source: Modener Markt. December 1970.*

The size of the centre is determined by its catchment area and such centres generally cater for the motorized consumer. The Elbe-Einkaufszentrum in Hamburg provides a good example of this. Opened in 1966 on a 70,000 m² site, this was the first German regional shopping centre to be built in an area of high population density. The total catchment area was estimated at 300,000 people. Surveys have shown that the average travelling time taken to reach the centre has increased from ten minutes in 1966 to eighteen minutes in 1970 and that about one-half of customers visit the centre with their car.[10] There is no hard and fast rule for the positioning of such centres and they exist in a variety of locations, all of which are out-of-town; for instance residential areas, suburbs, edge-of-town locations; but those serving a truly regional function will be found in peripheral locations.[11] By June 1970 West Germany had 620 hypermarkets and in March 1972, twenty-three regional shopping centres.[12] Turnover figures for shopping centres are difficult to obtain and the problems of definition tend to obscure the hypermarket situation. The

German Institute of Self-Service has, however, calculated that about 7% of total retail turnover in 1970 was accounted for by business forms that did not exist before 1965; that is, predominantly hypermarkets.[13] The same survey also showed that these business forms accounted for 9·5% of total food turnover in 1970.

One might ask what were the factors which prompted so many retailers to move out-of-town. Clearly retailers do not seek new locations without good reason and we can select three categories of motivation which, taken together, seem to afford a convincing argument:

(a) *Demographic:* a feature of urban development in recent years has been the relative stagnation of city areas and greater population concentration in peripheral areas. The population of core towns in urban regions in Germany increased by 1·7% in the period 1961–8 whereas the corresponding increase in those areas bordering the urban regions in the same period was 19·8%. The rural exodus becomes less important from year to year and one can now even talk of an urban exodus.

(b) *Economic:* rising land- and rent-prices in city centres were making such locations impractical for many retailers. The hardest hit were those people working in conditions of keen competition at low profit margins; that is, principally food retailers. Lower overheads make possible a more aggressive pricing policy which in turn gives a competition advantage.

(c) *Customer:* customer attitudes had been changing. A whole host of factors—the population shifts mentioned above; increasing ownership of cars and domestic appliances, particularly refrigerators; rising proportion of women going out to work; increasing disposable income; desire for more sophisticated leisure activities; worsening traffic congestion in urban centres—combined to produce a situation in which the consumer was making fewer shopping trips, spending more on each trip and travelling greater distances to do his shopping.

The importance of the car as a shopping aid has been highlighted in a number of studies. The German Institute for Applied Consumer Research has found that 61% of all hypermarket customers use their cars and *Der Spiegel* has reported that 82% of a survey sample used their car for shopping purposes.[14] The importance of the gradual acceptance of tinned and frozen foods and general improvements in food packaging in recent years should not be underestimated.[15]

The out-of-town debate in Britain seems to hinge on the effect that hypermarkets and other developments will have on town-centre trade.[16] German evidence does not suggest that existing city centres have suffered.[17] We have already noted that economic pressures have forced many retailers to abandon in-city locations and that these were mainly retailers operating on low profit margins. There has been in Germany the realization that some form of functional division must be made between in-town and out-of-town shopping if the town centre is to remain viable. The centre, therefore, now tends to concentrate on long-term requirements and luxury articles, whereas short-term requirements and daily needs are catered for out-of-town.[18] This system seems to be working and there is no evidence of chronic town-centre decay on an American scale.

The future pattern of West German retailing will be strongly influenced by the out-of-town idea and it is clear that the hypermarket in its many forms is going to be an important component of the German retail scene for many years to come, even though it will change its face. While clearly still of importance, the initial advantage that hypermarkets had over most other forms of retailing, that of price, is no longer the attraction that it once was in the German context. As the consumer becomes more sophisticated in his tastes, price takes second place to choice and this is where the second genera-tion of hypermarkets referred to earlier will come into their own. The trend will be towards the larger out-of-town unit offering a department store product range coupled with the convenience of an out-of-town location. The Karstadt department store group, which until recently has pursued a 'city only' policy, is running self-service department stores in out-of-town locations in Northern Germany, and other department store groups, particularly Kaufhof, are designing special stores for regional shopping centres while in no way neglecting their city interests.

A brief case study here cannot hope to do justice to a topic as complex as German out-of-town shopping. It has succeeded in its aim if it has highlighted the following points:

(a) That out-of-town shopping is a complex phenomenon of which the hypermarket is only one part;
(b) that there is a place for both out-of-town developments and in-town centres;
(c) that the future pattern of German retailing is inconceivable without the concept of out-of-town shopping; and
(d) that consumer behaviour is becoming increasingly important in retail management decision.

This is how one eminent German economic journalist, Werner Osel, sees the future:

the German citizen of the 70's, wants everything: a wide assortment of goods, first-class quality, pleasant shops, unrestricted shop hours and low prices so that he can still afford an expensive holiday without having to go into his savings. Confronted with this situation, the tradesman has to try to realise as many of these desires as he can; some will emphasise value for money, some wide choice and others quality. The retail trade will have to use a wide variety of weapons in the battle for the consumer. There is not and never will be a patent solution as the consumer and his desires operate on many different levels.[19]

CASE STUDY TWO

Comparative study of distribution systems for gasoline in Great Britain and France
Research workers in the social sciences have used a number of different methods of finding out more about their subjects. One of the most fruitful of these methods has been the *comparative approach*. This has been used successfully in other fields; anthropology, psychology and political science. In each case the operation of two or more systems in different environments has been compared, and explanations sought for any similarities and differences found.

Comparative marketing and distribution analysis is not a particularly new idea; indeed a number of useful studies of markets in different countries have already been carried out.[20] Their particular practical importance is that such an approach can be of direct help to firms who operate in different markets and may seek to apply similar marketing techniques or use similar channels successfully in subsequent countries.

The comparative approach can only meaningfully be used if the comparison is made of systems that are comparable.[21] It is important that each system is defined as closely as possible and without too many unquantifiable elements.

We have had two main objectives in mind whilst carrying out this comparative marketing logistics research project.[22] The first was to develop a methodology which could be used by companies to help them analyse and assess possible logistics systems for their products in other countries. This of itself would be a necessary and feasible first step for any total marketing system comparison. The second and more academic reason for carrying out this project was to use the comparative insight to learn more about distribution systems themselves and to develop our body of knowledge in marketing logistics.[23] The dramatic transformation seen in this industry in the past two years makes it one of keenest interest to us all.

Our choice of petrol or gasoline distribution offered considerable advantages for an early study of this sort. There was little product differentiation between manufacturers; wholesalers were not a very important channel; there was considerable scope for sophistication in distribution techniques; and there were relatively few firms in each country, which together controlled very large market shares. The countries chosen for the initial comparison were Britain and France as, although they were of comparable size, there were thought to be considerable differences in the style of company operations in these countries.[24]

As well as using existing and published information about the distribution and marketing of gasoline in the UK and France,[25] a questionnaire was developed which could be administered to senior marketing and/or distribution managers in oil companies. All the large and medium companies were approached in the two countries and interviews were arranged with the twelve major companies in Britain and a similar number in France. This figure represents over 90% of the British market and a similar degree of coverage for the French market.

We investigated three aspects of the companies' distribution system. Firstly the channel relationships which each oil company had with its service stations: this was done by isolating data on vertical company ownership, company control over distribution, re-ordering, promotion, new site location, the terms of contracts, restrictions on diversification and accessories and participation in point-of-sale promotions and so forth. The second phase of investigation dealt with the physical movement of the product. How many depots or exchange points did the companies have; what modes were used for primary and secondary distribution; how sophisticated were distribution costing procedures; what optimizing techniques were used for increasing the efficiency of the distribution system; and what service levels did companies achieve or try to achieve? Finally, we looked at the environment in which the distribution system functioned. What were the influences which government, both national and local, had on the system design; what influence did trade associations have on the oil companies; and what was the competitive position of each oil company as viewed by each other?

Our findings for gasoline in Britain and in France are shown below:

MARKETING LOGISTICS SYSTEM FOR GASOLINE IN THE UK

A.   Environment to the system
The government's attitude to the competitive conditions for the gasoline market in Great Britain has been expressed through acceptance of the Monopolies Commission Report[26] of 1965, which made five main recommendations:

1. There was to be a restriction on the number of company-owned sites (in fact dropped after two years).
2. Agreements with dealer-owned sites were restricted to five years.
3. The exclusion of stocking competitive lubricating oils was prohibited.
4. There was disapproval shown of carrying only own-branded accessories.
5. Agreements with company-owned sites were limited to three years.

Instead of legislation, all the oil companies agreed to abide by the recommendations and spirit of the report. The other important way in which the government affects the oil companies is the size and method of excise duty levied. The oil companies have to bear the financial burden of paying the duty as the product leaves the refinery and before they are paid for the product.

Local government, which controls planning restrictions, has a very important influence not only on the building of new sites, but also on the development and rebuilding of existing sites. The restrictions are so severe that permission is granted for about 1 in 50 proposed new sites each year.

Trade associations are not seen by the oil companies as having an important influence on the logistics system. The Institute of Petroleum, to which all the companies interviewed belonged, acts more as a technical discussion forum and advisory body than as a political and coordinating policy influence. The Motor Agents Association has little influence on the oil companies except where it may act on behalf of one of its members to help resolve a problem which that member has encountered in his negotiations with an oil company.

The competitive environment[27] is characterized by the relatively very strong market position of the two largest oil companies. The Shell-Mex–BP group and the Esso group together have about 65% of all retail sites. The twelve companies interviewed in this survey represented about 91% of all retail sites and probably about 95% of all sales of gasoline. In the last few years the position of the largest two has been somewhat eroded by the increase in market share of the 'mini-majors', or those large world-wide oil companies which are as yet relatively unimportant in the British market. Competition is particularly intense in The Corridor, which is a forty-mile wide area of the country lying across the London–Birmingham–Manchester axis, which accounts for about 60% of all sales. It is in this area that most smaller companies seek to establish themselves initially.

B. Channel relationships and the execution of channel functions

Wholesalers and other types of intermediaries are very unimportant in the distribution of gasoline in the UK. They are only used to a significant extent in geographically isolated regions where distribution costs are much higher than average. They account for less than 2% of the market. There are four main channels of distribution which are important in the British market.

Percentage of sites

26	Company-owned sites with tenants on long-term agreements.
2	Company-owned and operated sites.
72	{ Dealer-owned sites with long-term agreements. { Dealer-owned sites with short-term agreements.

The relative importance of the company-owned sites is considerably greater than the above figures might indicate as those sites which are company-owned are usually high-volume sites. Company-owned and operated sites are often very-high-volume sites.

The terms of the agreements are limited by the Monopolies Commission. The manager in a company-owned and operated site has least control and may lose his job if he does not conform to the company's requirements. The tenant on a company-owned site has a higher degree of responsibility and control. A dealer on his own site has even more discretion and is less bound to cooperate with the oil company, particularly if his supply agreement is short-term. In practice the only reprimand that is common to ensure that each site achieves satisfactory standards in its operation, upkeep and service, is the chivying and bullying of the oil company's representatives. One fairly small company now operates a 'good housekeeping' bonus at the discretion of the oil company which is only given if standards are achieved.

There was considerable variation in the different ways companies used to find and select possible new sites to purchase or supply. The sophistication varied from simple gallonage estimates to the use of computerized models which not only predicted return on the investment required, but in some instances performed a sensitivity analysis on these predictions to take account of possible inaccurate estimates. In some companies these new site decisions were initiated by the sales organizations, but in others there was a 'new development' department whose sole responsibility was the acquisition and selection of new sites. New site decisions play an important part in the oil companies' 'search for new markets'. Other components of this search function are mass-media advertising, below-the-line advertising and maintenance of decor and logo standards so as to be as effective as possible.

On below-the-line promotions, the oil companies had to persuade tenants and dealers to undertake the promotion. This usually not only involved willingness to handle the extra merchandise or leaflets, but also involved a financial burden being taken by the dealer or tenant, as he was usually expected to contribute a considerable proportion of the cost of the promotion. This contribution was often as high as 50% and thus represented a financial risk to the dealers. Nevertheless, participation rates as high as 90% of all dealers were quoted by a number of companies for recent promotions.

Although most companies maintained that they were not active price-cutters, nearly all were prepared to cut prices in localities where price competition was seen to be very severe. In such circumstances, it was quite common for the oil company and the dealer to share the cost of the price-cut at some prearranged proportional share. With the abolition of retail price maintenance, dealers are free to set their own prices. Nearly all the companies, however, took a close note of pump posted prices and would continue to advise dealers as to their attitude to the dealer's prices.

The credit function in the channel did not vary very much between different companies. Most companies tried to obtain a no-credit relationship with their outlets. They tried to obtain a cash- (or cheque-) on-delivery situation. Where this was not achieved, a 'load-over-load' credit was most common. Monthly or other terms were much less common. There was some evidence that some companies which dealt with groups of garages granted larger credit when dealing with these groups.

C. The physical movement of product from refineries to customers

The oil companies were responsible for all movement to the outlets. This was usually achieved in a two-stage process. The primary distribution was from the refinery to various numbers of terminals situated across the country. This primary distribution was usually carried out by pipeline, coastal shipping or railway. The secondary distribution to outlets was carried out by road haulage. A few depots were fed by road haulage but not many. The practice of exchange agreements between oil companies obviated the need for each company to perform the primary stage of distribution. These agreements allowed one company to draw product from a second company's depot in exchange for reciprocal arrangements at a different depot belonging to the first company.

Some companies owned all their delivery tankers, but others rented up to one-third of their fleet from outside operators. There were varying degrees of standardization of their fleets and servicing was carried out centrally by one company, but more usually was carried out regionally either by contract outsiders, by their own servicing department or a combination of both.

The costing and control of the distribution of product was fairly sophisticated and most companies claimed that they took a total-cost approach to distribution, and knew the actual cost of getting product to any particular place. All companies included, in this cost, the primary cost of distribution and the secondary transport cost; however, not all companies included depot storage, management costs, depot inventory charges and loss and insurance. Few companies included data-processing costs and distribution–management costs. No company formally included some estimate of out-of-stock costs, although most agreed that it could be viewed as a cost of the distribution system.

Delivery service offered to outlets varied between twenty-four and forty-eight hours of the order being placed by the customer. In nearly all cases, the re-ordering decision was solely at the discretion of the dealer or tenant. Two instances of pre-programmed re-ordering were found, but these were experimental schemes. Stock-outs at depots only occurred rarely and were nearly always due to external causes, such as rail or terminal staff strikes. Even when they did occur, other arrangements for supplying the product were usually made.

Very advanced computerized models were used by many companies to help them in their distribution management. Computerized vehicle scheduling was being tried experimentally by about half the companies interviewed.[28] Only a few had adopted this form of truck scheduling instead of manual scheduling. About half the companies used a model to decide on either the location of depots or the allocation of existing depots to particular customers. A few companies used models which represented the total distribution system and which were used for future planning of market growth and supply coordination.

MARKETING LOGISTICS SYSTEM FOR GASOLINE IN FRANCE

A. Environment to the system
The French gasoline market is characterized by the very strong influence which the government exerts on the mechanism of competition in the market. The government grants licences to each firm to market its product through a specified maximum number of sites for each three-year period. Thus the government controls the market share of each company and restricts the number of new sites which each company may obtain. The government reaches these figures by a recognized procedure which leaves room for competition between firms because of the fact that each company is given a maximum market share it would be allowed to reach, but is unlikely to do so. All the companies are competing inasmuch as they are trying to achieve targets at the expense of the others. Planning restrictions are not very limiting. Taxation is a large part of the retail price, and is paid by the oil companies. Value-added tax is paid by the retail outlets in addition.

There are five or six large petrol companies each with between 10 and 20% of the market. There are also 'revendeurs' or distributors who account for 10% of the market. Hypermarkets offering cheap own-brand gasoline is a recent and significant development in the market. As far as the actual outlets are concerned, only about 25% may be called service stations, the rest are garages where the repairing of cars and their sales is a more important activity.

In French law there exists what is known as a *fond de commerce*. It means that a place of business can be discussed in law and valued to include all the aspects of the business including good will. Thus agreements with dealer outlets can legally be very specific about what trade and terms are carried out.

The oil industry trade association is not very powerful or particularly influential on its members. However, the two retail trade associations have each in certain instances been able to effect quite major changes in the oil companies' behaviour in favour of their own members. One association has as its members garage-owners, and the other tenants or dealers at service station sites.

The oil companies have agreements with all the major car manufacturers in France. This means that each manufacturer recommends the products of a particular oil company to be used on its cars.

B.   Channel relationships and the execution of channel functions

Revendeurs or distributors account for 10% of the market. About 15% of outlets are company-owned. Around 75% of outlets are garages rather than service stations. Very few outlets are company-owned and operated, probably less than 2%.

On company-owned sites the tenants have contracts to sell products at specified prices. Their contracts are six-monthly or yearly. The scope and extent of services a tenant can offer is limited by law. On dealer-owned sites the contracts are usually for about ten years and are commonly of two types. Either the dealer is paid a lump sum in advance, which will represent the rebate he may expect to receive for a large proportion of his fixed-time-length agreement. The other type of agreement is where a lump sum is paid in advance and the contract lasts until the rebate reaches that sum. The tanks and the pumps are usually lent to the dealer and may become his property at the end of the contract. The dealer decides when to re-order and how much. A dealer on his own site has as his only obligation to buy exclusively gasoline at a certain rate. Beyond that, he has very full discretion as to how he runs his business.

Different companies have different degrees of centralization in the control of new site purchase. The criteria are basically profitability, although some companies, eager to achieve the targets which the government has set them because it will enhance their future market position, are prepared to seek volume as a first priority. The market as a whole is growing at 8% per year, but new service stations are getting a 12–15% growth rate per year.

Promotion campaigns if they are to be successful have to be sold to the dealers in order to encourage them to cooperate. Where dealers have to contribute in financial terms to the promotion it is usually less than 50% of the cost. The oil companies organize campaigns for different sectors of the market and they are geared to those sections. Promotions are tested before being launched as a campaign. In some instances only good service stations are asked to participate. Of those asked as many as 95% may agree to cooperate for this type of promotion.

For the oil companies to give credit in some form or other is quite a common occurrence. Cash-on-delivery is the policy for some stations. On dealer-owned sites, an advance on rebate is usually given. Even on company-owned sites, a loan arrangement is often arranged with a bank because the tenant has to finance the stock of gasoline which may be £3,000. Own-brand petrol is supplied by most companies and in these circumstances credit is often given.

C. The physical movement of product from refineries to customers
Pipelines are used for the distribution of refined product to depots. There are joint pipelines shared by a number of companies, and also private pipelines owned and used by one company. Exchange agreements are quite common. Rail is the most important mode of delivery for primary distribution followed by coastal ships and pipelines. Road-fed depots are very few. The road haulage fleet used for distribution to outlets has a high proportion of vehicles not owned by the oil companies; this may be as high as 65%.

In the costing and control of the distribution function, the larger companies interviewed included in their costing a system approaching a total-cost one. They included primary and secondary transport costs, depot storage management, depot inventory charges and loss and insurance. There is in fact a legal obligation to carry so many months' supply at each depot. Distribution management is usually charged as a Head Office overhead. Whilst no charge is made for out-of-stock situations, in one firm, if a customer takes less than has been expected, a charge is made on to the operations department.

The delivery service offered is usually forty-eight hours for gasoline and two to eight days for lubricants. Long weekends seem to cause supply problems, partly because some sites which are underneath buildings are not allowed to extend their storage capacity. These sites may have too little stock. The dealers are responsible for re-ordering, although quantity drop sizes may be written into their contracts.

Computerized scheduling of vehicles is done by some companies although one company uses a computer to check if a delivery which has been carried out has been done in the most efficient way. Other models are used for locating depots and for re-assigning depot zones.

COMPARATIVE INSIGHT FOR LOGISTICS SYSTEMS

A. System similarities
The oil companies' role as distributor and marketeer for the vast majority of gasoline in both markets, is a consistent feature. They take prime responsibility for finding new sites, initiating promotions and establishing their image in the market.

The physical movement of product is carried out in a very similar way with rail, pipeline or coastal primary distribution and road vehicle for secondary distribution. The control of distribution is fairly sophisticated in both markets with an approach not far off a total-cost approach. Computerized models for vehicle scheduling, depot location and allocation would appear to be similarly advanced in each market.

B. System differences

There are more company-owned sites in the UK and there are far more garage-type outlets in France. The basis of agreements with dealer-owned sites is quite different in France, where payments of rebate are made in advance and where the oil companies exert less influence as to the style of management of the sites. However, on the company-owned sites, a tenant in Britain has more responsibility, discretion and tenure than he would have in France. Dealer-owned sites in France are less prepared to participate in national promotions. Credit is more common in France.

Distributors are more important in the French market, and own-brand petrol is now a significant feature of the market, which it is not yet in Britain. The investment which the oil companies have made in the distribution system is of a different type in each market. In Britain they have invested heavily in acquiring their own sites. In France payments in advance to dealers must be a large proportion of their investment. In Britain there is a higher proportion of company-owned vehicles than in France.

C. System environment differences

The most important difference is the completely different attitude of the government in the way it influences each industry. Legal differences are also significant where they affect the terms of agreements between channel members. Retail trade associations are more influential in France than in Britain. Restrictions in the building of new sites are very severe in Britain, but not very important in France. There is less difference in the size of the important oil companies in France than in Britain, where two companies dominate the scene.

D. Conclusion

At the ultimate conclusion of this comparative study, it is hoped to relate the system similarities and differences more closely to their causes in the environment of the system. However, it may be seen from the above how a rigorous comparative system analysis can yield insights into the operation of marketing logistics systems, which would not have otherwise become apparent. As well as the academic value of being able to take an objective viewpoint in analysing a system, there are practical gains which may be achieved by carrying out such an exercise. A company can get a useful insight into its own operations by viewing them from a comparative approach. Furthermore, the suitability for adoption of successful practices in one market to another should be more easily gauged by using this sort of analysis.

By taking a distribution system focus for this comparative study, the results are of more relevance to an easily definable system than if a more general comparative marketing study had been undertaken. However, the results of an approach such as this are a good basis for further comparative studies of other aspects of international marketing, such as comparative consumer behaviour. Such linked comparative studies would be useful not only to academics but also to firms engaged, or likely to be engaged, in international marketing.

It is hoped that the methodology developed in this project would be as appropriate for comparative studies of products other than gasoline. It is for this reason that it is important that the distribution system is clearly identified. The experience of having carried out this comparative marketing logistics study for gasoline in two markets should be of considerable value to a follow-up study for different markets and products, as well as helping to show the way towards improved channel productivity.

We have attempted to demonstrate that a static examination of European distribution systems alone can never be sufficient for effective management planning. Within the context of an enlarged EEC of nine nations, it is our firm belief that much greater attention must be paid to the systematic analysis of total marketing logistics systems and of the role of channel members as well as manufacturers within them. The two case studies reported above demonstrate one way in which we can proceed; that is, via a rigorous comparative approach. There are a host of other valid directions for development besides.

REFERENCES

1. Bucklin, L. P., 'Postponement of speculation and the structure of distribution', Journal of Marketing Research, 2(1), 1965, pp. 26–31.
2. Terry, W. M. and Watson, R. B., 'A systems approach for the selection of distribution channels', cited in Montgomery, D. B. and Urban, G. L., Management science in marketing, pp. 239–41, Prentice-Hall, 1969.
3. Le Kashman, R. and Stolle, J. F., 'The total cost approach to distribution', Business horizons, pp. 33–46, 1965.
4. Bowersox, D. J., Smykay, E. W. and La Londe, B. J., Physical distribution management. Macmillan, 1968.
5. Tietz, B., 'The future development of retail and wholesale distribution in Western Europe: an analysis of trends up to 1980', British (now European) Journal of Marketing, 5(1), 1971, pp. 42–55.
6. Der Einzelhandel in der BRD Teil 4, Axel Springer Verlag AG, 1971, pp. 36–7.
7. Der Einzelhandel in der BRD Teil 4, Axel Springer Verlag AG, 1971, p. 35.
8. Adapted from figures given in Konzentration im Handel; Der Spiegel, 12/1971, p. 54.

9. Taken from *Moderner Markt:* December 1970.
10. *Presseinformation anlässlich der Eröffnung des Elbe-Einkaufszentrums in Hamburg,* Beratungsgesellschaft für Gewerbebau, Hamburg, May 1966. *Blick zurück ohne Zorn,* Mitteilungen der Handelskammer Hamburg, May 1967. *Elbe-Einkaufszentrum*—5 Jahre alt, Handelskammer Hamburg, 1970.
11. The Main-Taunus-Zentrum between Frankfurt and Wiesbaden and the Ruhr-Park-Zentrum near Bochum were the first German regional shopping centres and are also good examples of the 'auf der grünen Wiese' concept.
12. Hypermarkets as of June 30th, 1970. DIHT survey quoted in *Der Einzelhandel in der BRD Teil 4,* Axel Springer Verlag AG, 1971, p. 44. Shopping centres as of March 31st, 1972. DIHT figures taken from *Handelsblatt,* June 19th, 1972.
13. *Der Einzelhandel in der BRD Teil 4,* Axel Springer Verlag AG, 1971, p. 36.
14. *Der Einzelhandel in der BRD Teil 4,* Axel Springer Verlag AG, 1971, p. 46. *Der Deutsche und sein Auto: Eine SPIEGEL-Umfrage,* Der Spiegel, 53/1971, p. 42.
15. *Discount-Entwicklung in der Bundesrepublik: Der Verbrauchermarkt.* Werner Oehler, Albert Backs, Hauptgemeinschaft des Deutschen Einzelhandels, Cologne, 1968, p. 8.
16. Both sides of the hypermarket argument in Britain are well presented in 'Shopping goes out-of-town', Business Brief, *The Economist,* April 15th, 1972, pp. 60–1.
17. *Neue Märkte und Chancen des Einzelhandels.* Tertial-Bericht für den Einzelhandels 3/70. Hauptgemeinschaft des Deutschen Einzelhandels, Cologne, 1970.
18. This is obviously an over-simplification of the situation but shows the basic division expected in future. Such a development will be accompanied by phenomena such as the convenience store.
19. *Der harte Kampf um den Kunden geht auch in Zukunft weiter.* Werner Osel. From *Zukunft der Wirtschaft.* Fischer, Frankfurt, 1971, p. 106.
20. Bartels, R., *Comparative marketing: wholesaling in 15 countries.* Irwin, 1963.
21. Cox, R., 'The search for universals in comparative studies of domestic marketing systems', in Sommers, M. S. and Kerman, J. B. (eds), *Comparative marketing systems.* Allyn and Bacon, 1971.
22. Liander, B., *Comparative analysis for international marketing.* Allyn and Bacon, 1967.
23. Boddewyn, J., *Comparative marketing and management.* Scott Foresman & Co., 1969.
24. David, J. A., Callow, C. and Morrison, J., 'European marketing remains', *Oil and Gas International,* 7(4), April 1967.
25. Harris, W. J., 'Retail petrol outlets in the UK', *Petroleum Review,* April 1967.
26. The Monopolies Commission Report on Petrol Supply to Retailers. HMSO, 1965.
27. Institute of Petroleum Information Service, UK, *Retail Petrol Outlets,* March 1970.
28. Gillies, G., 'The planning of tank truck deliveries', *Petroleum Review,* April 1971.

CHAPTER 6

Distribution and Retailing in the Eighties

During the sixties, the consumer experienced a period of increasing prosperity during which disposable income increased, and was seen to have increased. This is reflected in the growth of home-ownership, and ownership of cars and other consumer durables. Employment patterns have changed, with a marked increase in the proportion of professional and managerial workers and a decrease in the proportion of the unskilled. At the same time the age-composition of the population has also changed. There has been an increase in the proportion of the very young and the elderly.

The population has been affected by both external and internal migration. While it can be established that the net external migration figure is negative, the overall effect in recent years has been to increase the numbers of non-Europeans in the UK. Internal migration has resulted in intra-regional population shifts from urban/industrial areas towards suburban/rural locations. Such inter-regional shifts that have occurred have not been large, with the South and South-East absorbing most of the migrants. Again, it must be emphasized, there has been no large movement.

Educational standards have increased during the period. Passes at O and A level increased; university degrees awarded doubled and more children stayed at school longer. People married younger, divorced and remarried more often, and tended to have larger families.[1]

Incomes increased at an average rate of 8·5–9·0% per annum, with a shift in distribution favouring the medium and lower paid. Wives' incomes and pensions have shown large proportional increases (of the total) whilst incomes from profits and investments have declined.[2] Incomes vary regionally. Highest incomes are earned in the South-East; the lowest are in Northern Ireland. The regional differences have diminished over the 1960/70 period.[3]

Consumption patterns have changed. Overall food expenditure in 1970 accounted for 20·6% of the household budget: in 1960 it had accounted for 25·3% (both at current prices). Expenditure increased on housing, motor vehicles and their maintenance, and alcoholic drinks. While food expenditure increased in real terms by 10·3%, that increase compares with an overall real increase in expenditure of 26·9%.[4] Consumption patterns are seen to vary regionally, by income, and by family size.[5]

Shopping habits also vary. Younger women prefer the Multiples type supermarketing operations, while older housewives—45–55 years and over—strongly favour the Co-ops. Regional differences occur. The Co-ops are more favoured in the North, the Midlands and Scotland, while the South-East is the Multiples' best territory. It must of course be remembered that this is influenced by the distribution of outlets and that the Multiples are more concentrated in the south of the country, although they are opening new stores in the other areas.[6]

It is difficult to be positive and to point to any likely cause-and-effect relationships between consumer changes and physical distribution. What is much more likely is that the shoppers' preferences for economy, convenience, and choice have influenced the structure of retailing and thereby have played a part in shaping physical distribution and other activities. Thus we must now look in more detail at the changes in grocery retailing. The changes that have occurred in grocery retailing during the 1960/70 period have had two types of effect. The direct effects have been those which have had identifiable impact on manufacturers' policies and operations. Others, while not as obvious and more indirect in their nature, have none the less had an impact.

Organizational changes in retailing and the concentration of retail buying have brought about considerable changes in the market shares controlled by the main types of grocery outlet. The Co-ops' share has fallen from 21 % to 15 % while the Multiples have increased their share from 28 % to 42 %. The Independents have shown the biggest change, a decrease of 18 %. Meanwhile Symbol Independents have expanded their share from 13 % to 23 %. This change has been accompanied, and aided, by a considerable number of mergers and acquisitions. At the same time the total number of outlets has decreased. The result has been a shift of channel power from the manufacturers to a few large multiple retailers, who have been able to squeeze the manufacturers hard for price and service concessions.[7,8]

Another direct change has been the switch to self-service from counter-service, which has enabled the larger operators to offer the economy, convenience and choice implicit in shoppers' behaviour. Larger units have meant that retailing productivity has increased. Pricing policies and service have met the demands of an increasing number of customers and larger units have continued to grow larger. The consequence has been that retail operations have increasingly made use of capital equipment and manufacturers have had to align their policies and operational activities with these changes.[6,7]

Cash-and-carry has also had a direct effect on manufacturers. Not only has cash-and-carry enabled them to continue to service their small customers who have become uneconomic to call on, but it has opened up and made accessible the institutional and catering market segments.

Recent trends in urban planning suggest another direct effect: this of course is the slow decline in High Street shopping and the move towards out-of-town and other off-centre forms of retailing. Trends suggest the following to be emerging:

(a) A decline in the popularity of the High Street supermarket type of outlet.
(b) A move towards the suburbs in an attempt to develop convenience store operations comprising neighbourhood, 1,000 ft^2, self-service units retaining a personal service atmosphere.
(c) Off-centre locations, retailing units of between 10,000 and 25,000 ft^2 situated outside a central or suburban shopping area and providing substantial parking facilities. These stores may sell foods and/or non-foods.
(d) Free-standing superstores, retailing units with at least 25,000 ft^2 selling area, situated outside the conventional commercial centres and located on the edge of, or outside, a town. Food and non-food items are sold by self-service and the store is surrounded by large parking facilities.
(e) Out-of-town regional shopping centres, situated outside the built-up area of a town, providing all forms of general merchandise, clothing and furniture, and almost all the retail facilities available in a town centre. A population of at least 100,000 to 250,000 is required to support this type of outlet, which operates in a building area of from 100,000 ft^2 upwards. The minimum site area is about 40 acres with an average of 400 car parking spaces. The centre contains at least one department store.[10,11]

The growth of retail advertising is one of the more significant indirect factors. Advertising expenditure has increased some sevenfold between 1966 and 1970 and suggests that retailers are taking some of the initiative in promotions and are conscious of an opportunity to build their own images. This further suggests that manufacturers have had to become increasingly aware of service level requirements and delivery times, and variances required in response to service requirements from the large Multiples.[12]

The large increases in own brand sales have made them a major indirect factor in grocery sales. It has been estimated that 13 % of all sales of packaged goods are now of own-brands. Fine Fare have 20 % of turnover in own brands; Tesco 20 % and Sainsbury 50 %. The Symbol Independents are lower: Spar/Vivo have 11 %, but are increasing; VG reported a 35 % increase in own-brand sales during 1970. At the same time the share of advertised brands of twenty major grocery product classes remained at a constant 78·3 % of consumer sales (£) between 1965 and 1969. The major brands increased their sales volume some 3½ times more than other brands.

The growth of convenience foods has been another important indirect factor. This is particularly so for quick-frozen products. During the period 1963–9 expenditure on convenience foods expanded at a rate which was 10 % faster than all other foods. Quick-frozen foods had a rate of expansion of almost 70% more than other foods. Clearly those manufacturers producing convenience foods have had to keep pace with expanding sales and their distribution systems, more than almost any others, have changed to meet the new circumstances.

THE LOGISTICS IMPLICATIONS OF CHANGES IN RETAILING

For some of the topics discussed in the previous section it is possible to point to some likely cause-and-effect relationships. Fig. 6.1 demonstrates the

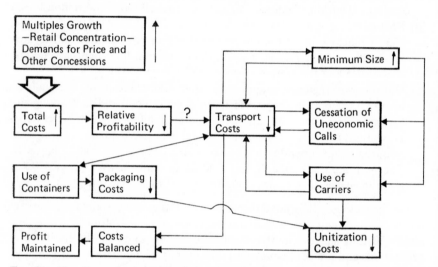

FIG. 6.1   *The effects of organizational changes in retailing and the concentration of buying-power on manufacturers' distribution systems.*

effects of organizational changes in retailing and the concentration of buying power on manufacturers' distribution systems. With profits squeezed by the demands of large retailers for price and service concessions, costs increase relative to existing profit levels. Manufacturers have achieved economies by lowering transport costs through implementing minimum drop size policies; cutting out uneconomic calls; and using specialist carriers. Packaging costs have been reduced by using carriers and containers. Thus the turnover/cost relationship has been restored but with resultant changes in the manufacturers' physical distribution systems.

The effects of cash-and-carry on manufacturers' distribution systems can also be modelled, and these are suggested by Fig. 6.2. The high costs involved in uneconomic calls have forced manufacturers either to drop small accounts or to raise minimum drop sizes. This, together with the move by manufacturers

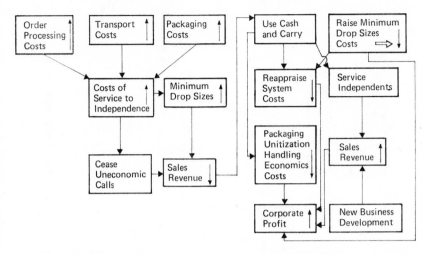

FIG. 6.2   *The effects of cash-and-carry on manufacturers' physical distribution systems.*

to go direct to large retail buyers, presented conventional wholesalers and small Independents with problems. Cash-and-carry came as a salvation to both by offering existing wholesalers an opportunity to reorganize and stay in business and the Independents a source of small order/low cost supply. It also generated new business. Manufacturers were afforded an opportunity to continue servicing the small Independent and to increase sales to new customers; that is, caterers and institutional buyers, butchers, newsagents.

The effects of urban congestion and the demand for service on the costs of servicing High Street retail outlets are shown as Fig. 6.3. Retailers' costs have risen due to the effects of the credit squeeze, and old warehousing facilities,[13] which together with the fact that some manufacturers use a short-order cycle time period as a sales aid, result in demands from retailers for more frequent deliveries. Urban congestion compounds the problem and the result is an increase in service costs for the manufacturers and an unacceptable effect on profitability. System costs have then been reduced by resorting to an increased minimum drop size; reduced delivery frequencies; discount/order size incentives, and the use of distribution services. Reduced costs from out-of-town deliveries in larger volumes and in less congested locations have helped to reduce or at least maintain system costs relative to the increases elsewhere.

An indirect effect, that of the growth of retail advertising, is featured as Fig. 6.4. Here, because retailers are taking the initiative in promoting branded products, manufacturers can find that all activities, and therefore cost centres, experience cost increases in meeting the desired service levels.

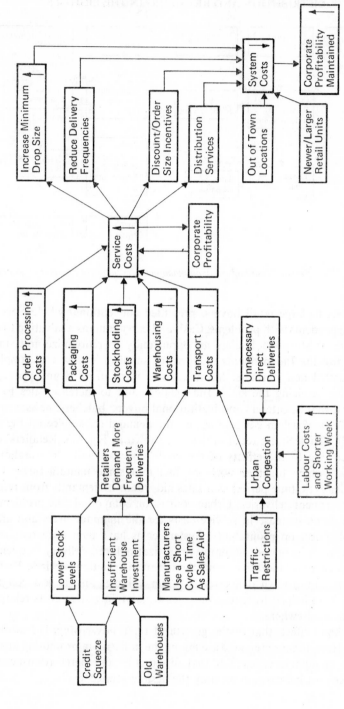

FIG. 6.3   *The effects of urban congestion and the demand for service on the costs of servicing High Street retail outlets.*

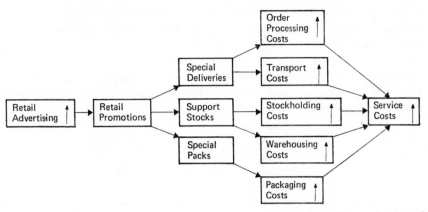

FIG. 6.4   *The likely effects of increases in retail advertising on manufacturers' physical distribution systems.*

The effects of increasing own-brand sales and the economies of scale due to large orders requiring less service can be seen as Fig. 6.5. It suggests that, relative to other business of the same turnover, own-brand sales result in relatively lower costs and improved corporate profitability. However, some manufacturers suggest that the economies of scale effect holds only up to a certain level and that beyond it a number of diseconomies occur; for example,

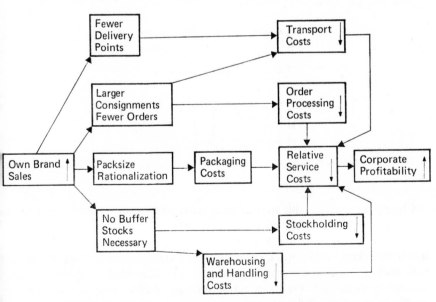

FIG. 6.5   *The effects of own-brands on physical distribution systems.*

warehouse cube utilization decreases due to the large range of pack sizes and container shapes involved when servicing a large number of different own-brand customers.

Finally, in Fig. 6.6, the effects of the growth of quick-frozen foods on distribution system costs are depicted. Specialist distribution requirements and the service support needed with new products in an intensely competitive situation have resulted in persistently high distribution costs.

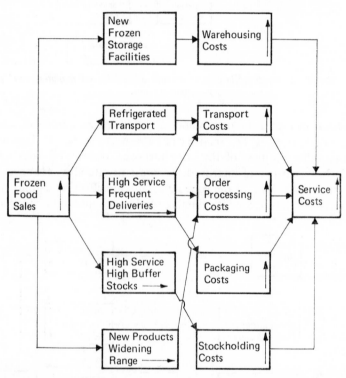

Fig. 6.6 *The effects of the growth of quick-frozen foods on distribution system costs.*

Clearly it is not possible to determine these relationships exactly. Nor is it possible to determine their effects on costs. However, it is useful to trace the relationships and to establish that the changing retailing environment has had some effects on physical distribution and much more important to realize that such change is a dynamic process. Thus it is vital to determine as accurately as possible the likely future changes, and to estimate how these are likely to affect the firms' operations, revenue and profits.

FORECASTING LOGISTICS AND RETAILING CHANGES

The importance of choosing the right technique

Planning relies heavily on forecasting and it is obvious that the usefulness of any proposed planning system depends upon an accurate prediction of the future. This is a statement of the obvious but it is relevant in light of the fact that many techniques exist, and choice from among them must aim at selecting that which best serves our purpose.

In recent years there has been a change in attitude towards public and private planning which:

> ... has extended customary planning horizons to a more distant future and replaced haphazard intuitive gambles, as a basis for planning, by sober and craftsmanlike analysis of the opportunities the future has to offer.[14]

The result has been development of a number of technological forecasting techniques all of which have specialist uses and applications and have been reviewed in this context by Cetron and Monahan.[15] They suggest five definable categories of technological forecasting techniques:

(i) Trend extrapolation
(a) *Simple extrapolation*—assumes that whatever happened in the past will continue in the future, provided there are no disturbances; not particularly accurate but has the advantage of objectivity.
(b) *Curve fitting*—technological progress appears to proceed in an exponential manner, with a period of slow growth as problems are resolved and money becomes available; eventually a limiting factor is encountered and the curve asymptotically approaches some upper value.
(c) *Trend curves*—there are a number of trend curves:
  1. linear increase, flattening as the limit is approached;
  2. exponential with no limit in the time frame under consideration;
  3. 'S'-shaped, logistics type curve;
  4. double exponential, with subsequent flattening.
(d) *Systematic curve fitting*—to calculate and project trends quantitatively, one or more empirical equations can be used:
  1. straight line $y = a + bx$;
  2. parabola $y = a + bx + cx^2$
  3. exponential $y = ae^{bx}$

If the empirical data to be used are reliable the above equations may be used, together with the technique of least squares to project future values of significant parameters.

(ii) Trend correlation analysis

The trend of a complex and difficult technical parameter may be more easily expressed as a result of its relationship to two or more trends.

Whereas time-dependent trend extrapolation attempts explicit forecasting, interrelationships between parameters can be explored on a much more general level if they do not have to fit into a specific time frame. In order to use two or more trends to determine a third, the predictor must have available a number of primary trends which are related to the technical field of interest. To these must be added a knowledge of probable relationships that might arise from combinations of such variables which influence the desired technical improvement. The trends of the primary variables may be projected on the basis of techniques which appear appropriate. The prediction is then completed by projecting the unknown variable on the basis of the relationships between the primary variables.

(a) *Precursor events*—this forecasting method uses the correlation of progress trends between two developments, one of which leads the other. There is a clear need for the development to be related.

(b) *Correlation analysis*—covers problems dealing with the relationships between two or more variables, and specifically the degree of a certain special type of relationship among them. This method makes use of regression analysis and, when consistent correlations can be found, the method offers an objective approach to forecasting. Multiple regression and multiple correlation handles more than two variables.

(*iii*) *Analogy*

(a) *Growth analogy*—makes the assumption that technical progress proceeds in an exponential manner and dates back as far as 1907 to the theory advanced by Henry Adams. There are a number of models proposed based on this assumption, and the basis may be a useful approach to research and development in a specific field or within a small or medium-sized group.

(b) *Historical analogy*—attempts to study the impact of a new technology on functional capability by looking back into history and observing the growth curves relating to the same or a similar technology.

This method of forecasting is of use primarily in dealing with technological problems.

(*iv*) *Intuitive forecasting*

One of the most direct and widely used methods of generating a forecast is to sample the opinions of one or more persons who are knowledgeable in the area under consideration. If more than one forecaster is involved then a forecast is built from a consensus or a composite of estimates.

(a) *Individual or 'genius' forecasting*—there is considerable merit in a forecast made by a single individual who is expert in his specialist area and has a synoptic view of the functional area to which his expertise has direct application.

(b) *Consensus*

1. Polls—because one single estimate may be poor, an attempt may be made to 'cancel out' errors of a number of estimates by combining the judgements of a number of individuals active in the field. If the sample is a poor one these errors may not necessarily be 'cancelled out'.

2. Panels—bring individual experts together and provide for an interaction of their different opinions. There are problems here of a behavioural nature, for example, the 'senior' expert or perhaps one with most leadership can overwhelm the remainder.

3. Delphi technique—eliminates the committee activity in favour of a programme of questionnaires designed on a sequential basis. The first questionnaire attempts to establish median values of a variable and this together with extreme values are passed back to the members. Those who made extreme estimates are asked to edify the remainder on why they made such estimates; this information is included together with the other feedback data. The procedure continues in like manner until a consensus is reached.

Clearly some of these techniques are more appropriate than others to specified problems. The problem of forecasting retailing futures would seem best dealt with by the Delphi method. This can best be shown by considering the inadequacies of the other methods.

As far as trend extrapolation is concerned, the basic assumption is 'what happened in the past will continue'. Since retailing is undergoing changes and is faced with many innovations in organization and product development this assumption clearly does not obtain.

Trend curves cannot allow for unquantifiable data and much of what has caused change and is likely to cause change in grocery retailing is of this nature. Hence it may be possible to fit a curve to the growth of concentration; that is, decrease in buying points, but it is unwise to project this into the future because further merger and acquisition activity may be subject to Monopolies Commission review, etc. There are any number of social, legal and economic factors which cannot be foreseen at present but which may in the course of time have effect; these cannot be considered by a statistical relationship or technique.

The analogy method would appear to be most applicable to scientific applications, although Bass,[17] has used the epidemic phenomenon to forecast sales of consumer durables. In this instance, however, the pattern of the forecast is predictable if the time and quantity values are not.

This narrows the choice. The individual or genius forecast is not suitable in our case due to the fact that there are many aspects of grocery retailing not known, nor can they be expected to be known, by just one person. The use of a poll for a once-only estimate has the obvious problems that were mentioned above. The panel technique has the problems mentioned, but in addition also has the disadvantage of requiring panel members to be in one place at one time. For an accurate useful forecast the type of panel member required is unlikely to be available at the same time as his fellow members, nor is he likely to be able to devote the time required in one session. This eliminates all but Delphi which is a perfectly adequate technique.

Why Delphi?

The Delphi method is chosen because it attempts to make effective use of informed intuitive judgement, deriving its importance from the realization that projections into the future are largely based on the personal expectations of individuals rather than on predictions derived from a well-established theory:

> Even when a formal mathematical model is available, the input assumptions, the range of applicability of the model, and the interpretation of the output are all subject to intuitive intervention by an individual who can bring the appropriate expertise to bear on the application of the model.[14]

A closer look at the mode of operation among experts strengthens Delphi's case. A panel of experts is carefully selected and asked to estimate either the year that some particular phenomenon is likely to occur, or, to make an estimate of values of a phenomenon. The response estimates are most likely to spread over a sizeable time or value range. A follow-up questionnaire is fed back to the respondents with a summary of the distribution of these responses, stating the median and—as an indication of the spread of opinions—the interquartile range (that is, the interval containing the middle 50% of the responses). The respondents are then asked to reconsider their previous answers and revise them if they so desire. If a new response lay outside the interquartile range, the particular respondent is asked to state his reason for thinking that the answer should vary that much from the majority judgement.

The effect of this is to cause those without strong judgements to move estimates closer to the median. Those who consider that they have a good argument to support their opinions tend to retain their original estimates and in fact defend them.

In the following round responses are again summarized, and the respondents are given a concise summary of the reasons supporting extreme positions. They are then asked to revise their second round responses, taking into consideration the extreme reasons and giving them whatever weight they feel justified. Any respondent with an answer that remains outside the interquartile range is asked to state why he has not been persuaded by the opposing arguments.

By this anonymous debate-by-questionnaire, the Delphi method can draw on the benefits of the committee approach (the advantage of perceiving the line of reasoning of others), whilst avoiding the social compromise which normally occurs at a meeting.

> Individual views can be argued, abandoned or sustained behind the mask of anonymity, without loss of face and without being affected by the personality, reputation or seniority of the protagonists. The method also permits the individuals participating in the panel to consult with their colleagues (not fellow panel members) should this be deemed desirable.[15]

It would be wrong to assume that Delphi is all to our advantage; it is sometimes suggested that:

> ... the opinion that consensus is not forced by social pressure on the deviant when face-to-face confrontation is avoided is not wholly convincing. Less convincing still is the aggregation of all the views of all panel members as though they are all of equal value.[15]

This first problem we must live with, at least in the knowledge that if it is not eliminated it is lessened. But a second problem can be dealt with. Clearly some experts are more expert than others concerning particular aspects of the topic under investigation and therefore their opinions should be weighted, and this can be done by asking the respondents to rate their own competence in each sector, or on each question to which they respond. Should they consider themselves unequipped in any particular area they should make a nil return.

Finally, the capacity for future development gives added appeal to Delphi. Mandanis[16] discussed the possibility of computer analysis of any type of information inputs:

> ... with sophisticated computer programming it [Delphi] will be able to utilize any form of information: from proven to exploratory models; from algorithmic to heuristic rules; from actual to synthetic data. Opinions will be traceable to their respective premises, and be amenable to detailed scrutiny. The output from such enriched Delphi experiments need not only be a consensus, or dissensus on matters explored. Perhaps more importantly, it will be a learning experience which the participants could not acquire by any other means. For example, in business, it can take the form of a detailed understanding by corporate executives of the reasoning that underlies their respective staffs' recommendations; conversely, it can help the latter appreciate, more intimately, the biases and style of those they counsel.

Previous experience with Delphi

Delphi has not been restricted to technological forecasting only. There have been a number of successful applications in other fields, however, a literature search reveals technological forecasting to be by far the widest. The range of applications is quite varied and includes:

Education[17]

Medicine[18,19]

Social development[20]

Public policy development and application[21,22,23]

Transportation[24,25]

Personnel planning[26,27]

The role of the mentally retarded[28]

Civil defence[29]

National planning[30]

Information processing[31]

A review of other applications, more orientated towards business planning, is probably worth while at this stage.

LTV (Ling–Temco–Vought) began using Delphi in 1968.[32] Their forecasts consisted of almost a hundred events and were incorporated into corporate plans through R & D planning cycles. To broaden the base of the exercise, non-technical panelists were used and this increased the awareness of the panel to economic, marketing, and environmental factors. The resulting forecasts were made with estimates of probability and indications of which LTV divisions would be primarily affected by each event.

TRW's experience with Delphi began in 1966–7 and has covered diverse fields—space, military, transportation, housing, communication/education, materials, power, and biology/oceanography—and contained hundreds of events. TRW use 'mapping'—a map of the technological future displaying technological alternatives and their environmental consequences in such a way as to enable the coupling of near-term technical activities to long-range forecasts.[33]

Goodyear simplified the Delphi process into three steps. In the first step a group of experts from the principal organizations influencing the tyre industry were requested, by mail, to list the most important developments they anticipated over a selected time horizon (up to the year 2000). The organizations included: tyre companies, fibre companies, chemical companies, carbon-black companies, industry consultants and trade journalists. From these a relatively few event questions of particular importance were selected. The study was completed by several questionnaire iterations of a revised list.[34] The Hercules Powder Company Ltd conducted an exercise, during the period 1968–9, to forecast future patterns of the UK chemical industry.[35] The exercise consisted of three rounds. In Parker's opinion its accomplishments were:

> ... we have a composite picture, of a kind that did not exist before, of the expected future profile of the broad UK chemical industry. It represents the

triple distilled views of a body of pretty authoritative people. There is a wide measure of agreement about the orders of size of the major segments of the industry, which suggests that the forecast may well be reasonably valid.

In addition, we have a strong indication of the most probable major developments of outlets which are likely to be instrumental in bringing about the foreseen growth. We can identify some fields where change and innovation are virtual certainties, and others where research effort would probably fail to pay a dividend.[35]

Parker's exercise is of particular value and interest because in his subsequent documentation he also describes the problems that arose and how they were dealt with.

Validating Delphi

Clearly, the only possible method of validation for a Delphi futures exercise is to wait and see. However, other possibilities exist and have been used.

The early work of Helmer, Gordon, Dalkey and others, published by RAND, dealing with almanac studies, suggests validation for Delphi in as much that the iteration process achieved results which when compared with the factual data were acceptable. However, this in itself is not totally satisfactory and some alternative is desirable.

Ament's study was one of the first to examine the validity of Delphi forecasting in a manner similar to the almanac studies. The study examined the results of a 1964 Delphi forecast and found that approximately 50% of the events were either accurately forecast or were forecast for the same date by a similar 1969 forecast. Also it showed the influence of environmental change. The 1964 forecasts of space events were made under an implicit assumption of funding at the 1964 level and growth rates. The subsequent changes in funding levels had obvious effects on the forecasts and suggests improvements such as more complete coverage of various sources of experts.[36]

There are other problems and Fusfield and Foster[37] suggest these as a range of questions:

(i) What is the psychological bias of the year 2000?
(ii) What individual characteristics, if common to a panel, influence its forecasts?
(iii) Does the position of an individual in his career or life tend to bias results?
(iv) What kind of perceived risk-taking is involved in the minds of Delphi panelists?
(v) Is it possible that consideration of future events beyond a certain range is too 'inexact' a science and not a legitimate part of planning?
(vi) Do Delphi panelists take full cognizance of the fact that their forecast may somehow influence the event?

(vii) What are the confidence limits that can empirically be placed or justified for Delphi forecasts?

The authors comment on these questions by saying:

The answers to these and other questions raised by the preceding discussion are not readily available. However, a consideration of their possible effects is paramount to the truly effective use of Delphi forecasting, and they should, therefore, be resolved in some form by the corporate planner.[37]

Delphi as a tool for corporate planning
Fusfield and Foster suggest five areas, consideration of which would be fruitful in the successful application of Delphi to Corporate uses:

(i) The planner must match the type of output desired with the alternative outputs which Delphi can produce. Because of its limitations and unanswered problems, Delphi may produce naïve and intuitively obvious results, promising more than can be delivered, making forecasts that are not used, or helping to allocate investment funds on an unsound basis.

(ii) The amount of uncertainty that can be tolerated must be considered. A possible measure is to use the interquartile range as a measure of the dispersion of responses. For example if the interquartile range increases as the median increases there may be a point at which the range limits the usefulness of the forecasts. Therefore, assessments of the utility of forecasts with various interquartile ranges should be made prior to establishing a Delphi-based planning system.

(iii) The possibility of using Delphi in conjunction with other forecasting techniques. Possibilities include trend analysis, mapping, and monitoring the environment to obtain a highly reliable forecasting system.

(iv) Consideration should be given to research planning or the industry development cycle. The research cycle can supply dates that will serve as targets upon which to focus a forecast. Alternatively, the industry development cycle may suggest aspects of developments that should be explored; for example capital funds, constraints, sources, opportunities, etc.

(v) The forecaster may wish to incorporate forecast stratification whereby the project is broken down into overlapping subgroups which may be addressed by groups of self-rated experts. The overlapping will permit the development of internal consistency while the use of subgroupings will yield greater accuracy.

Fusfield and Foster highlight the primary advantage of Delphi:

... one of the major advantages of Delphi is that it stimulates thinking and involves management in the forecasting process.[37]

Delphi as an aid to physical distribution system planning
The discussion thus far has been aimed at establishing Delphi as a worthwhile forecasting method for business planning. It is necessary to be more specific and to establish its acceptability for use as an aid to physical distribution system planning.

This is best done by considering what output information is required of the forecasting system. Here information is required on the likely developments of:

Product types and throughput
Organizational change
End-users—change in type and habits
Changes in specific product types
Changes in outlets—characteristics

These elements are basic to physical distribution system design which has as its basic goals the creation of time and place utility in products. However, to do this effectively it is necessary to determine who will cause change and just what that change may be.

It is too much to expect this information input to be determined from the application of statistical techniques to existing data. Existing data are useful in as much as they will give indications of what has happened in the recent past and currently and this information can be analysed for a basis from which an estimate of the future can be made. But this is the limit. Future developments depend on changing environmental factors, many of which cannot be quantified directly but nevertheless do have quantifiable end-results. For example, a shortage of investment funds will manifest itself in the channelling of whatever amounts are available to those companies which are capable of offering investors the best return. Viewed in the context of forecasting for planning it is necessary to discuss and consider this type of influence. In the grocery business (to take this example further) it is possible that in such circumstances (shortage of investment funds) the more efficient larger units, for example the Multiples, will be able to attract the funds needed for expansion. They will do this because of two factors. First, their past records; and secondly because of their future plans, ownership of assets, management expertise, etc., much of which is known to persons connected with the grocery business. Furthermore, the longer-term effects of social, economic, political and technological change are best known by these people because their own prosperity is very much governed by those factors.

It follows that in order to use this material the forecast should involve these experts and their views. Delphi offers this facility. It is useful because it enables those aspects to be identified and subsequently to be discussed. Evidence has been presented which suggests that the iteration processes arrive at results which are acceptable.

Therefore, bearing in mind Fusfield and Foster's suggested criteria for using Delphi as a 'tool for corporate planning', an exercise was designed with the following objectives and in the following terms:

(i) A consumer service mission has been identified for a grocery company and a desk research exercise will be conducted to establish the basis for the Delphi scenarios.

(ii) The scenarios will identify and seek forecasts of those aspects most likely to exert a major influence on physical distribution service.

(iii) A time horizon of a total of approximately twenty years will be used.

(iv) Forecast stratification will be used in order to obtain more accuracy. Corporate planners, senior marketing management and similar knowledgeable people from the trade press and associated industries, academics and consultants will be approached to obtain a forecast of activities in grocery retailing.

Senior distribution directors and managers were approached in a separate exercise aimed at forecasting 'philosophical change' within corporate physical distribution management.

Thus, for grocery retailing the following scenarios were established:

(i) Quantitative estimates of:
consumer food expenditure
convenience foods
own brands

(ii) The organizational structure of grocery retailing

(iii) The locational structure of grocery retailing

(iv) The nature of shopping habits

(v) Consumer durables ownership patterns

(vi) Development in store size trends and self-service

(vii) Cash and carry developments by:
volume
customer
products sold

(viii) The sales development of products from other EEC members.

For physical distribution both retailers and manufacturers were approached to estimate future dates for:

(i) The acceptance of PDM (physical distribution management) as the integrated control point for:
inventory
warehouse facilities
transportation
unitization
product communications

(ii) The widespread appointment of Distribution Directors
(iii) Total materials control
(iv) Computerized inventory prediction programmes
(v) Linked inventory control systems and inter-organizational data systems
(vi) Containerization
(vii) Out-of-hours deliveries
(viii) A National Pallet Pool
(ix) Cooperative distribution between manufacturers
(x) National consolidated distribution services

During the autumn of 1972 and spring of 1973, an extensive Delphi exercise extending to three rounds was run both with grocery manufacturers and with major retailers. The methodology employed was as indicated above. The results of the Delphi exercise are analysed in the section which follows and then tabulated in Appendix 2.

A DESCRIPTION OF THE FORECAST RESULTS

Grocery manufacturers' physical distribution systems can be expected to undergo considerable change during the next decade. The causes of this change are two-fold. First PDM (physical distribution management) as a discipline is becoming accepted at an accelerating rate and management at all levels is becoming aware of PD not only as a single cost centre but as a source of revenue. Secondly, techniques and facilities are being developed which aim to reduce system costs and at the same time enable individual systems to cope with continually increasing demands for service.

The results of our Delphi exercise have put dates to future developments in physical distribution. They have also put quantitative values to developments of a number of aspects within grocery retailing for the years 1980 and 1990.

Physical distribution futures—manufacturers' views
In the not-too-distant future (1976) it is anticipated that the majority of companies in the grocery industry will have distribution directors and that by 1977 physical distribution management will involve complete responsibility for inventory management, warehousing and materials handling facilities, unitization policy, transportation, and communications. By this time it is further anticipated that both strategic and tactical policies will be made with full cognizance of the interrelationships and interdependence of purchasing, production planning, marketing planning, and distribution planning. These are not insignificant changes in management attitudes. In fact when the

Distribution Futures—
Manufacturers' Forecasts

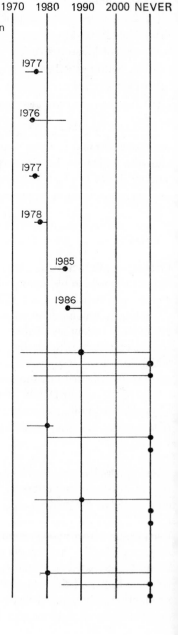

1. Physical distribution management will involve responsibility for the integration and coordination of inventory management: warehousing and materials handling facilities: unitization: transportation and communications by the majority (75%) of companies by:

2. Physical distribution management will report at board level in the majority (75%) of companies by:

3. In the majority of companies (75%) purchasing, production planning and distribution planning will be integrated for the purposes of tactical and strategic policy decision making by:

4. Analyse-and-Predict-Programmes for inventory control will be in use with the majority of companies (75%) by:

5. Linked inventory control systems will be utilized by the majority (75%) of companies by:

6. Automated warehousing will be in use with the majority of companies (75%) by:

7. Public warehousing will be used by the majority (75%) of companies for

   25% of warehouse requirements by
   50% of warehouse requirements by
   75% of warehouse requirements by

8. The majority of companies (75%) will use inter-modal containers for:

   25% of shipments by
   50% of shipments by
   75% of shipments by

9. The majority of companies (75%) will be using containers for:

   25% of shipments by
   50% of shipments by
   75% of shipments by

10. Freightliner will be used by the majority of companies (75%) for:

    25% of shipments by
    50% of shipments by
    75% of shipments by

11. Out of hours deliveries will be enforced:

    Between   6.00 p.m.-10.00 p.m. by
    Between 10.00 p.m.- 6.00 a.m. by

12. Government/Local Government control of bulk
breaking can be expected by:

13. Manufacturer/Distributor Inter-Organizational
Data Systems will be used by the majority (75%)
of manufacturers by:

14. A National Pallet Pool will be working by:

15. The majority (75%) of manufacturers will link bulk
(quantity) discounts to economic drop sizes by:

16. The majority (75%) of manufacturers will link
discounts to out of hours deliveries by:

17. Standardized packs for product groups can be
expected by:

18. The majority (75%) of companies expect vehicle
loading to be computer controlled by:

19. The majority (75%) of companies expect packages
for evaluating and planning physical distribution
systems to be available and used by:

20. The majority (75%) of companies expect to
cooperate with each other and operate consolidated distribution for:

    25% of shipments by
    50% of shipments by
    75% of shipments by

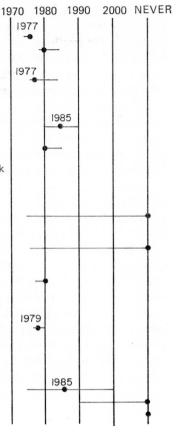

'average' company is considered it is going to take considerable rigorous self-appraisal and reorganization to meet these dates.

In terms of 'hardware', PD systems are likely to show significant change. It is estimated that EDP systems will continue to be developed and that by 1978 most manufacturers will be using Analyse-and-Predict programmes for inventory control. By 1985 it is foreseen that manufacturers' and retailers' inventory systems will cooperate jointly to control respective inventory levels and re-ordering. Inter-organizational data systems are expected by the same date. Extensions of EDP applications into vehicle loading programmes (1980) and system planning and evaluation programmes (1979) are anticipated. Warehousing developments are likely to be slow. The widespread use of automated warehousing is unlikely until 1986. Most manufacturers appear to consider their own warehousing facilities are, and will continue to be, pre-ferable to leased public warehousing.

Extensive use of containerization appears unlikely. A maximum of 25% of shipments will be containerized and this is unlikely before 1980. Intermodal containers are less likely to be used extensively and it is likely to be 1990 before 25% of the shipments move this way. Freight-liner will not obtain a large share of the grocery manufacturers' business. It is estimated that by 1980 some 25% of shipments may use this mode but that any further increase is not likely.

Government intervention in the control of deliveries is considered very likely (there were few 'nevers') and in the not-too-distant future. By 1977 it is expected that in urban areas deliveries will be enforced between 6 p.m. and 10 p.m. and that by 1980 this could be extended to between 10 p.m. and 6 a.m. It is also possible that by 1977 controls over the location of bulk breaking and deliveries may be implemented by the government or local government. The problems surrounding a National Pallet Pool seem unlikely to be solved until 1980.

Cost control is likely to cause manufacturers to consider linking bulk (quantity) discounts to economic drop sizes by 1975. However, linking discounts to out-of-hours deliveries is unlikely. Also unlikely is any attempt towards pack size standardization in any unitization programmes.

Cooperation among manufacturers to combine facilities in deliveries is not likely to be extensive, with only some 25% of goods movements so affected by 1985. The acceptance of distribution services such as those offered by Cory or SPD is not likely to be widespread. Only 25% of manufacturers' shipments are expected to take this form and this only by 1986.

Physical distribution futures—retailers' views
Grocery retailers' opinions do not differ materially from the manufacturers. They anticipate earlier acceptance of the PDM concept by some two or three years and suggest that large companies have already implemented the concept. The retailers also consider that Analyse-and-Predict programmes will be implemented earlier and suggest that large companies are using these programmes now. However, the estimate for linked inventory control systems coincides with the manufacturers' estimate. Inter-organizational data systems are expected to operate earlier between manufacturers and large retailers.

Some difference of opinion concerning manufacturers' use of containers is apparent. Retailers consider that manufacturers will make much more use of containers at earlier dates. The retailers consider that control by government of deliveries is likely later, with more opinion weighted towards no action at all. Deliveries enforced between 10 p.m. and 6 a.m. are considered unlikely ever to occur. Discount incentives by manufacturers are not

Distribution Futures—Retailers

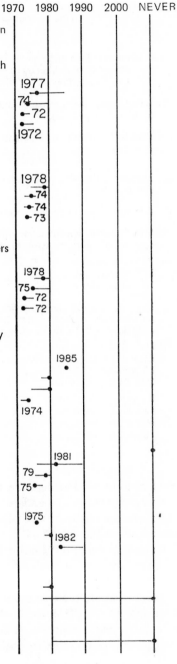

1970 1980 1990 2000 NEVER

1. Physical distribution management will involve responsibility for the integration and coordination of inventory management; warehousing and materials handling facilities; unitization; transportation; and communications in companies with turnovers of:

   Up to £10 million by
   £10 million-£50 million by
   £50 million-£150 million by
   Over £150 million by

2. Physical distribution management will report to the board in companies with turnovers of:

   Up to £10 million by
   £10 million-£50 million by
   £50 million-£150 million by
   Over £150 million by

3. Analyse-and-Predict-Programmes for inventory control will be in use by companies with turnovers of:

   Up to £10 million by
   £10 million-£50 million by
   £50 million-£150 million by
   Over £150 million by

4. Linked inventory control systems will be used by companies with turnovers of:

   Up to £10 million by
   £10 million-£50 million by
   £50 million-£150 million by
   Over £150 million by

5. Automated warehousing will be used in companies with turnovers of:

   Up to £10 million by
   £10 million-£50 million by
   £50 million-£150 million by
   Over £150 million by

6. Manufacturers will be using containers for:

   25% of their shipments by
   50% of their shipments by
   75% of their shipments by

7. Out of hours deliveries will be enforced:

   Between 6.00 p.m.-10.00 p.m. by
   Between 10.00 p.m.- 6.00 a.m. by

8. Government/Local Government control of bulk breaking and out of hours delivery can be expected by:

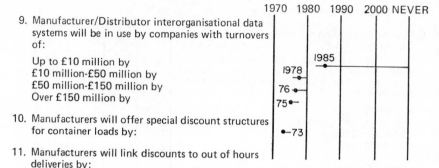

1970 1980 1990 2000 NEVER

9. Manufacturer/Distributor interorganisational data systems will be in use by companies with turnovers of:

   Up to £10 million by   1985
   £10 million-£50 million by   1978
   £50 million-£150 million by   76
   Over £150 million by   75

10. Manufacturers will offer special discount structures for container loads by: 73

11. Manufacturers will link discounts to out of hours deliveries by:

12. Standardized packs for product groups can be expected by: 1985

13. A National Pallet Pool will be working by: 1976

14. Manufacturers will cooperate with each other and operate consolidated distribution for:

   25% of supplies by   1977
   50% of supplies by
   75% of supplies by   1985

15. Nationwide consolidation services using computerized distribution centres will operate by companies with turnovers of:

   Up to £10 million by   1977
   £10 million-£50 million by   77
   £50 million-£150 million by   78
   Over £150 million by   77

   By manufacturers for:
   25% of shipments by   1975
   50% of shipments by   78
   75% of shipments by   1988

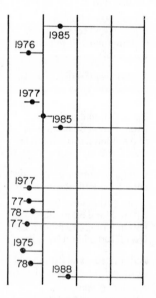

considered likely. Furthermore, the retailers' group agreed with the manufacturers' group that pack standardization is also unlikely. The retailers, however, are more optimistic towards the problems of a National Pallet Pool and consider it viable by 1976.

Consolidation of distribution by manufacturers is considered likely sooner and for larger goods volumes. Equally, the retailers consider that manufacturers will make more use of distribution services at earlier dates.

These then are the changes that are anticipated in PD systems due to the development of PDM as a discipline and the continued application of techniques and equipment. It is possible, however, that more far-reaching changes will be imposed by changes in the retailing environment.

Retailing futures

By 1980 weekly food expenditure, as a proportion of total consumer expenditure, will fall from the 1970 volume of 21·3% to 19% and by 1990 to 15·5%. Convenience foods sales will increase from a 1970 proportion of 27·8% of total grocery sales to 33% in 1980 and 36% in 1990. Frozen foods are likely to show most increase with an estimated 50% increase on 1970 sales by 1980, and a 100% increase by 1990. AFD foods are expected to increase by 25% by 1980 and 50% by 1990. Other types of convenience foods will increase by 15% and 30% for the same periods.

Market shares of retailing organizations will change. They can be expected to be:

	1980 (%)	1990 (%)	(1970) (%)
Multiples	50	58	42
Co-ops	15	13	15
Symbol Independents	20	19	23
Independents	15	10	20

The food sales of the variety chain operations are expected to increase. By 1980 a 20% increase is anticipated, and 40% by 1990.

Non-food sales are expected to increase for most types of outlet to represent:

	1980 (*percentage of total turnover*)	1990 (%)
For Multiples	10	20
For Co-ops	15	15
For Symbol Independents	5	5
For Independents	3	5

The future development of grocery sales through differing outlet types and locations will vary for each type. For example, sales through supermarkets in central shopping areas can be expected to show a 10% increase on 1970 volume by 1980, but are not expected to increase further by 1990. For superettes in central shopping areas no change is expected. Sales by supermarkets in out-of-town locations can be expected to increase by 50% to 1980 and by 80% to 1990. 'Super stores' in out-of-town locations will show the largest increases—a 100% increase by 1980 and 200% by 1990. Suburban supermarkets will also show large increases. By 1980 they can expect to increase sales by 40%. However, the increases are expected to be smaller and will represent 50% of the 1970 values. Superettes in suburban areas are expected to show no changes. Regional shopping centres are expected to grow rapidly. Fifteen are anticipated by 1980 and a total of twenty by 1990. Hypermarkets will also grow at a rapid rate with thirty in existence by 1980 and seventy-five by 1990.

Shopping frequencies will change. By 1980, only 19% of housewives will be shopping daily with a fall to only 14% by 1990. In 1970 the figure was 23%. Those shopping every two or three days per week will also be fewer, that is 34% by 1980 and 30% by 1990; the 1970 figure was 38%. Some 11% of housewives will still be shopping every four or five days per week in 1980 and 1990.

Consumer durables ownership can be expected to increase. Washing machine ownership, as a percentage of households, was 64% in 1970. By 1980 it will be 75% and by 1990, 80%. For refrigerators the increase is likely to be similar; 75% in 1980 and 85% in 1990 from 63% in 1970. Food and drink mixers are likely to show the largest increase rate, from 24% of households in 1970 to 35% in 1980 and 50% in 1990. Dishwasher ownership will increase from a low 1%, to 5% by 1980 and 15% by 1990. Families owning two cars will increase from 6% in 1970 to 10% in 1980 and 20% in 1990. Those with one car will increase from 45% in 1970 to 58% in 1980 and 68% in 1990. Telephones will increase from a 1970 figure of 35% to 45% in 1980, and 65% in 1990.

Own-brands will increase, with the Multiples increasing their 1970 proportion of total sales (average for all Multiples) of 12–14% to 20% in 1980, and 24% in 1990. The Co-ops can be expected to show the largest growth: from 9–11% in 1970 to 15% in 1980 and 20% in 1990. The Symbol Independents' own-brands activities will be much smaller. At present 2–3% of total sales, they are expected to be 5% in 1980 and 8% in 1990.

Cash-and-carry is expected to plateau during the 1980/90 period. Turnover is expected to reach 18% by 1980, from 13–14% but will decline slowly by 1990 to 17%. Customer types using cash-and-carry outlets will change. Currently, grocers and other general stores comprise 40% of customers. By 1980 this is likely to be 35% and by 1990, 30%. Sales to caterers will increase, from 40% in 1970 to 45% by 1980. By 1990 48% of cash-and-carry customers are expected to be caterers. No change is expected in the 10% share of confectioners, tobacconists and newsagents. A small increase is expected in the 10% share of greengrocers, butchers and other non-food retailers to 12% in 1980 and 13% in 1990.

The product mix sold in cash-and-carry outlets will change. Groceries are likely to decline from 63% of the total to 55% in 1980 and 48% in 1990. Wines and drinks will show an increase from 10% to 12% by 1980 and 15% by 1990. Confectionery sales are not expected to show change; currently 10% they are expected to remain at that figure for 1980 and 1990. Tobacco product sales are likely to decline slowly over the period from 8% in 1970 to 7% in 1980 and 6% in 1990. It is expected that non-food products will increase from 7% in 1970 to 10% by 1980 and 12% by 1990.

Consumers will spend more in restaurants and take-home outlets. For restaurants increases of 25% and 78% are expected for 1980 and 1990. Take-home sales will grow faster, 45% and 88%. Again the base year is 1970. Sales through self-service stores will also increase. In 1970 the proportion was 66% of total sales. By 1980 we can expect this to be 78% and for 1990, 85%.

Store size developments are forecast to show increases in the larger stores and relative decreases for smaller stores. Those stores over 25,000 ft^2 can be expected to show a 50% increase by 1980 and a 300% increase by 1990. Stores of between 15,000 and 25,000 ft^2, a 60% increase by 1980 and a 200% increase by 1990. Stores of between 8,000 and 15,000 ft^2 will not increase as rapidly; 15% by 1980 and 30% by 1990. Stores in the 4,000–8,000 ft^2 size will increase by 10% in 1980 and 20% by 1990. No change in the number of 2,000–4,000 ft^2 size stores is expected by 1980 but a relative decline is expected, some 10% by 1990. Small stores, 2,000 ft^2 and smaller, are expected to decrease in number, 15% by 1980 and 20% by 1990.

Sales of grocery products manufactured by other EEC member countries are expected to increase by 20% for 1980 and by 70% for 1990.

How will the retailing futures influence physical distribution?
In attempting to explore the implications of the futures that our experts have forecast, a series of questions has been prepared. It behoves each reader to examine any implications and likely impact on his or her own business.

Qu: What effect will the continuing reduction of consumer expenditure on food have on system throughput and capital utilization?

Qu: Will the increased demand for convenience foods change inventory policies, warehouse facilities and transportation?

Qu: What are the implications of the forecast growth in Multiples' sales? Does this mean even more service in terms of higher service levels, and therefore higher inventory carrying costs? Unitization programmes to meet the individual requirements of these even larger customers? Will deliveries be dictated to even finer limits? What other changes are likely?

Qu: The Variety chains are expected to increase their food sales by 20% by 1980 and 40% by 1990. All have large investments in down-town locations. Thus, can current congestion problems be expected to be amplified?

Qu: Just what does the increasing proportion of non-foods in retailing turnovers mean for manufacturers' PD systems? Are more manufacturers likely to add non-food lines? If so, what problems will these present to PD managers in terms of their existing inventory, warehousing, transportation, unitization and communications policies?

Qu: A big question is posed by the forecast three-fold increase by 1990 of large out-of-town retail units. Does this mean more retailers will utilize central warehouses or that the current trends will be reversed and that direct deliveries to these and similar outlets will be favoured? Food retailing outlets in suburban areas will increase by 80% by 1990. Again delivery patterns and stock-holding policies will be required to change. What changes are likely? Who will be making them? Who will be required to make the investment? Furthermore, there are derived problems. For example, what sales aids will be required in the new large outlets, and what are the likely effects of these on PD system design?

Qu: Much the same set of problems must be posed concerning the effects of an increase in regional shopping centres and hypermarkets. In the case of these outlets are different service requirements—service levels, deliveries, unitization, order processing, invoicing—likely?

Qu: Housewives are expected to make fewer shopping trips for groceries. Does this mean they will buy larger amounts in larger packs? If so what are the implications for PD systems? Is it possible that inventory levels throughout the system may be fractionally lower? On the other hand could this be offset by the need to ensure higher service levels to accommodate the fewer visits of housewives?

Qu: The more affluent consumer will invest more in consumer durables. Ownership of refrigerators and food mixers is likely to increase appreciably over the next twenty years. Is it likely then that product ranges will change and for some manufacturers these will necessitate changes in PD systems? The most likely changes are in convenience foods products. It has been seen that frozen foods and AFD foods are likely to continue to develop at a high rate. Therefore is it likely there are to be system changes because of consumers' desire for and ability to store frozen foods? For example, are we likely to see a freezer boom or freezer space rental made available to the public—and if so what modifications are likely in the future to PD systems?

Qu: Car ownership too will have its effects. Not only is it likely to accelerate congestion problems and hasten legislation on deliveries and possibly the use of cars in city centres, but it is possible for the British housewife to begin to favour 'one stop shopping' at out-of-town locations, possibly midweek as opposed to weekends. Could this alter delivery scheduling? Does it mean higher service levels at all times—particularly midweek? What are the unitization (packaging) implications of housewives buying in larger volumes once she is relieved of the carriage problems?

Qu: Own-brand sales are expected almost to have doubled by 1990. Does this fact relieve or intensify manufacturers' PD problems? Does it mean lower inventory holding for manufacturers? More economic transportation? Lower order processing costs?

Qu: Cash-and-carry sales are expected to increase by 4% by 1980 but to decrease very slightly by 1990. This suggests a levelling off of their growth during the eighties. Furthermore, their pattern of sales is likely to change with caterers becoming more important and specialist non-grocery retailers increasing their business slightly. There are obvious logistics implications.

Manufacturers' planning should take into account the possibility of the change in sales pattern on such aspects as unitization; for example, a switch of emphasis towards catering packs is clearly likely and perhaps, too, there are changes in service level requirements. The products sold through cash-and-carry outlets will change. Groceries will decline in importance as wines and non-foods sales increase. Again there are logistics implications. It is possible that long-term unitization policies may need modification. If grocery sales decline and total cash-and-carry sales plateau, then it is likely that some retailers (those large enough) may be seeking alternative delivery programmes. Thus volume unitization will not be satisfactory and modifications will be required. Delivery problems under these circumstances would increase. There are obviously other possibilities. The most obvious is that the Multiples will move into this field (some of course have). In this case it is likely that not only will the manufacturers find changes necessary but so too will the retailers. Will they increase their investment in centralized warehousing and from these locations supply both their retail and wholesale activities? If so what service demands are likely? How will the PDM activities change to accommodate them?

Qu: Consumers are expected to increase their spending in restaurants and in 'take-home' outlets. Both can expect enormous increases but the 'take-home' outlets will grow faster. The grocery product manufacturer can expect changes. For example, he must consider the service requirements of the chain operators as these are the outlets likely to enjoy the growth. Have these been identified?

Qu: Self-service is a well-established concept. In 1970, 66% of sales were through self-service stores. By 1980 there will be 78% of sales made through self-service, and 85% by 1990. What are the implications here? Is it likely that overall costs can be expected to fall as the proportion of self-service stores increases, thereby permitting manufacturers to obtain economies of scale in such aspects of their operations as deliveries, packaging, order processing?

Qu: Much the same comment can be made concerning self-service store sizes. The large stores, over 25,000 ft^2, can be expected to treble by 1990. Can this increase, combined with a 20% decrease in stores of less than 2,000 ft^2, lead to increased efficiency in physical distribution throughout the process?

Qu: An increase in sales of other EEC members' products is likely—a 70% increase by 1990. The logistics implications here are numerous. One possibility is the development of distribution agreements among all EEC manufacturers, whereby a British manufacturer adds a non-competitive but similar product type of a French manufacturer to his product line for a reciprocal facility, thus lowering overall costs for each of them.

Qu: Finally we come to PD system planning. Is it feasible for manufacturers to group units with similar service requirements together into distribution missions: for example, is it possible that out-of-town units, large stores, hypermarkets, cash-and-carry operators, may each have specific service requirements which are most effectively and economically met by grouping them together and developing specific programmes to service them?

Qu: If this is a possibility then how would this approach affect such aspects of operations as *administration and organization*? How would organization adapt to this approach? What would the information requirements be? Indeed will change be necessary at all? *Facility locations:* Would changes in type, number and location be required? What are the capital investment problems? *Transportation:* Is vehicle size likely to differ? Will vehicle numbers increase? Or will carriers be used? *Unitization:* How can developments in containerization and packaging design be utilized? What are the likely effects of size and mode of handling? *Communication:* Would a missions approach require special EDP inventory control programmes? Would order processing and invoicing procedures need modification?

REFERENCES

1. *Social Trends No. 3*, HMSO, 1972.
2. 'Survey of personal incomes', Inland Revenue, 1970.
3. *Abstract of regional statistics.* HMSO, 1967 and 1971.
4. *National income and expenditure.* HMSO, 1972.
5. *Household food consumption and expenditure.* Ministry of Agriculture and Fisheries, 1960 and 1969.
6. *Prices, profits and costs in food distribution—Report No.* 165. National Board for Prices and Incomes, HMSO.
7. *Census of distribution of* 1966. HMSO, 1970.
8. A. C. Nielsen.
9. *Retail business No.* 164, Economist Intelligence Unit, 1971.
10. A. C. Nielsen.
11. Braham, M., 'Superstores', *The Observer*, October 3rd, 1971.
12. *Retail business Nos.* 153 *and* 165, Economist Intelligence Unit, 1970 and 1971.
13. *Report of the deliveries working party*, Institute of Food Distribution, October 1970.

14. Helmer, O., 'Analysis of the future: the Delphi method', in Bright, J. (ed.), *Technological Forecasting for industry and government.* Prentice-Hall, 1968.
15. Wills, G., *Technological forecasting.* Penguin, 1972; and Wills, G., Ashton, D. J. L. and Taylor, B., *Technological forecasting and corporate strategy.* Crosby Lockwood, 1969.
16. Mandanis, G. P., 'The future of the Delphi technique', in Arnfield, J. (ed.), *Technological Forecasting.* Edinburgh University Press, 1969.
17. Adelson, M., Alkin, M., Carey, C. and Helmer, O., 'The education innovation study', *American Behavioral Scientist,* **10**(7), 1967.
18. Bender, A. D., Stack, A. E., Ebright, G. W. and Von Haunalter, G., 'Delphi study examines developments in medicine', *Futures,* June 1969.
19. 'Medicine in the 1990s', Office of Health Economics.
20. de Brigard, Raul and Helmer, O., 'Some potential societal developments: 1970–2000', *IFF Report R7,* September 1969.
21. Enzer, Selwyn and de Brigard, Raul, 'Issues and opportunities in the state of Connecticut', *IFF Report R8,* September 1969.
22. Turoff, M., 'The design of a policy Delphi', *Technological Forecasting and Social Change,* **2**, 1970.
23. Schneider, J. B., 'The policy Delphi: a regional planning application', *Technological Forecasting and Social Change,* **3**, 1972.
24. McDaniel, A., 'Transportation forecasting: a review', *Technological Forecasting and Social Change,* 1971.
25. Moore, G. G. and Pornrehn, H. P., 'Technical forecasting of marine transportation systems 1970–2000', USC, June 1969.
26. Kimble, R., 'Delphic forecasting of critical personnel requirements', *US Army Electronics Command,* 1969.
27. Gordon, T. J., 'A study of potential changes in employee benefits', *IFF Report No. 1,* April 1969.
28. 'Recent use of Delphi on the role of mentally retarded in society', *SET Incorporated,* Los Angeles.
29. Turoff, M., 'A summary of the RAND civil defence Delphi', Office of Emergency Preparedness—Systems Evaluation Division, *Technical Memorandum 122,* February 1970.
30. 'Major continuing study of technological and economic developments directly related to Japanese national planning', Japan Techno-Economics Society.
31. International Federation for Information Processing, 'Delphi on the future of computers', *Science Journal,* August 1969.
32. McLoughlin, W. G., 'Technological forecasting at LTV', *Science and Technology,* February 1970.
33. Pyke, D. L., 'A practical approach to Delphi, technological forecasting and long-range planning', *American Institute of Chemical Engineers,* November 1969.
34. Kavac, F. J., 'Technological forecasting—tires', *Chemical Technology,* January 1971.
35. Parker, E. F., 'Some experience with the application of the "Delphi Method"', *Chemistry and Industry,* September 20th, 1969.
36. Ament, R. and Gordon, T. J., 'Forecasts of some technological and scientific developments and their societal consequences', *IFF Report No. 6,* September 1969.
37. Fusfield, A. R. and Foster, R. N., 'The Delphi technique: survey and comment', *Business Horizons,* June 1971.

CHAPTER 7

Marketing in Socialist Eastern Europe

This chapter reports on work prepared under grant from the Advertising Association which was an integral part of a wider programme of research at the University of Bradford Management Centre into Comparative Marketing Systems and the conduct of International Business. The authors have held the conversations with, and visited, marketing executives in the USSR, Poland, Czechoslovakia, Hungary, Rumania and Bulgaria, and have conducted a thorough review of the literature. The views expressed here, and any errors, are entirely our own responsibility.

There has been, for a decade now, a widespread belief in both the social democratic and predominantly capitalistic societies of Western Europe and North America that the socialist societies of Eastern Europe were drifting towards the prevailing American view of marketing. It is frequently suggested, for example, that the concept of customer sovereignty must increasingly predominate in Eastern Europe as discretionary income levels grow, implying that Adam Smith's view of the invisible mechanism for resource allocation will replace the considered social view from the centre. There seem to have been two particularly important triggers which have led to this belief. The first was Krushchev's historic change of direction after the death of Stalin. The second has been the continuing economic controversies which have rocked Marxist–Leninist thinking since fresh proposals were made concerning the role of profits in a socialist society by Professor Liberman and a group of his colleagues at Kharkov State University.

These are not, of course, the only two triggers which have effected a dramatic shift in thinking about the marketing activity within socialist societies, but they do encompass many of the issues which are significant about socialist marketing in Europe today. They symbolize the end of heavy industrial capacity as a socialist economic status symbol, and the emerging managerial revolution. They must be seen against philosophical background of socialist enterprises since the Russian Revolution.

MARXIST–LENINIST MARKETING

Karl Marx was no believer in the modern marketing techniques which are an integral pattern of the business life of Western societies today. His view of marketing was implicit in his labour theory of value. All value was perceived as deriving from labour, capital being simply stored labour. Value could only be added to goods in the act of distribution, therefore, by those necessary acts of labour which ensured the effective conduct of what today we might term the marketing logistics activity.

Accordingly Marx did not accept the virtual equating we see today of value with price. The difference between these two in a capitalist society was 'surplus value' which constituted the focus of his indignation. It was this surplus which capital expropriated; socialism demanded that it be treated as belonging to labour. It only emerged because the labourer was forced to sell his labour at subsistence level defined as a cultural minimum.

Marx dodged the question of utility as an element in value, although conceding that a product had to be demanded for it to be of any use-value at all. He implicitly assumed that supply created its own demand. (This was not an unfamiliar concept at a macro-level of economic analysis in the nineteenth century. It was known as Say's Law.) Stalin's era of planning, which lasted from 1928 until 1950, was posited on this assumption. For Stalin, adherence to Say's Law was quite explicit; for Marx it was implicit in his value theory but contradicted in his theory of trade cycle or crises. He recognized the naïvety of the dogma that because every sale is a purchase and every purchase a sale, the circulation of commodities implies an economic equilibrium. He placed the blame for crises on the inadequate purchasing power of the masses—a view contrary to the thinking current at that time, but a worthy precursor to the Keynesian revolution.

It has already been indicated that, apart from the marketing logistics activity, the process of distribution was viewed as unproductive by Marx. It can perhaps be more strongly put, all other marketing activities were but stage two in the process of exploitation of labour by which prices further outstrip the labour value of goods. He wrote:

> buying and selling costs are not incurred in producing the use-value of commodities, but in realizing their value. They are pure costs of circulation. . . . The labour employed in selling commodities, in packing and preparing them for the market, and in 'book-keeping' creates no value. It is merely engaged in realizing value created in industry. Transport, on the other hand, does create value.[1]

Non-productive, or pure, costs do not add to the value of the product, but are a social waste and parasitic in nature. Middlemen and intermediate agents who buy and sell deploy their labour, but it is unproductive. Marx perceived marketing channels where the ownership of goods was transferred as needless. Direct transfer of title was preferable in that it removed the opportunity for exploitation and the accumulation of capital by the expropriation of surplus value.

Marx's language terminology will be somewhat strange to Western marketing men, but the dichotomy on which he focused between productive and unproductive distribution is an issue with which we are all familiar, and which requires a great deal of attention in the years ahead, both in socialist and in Western societies. Against this background we shall now turn to examine Lenin's role as the operational interpreter and extender of Marxist value and distribution theory both before and after he came to power in the USSR.

Lenin faced major problems which were glossed over in the official directive of the Second Party Programme in 1919:

> In the sphere of distribution, the task of the Soviet Government . . . is undeviatingly to replace private trade by a systematic distribution of products. . . . The aim is to organize the population into a uniform network of consumers' communes . . . to distribute all necessary products, strictly centralizing the apparatus for distribution.[2]

Only the undeviating replacement of private trades by cooperatives (of which membership was compulsory) reflected Marx's views. The centralization and systematization of distribution were new ideological ingredients. Lenin freely conceded that Marx had not discussed the question of 'how and where products would be sold or how and where articles of consumption would be bought by the workers'.[3] Lenin's adherence, however, to the doctrine of Marx that true distribution was a supplemental or subordinate activity in the creation of value in a society meant that this area continued to be ignored.

Centralization and systematization were the basic weapons for the elimination of the 'abyss of small middlemen who are ignorant of market conditions and who created both superfluous shipping and excessive buying. . . . The proletarian government must become a sharp, zealous, daring manager, a careful wholesale trader'[4] in order to reduce the time and labour waste of capitalist distribution incurred by the myriad of speculators and brokers operating under market uncertainty. Lenin was able to find a clearer theoretical basis for his approach to socialization of distribution in Engels, whom he quotes in *State and revolution*. Certainly Engels identified clearly what today we would term a total approach to physical distribution:

> In due time, and without excessive frills, the proper quality of each good needed to satisfy the population is determined. Excessive middlemen will be unnecessary. Goods will be delivered directly to where they are needed. Delays and reshipping will be eliminated and shipments will be made with no waste.[5]

These were the basic theoretical foundations on which Lenin acted. The pre-1917 cooperatives were nationalized and became the basis for much of the gigantic pattern of state trading corporations which increasingly characterized the socialist system. But the ultimate issue of distributing to each according to his need remained unexplored in operational terms, and it is one of the great unresolved debates in socialist marketing to this day. The abolition of money as a means of exchange in a socialist society after the transitional dictatorship of the proletariat so confidently forecast by Marx in *Das Kapital*, and the residual mechanisms of socialist distribution remain unclear.

By 1921, the initial socialization of almost all private traders had been completed, but had to be reversed almost immediately because of peasant protests. This was the era of the New Economic Policy, which permitted private traders in distribution, but was a temporary setback to the Marxist–Leninist momentum.[6] No clear direction for economic management emerged until Stalin took an iron grip on Soviet society from 1928 onwards.

STALINIST MARKETING

Stalin, and the series of five-year planning periods over which he presided, marked the end of the New Economic Policy. His system had two key dimensions—industrialization and the collectivization of agriculture. Collectivization was deemed fundamental to the viability of the process of industrialization, in that the agricultural output surplus to peasants' needs had to be distributed on socialist lines to the industrial workforce. Stalin abolished the free market in agricultural produce which had existed under the New Economic Policy, and the concentration on heavy industry meant a reduction in the proportionate volume of consumer goods emerging from light engineering activities in the economy.

Rationing was both formally present and implicit in the pricing policies pursued for consumption goods during the Stalinist era. The market situation became analogous to what Western societies term production orientation. A sufficiently limited supply of consumption goods and engineered prices (reflecting the labour-value of production and the supplemental production of pure distributive activity) made Say's Law appear to work. Stalin's dictum that excess demand draws forth supply without inflation in a socialist society, because price and wage costs are under control, was seemingly made to work. No viable measure of dissatisfaction existed since needs were interpreted or determined (call it which you will) centrally. Hence, socialist society under Stalin had a centrally conceived view of utility, not an aggregated answer expressed through market forces. This outcome has been described by many western observers, most notably Felker in his far-reaching examination of *Soviet economic controversies*[7] as 'entirely devoid of concern for consumer welfare'. Such a criticism represents a partial view of a much longer total process through which Soviet society was passing. Concern for consumer welfare was vested in the Party as the guardian of socialist ideals, and the politicians rather than Adam Smith's invisible hands decided the social priorities.

	1924	1926	1928	1932	1940	1945	1950	1955	1960
Government stores	17	17	16	30	62·7	42	63·9	63·2	66·8
Cooperatives	35	42	60	53	23·0	12	24·1	28·1	28·8
Urban Kolkhoz									
markets	—	—	—	17	14·3	46	12·0	8·7	4·4
Private traders	48	41	24	—	—	—	—	—	—

SOURCE: reported in Goldman, M. I., *Soviet marketing*. Free Press of Glencoe, 1963, p. 46. (The urban kolkhoz is a market place where rural produce can be sold on the free market after collective farm targets have been met. They have experienced varying fortunes, as the statistics show. In the food sector of retail trade alone they made 51% of all sales in 1945 and as much as 26% in 1932.)

FIG. 7.1   *Percentage share of total retail sales in USSR.*

The structure of retail trade in the USSR has shifted considerably during the first fifty years of the life of that socialist society as indicated by the shares of total retail sales going through the three main types of outlets reported in Fig. 7.1.

KRUSHCHEVIAN MARKETING

The 20th Party Congress, of 1956, is a landmark familiar to most Western observers. It was the occasion for Krushchev's famous denunciation of Stalinism, but it is important to note that, whilst some Stalinist doctrines were rejected, others remained. An emphasis on heavy industry and collectivization policies was continued, with minor alleviations. Most importantly, however, debate was authorized concerning the mechanisms to achieve productivity and a more efficient allocation of resources, both in the agricultural sectors and in manufacturing industry. Closely linked with this was the rejection of Say's Law and Stalin's version of it. The quest for a socialist theory of utility began at last in earnest and the price mechanisms were engineered to introduce an element of purchase freedom or discretion for the customer. Sheer volume and rate of growth in production, which under a labour theory of value implied social progress, were seen as in need of supplementation by welfare criteria as measures of achievement. In his more extravagant claims, in the 1961 Party Programme, Krushchev claimed that socialism would pass through a transition phase towards communism where each would receive according to his needs rather than according to his work as under the socialist pattern of practice. 1971–80 was singled out as the decade when the abundance of materials will mean that communist ideals of the distribution of products can be attained. Hence, serious thought is being given to the issues of what we would term post-industrial society.

As the country advances towards communism, personal needs will be increasingly met. . . . The output of consumer goods must meet the growing consumer demand in full, and must conform to its changes. Timely output of goods in accordance with the varied demand of the population . . . is an imperative requirement for all the consumer industries. . . . Good shopping facilities will be made available throughout the country and progressive forms of trading will be widely applied. The material and technical bases of Soviet trade—the network of shops and warehouses . . . —will be extended.[8]

Such a transition to a communist society is succinctly summed up in what has been described as 'The Doctrine of the Universal Abundance of Products'. It has important implications for the contemporary socialist view of marketing in Eastern Europe and its elucidation by Anchishkin is worth careful study. He writes:

Universal abundance presupposes that each member of society will obtain a sufficient amount of high quality, comfortable, practical and handsome clothing . . . an abundant, high calorie and widely assorted food . . . abundance also means the full satisfaction of the needs of the ordinary cultural goods such as radios and television receivers, musical instruments, means of transportation . . . and finally, abundance presupposes the satisfaction of people's needs for housing and home comfort.[9]

The unfulfilled needs of members of a communist society will be personal rather than socially approved needs. Society will provide, as it already does, social sanctions to discourage needs which are not deemed acceptable. Hence, a relative concept of need satisfaction in line perhaps with learned needs concepts from social psychology will form the basis for the final achievement of communist goals. From each according to his ability, to each according to his socially acceptable needs, is the operational task to be achieved.

Socialist production, and the supplemental production which is distribution, are perceived as in need of improved managerial efficiency if the designated social goals are to be speedily achieved. This poses the fundamental question of how productive efficiency is to be measured in the socialist system. In the predominantly seller's markets which existed for consumption goods until the advent of Krushchevian marketing approaches, sheer volume of output was deemed an effective measure. Quality indices were scarcely considered, and prices were inflexible. The focus for the marketing problem became not the producing enterprise under the Krushchevian reforms but the trade outlet. Goods were delivered in planned quantities to retail stores who were expected to dispose of them to customers. As discretionary incomes began to emerge and consumer goods choice became possible, undisposed surpluses of unsaleable merchandise emerged. It became readily apparent that goods sold rather that goods produced must be the criterion of effectiveness in productive activity.

Pricing policies have traditionally presented a major practical problem within the socialist economic system. Prices based on the labour content of a product plus the supplemental production implicit in distribution depend on a consistent view being taken of the cost of labour. Arbitrariness in pricing can lead to all manner of distortions within the economy in terms of decisions on alternate means of achieving required loads. The case has been increasingly argued that prices should reflect both the actual costs of production and consumer preferences. Hence, profits would emerge which could act as an indicator of the efficiency of an enterprise.

In effect, the shift from a seller's market to a buyer's market in many consumption goods began to show up some of the theoretical inconsistencies in the pattern of Soviet economic planning and distribution which demanded attention. The initial response was to grant flexibility in the fulfilment of plans at the enterprise and wholesaler levels, but this new-found discretion was slow to be taken up. The fundamental problem gradually emerged as one requiring careful estimation of consumer demand within those fields in which production was deemed to be socially desirable. The distinction between the free market approach and the centrally determined social desirability of productive activity should be borne in mind.

Nevertheless, some attempt to identify what the centre should classify as socially desirable was aired in 1960 and introduced by the Supreme Soviet in 1965. This placed the onus on the production planners to first identify the nature of demand estimated for goods from within the state trading and cooperative trading enterprises. Furthermore, it is increasingly the practice for such trading enterprises rather than to be designated by planners as the outlet for predetermined output.

Such a shift in responsibility for the interpretation of social needs within a socialist society has many similarities with the trend of countervailing power in the marketing channels of Western societies today. Because of the very substantial size of the trading organizations involved in socialist societies, once harnessed this affords the opportunity for a major development in the task of effectively matching socially acceptable consumer needs to industrial productive capacity.

KHARKOVIAN MARKETING AND SOCIALIST PROFITS

The decade when Krushchev dominated socialist thinking in Eastern Europe was one of intellectual ferment. Its close, and his replacement by Kosygin and Brezhnev, saw the crystallization of as important a change in direction as any since Stalin's curtailment of the New Economic Policy in 1928. The name most widely associated with the switch of direction in the management of the Soviet economic system was Professor Liberman, with his colleagues from the Kharkov Economic Council. His concept of 'socialist profitability' as the yardstick for the effective operation of enterprises was finally promulgated by the Supreme Soviet on October 2nd, 1965.[10] Its key details required the improvement of economic guidance allowing for adaptive behaviour at the enterprise level; the perfecting of planning and economic incentives; the improvement of enterprise efficiency and increasing emphasis on the material interest of workers.

The implementation of these 1965 Reforms demands an enhanced professionalism at enterprise level in the exercise of management tasks. Socialist profitability as a yardstick provides an incentive for cost reduction. It affords an incentive for customer orientation since only sold output can contribute to profitability, and the retained profitability constitutes a fund at the discretion of the enterprise to reward labour above and beyond the planned wage fund determined by the state planning authority.

Liberman's interpretation of what this means has been fully described.[11] Profitability is seen as a twin concept—the rate of profit in relation to fixed and working capital, and the sheer volume of profit. The great majority of enterprise profits, which are the property of society since there is no private ownership of capital, are distributed and used in the interests of all in developing production in line with social requirements and affording social consumption of education, health services, culture, art and the like. However, between 8% and 15% is devoted to the establishment of incentive funds in the discretion of the enterprise. There are three such funds: the economic incentives fund with its impact on earnings via bonuses; the fund for social and cultural needs and housing of employees, the equivalent of what we term fringe benefits; and the fund for the development of production.

The fund for the development of production is particularly worthy of comment here in the marketing context. It provides not, of course, the new capital for major extensions of enterprise which are derived from the central planning authority, but the resources for product improvement and improvement in productive efficiency. This fund seldom falls below 2–3% of the fixed capital employed with direct profits supplemented by an allowance for depreciation. It can rise to 15% in certain industrial sectors.

Without a system of free prices, however, the profit concept which the Kharkovian approach implies is not necessarily going to achieve a maximization of utility in the sense that supporters of consumer sovereignty perceive it. The price levels which are still set by state planners determine the overall allocation of resources in the context of market response.[12] A shift is undoubtedly taking place in the USSR towards a social utility measure of value rather than the traditional labour value approaches. It is a trend which has moved further ahead in some of the Eastern/Central European socialist societies, most noticeably Hungary, Yugoslavia[13] and Eastern Germany.

The patterns of various facets of marketing in several socialist countries were described in a series of readily obtainable articles and books in the mid-sixties. Bartels[14] in particular explores the wholesaling system and Goldman[15] the whole pattern of marketing in the USSR at the start of the sixties which is usefully complemented by Miller's excellent study.[16] Polish retailing has been described in some detail by Walkers[17] and an interesting comparison with Red China is available from Richman.[18]

This extended discussion of the philosophical issues behind marketing activity in socialist societies has deliberately emphasized that which is germane to the empirical evidence which follows. For the first time since the twenties, management in the USSR has been afforded that degree of discretion in its work task which will encourage individual initiative and enterprise. A yardstick of performance has been fashioned which has quickened the interest at enterprise level in the marketability of output and in the creation of surplus value or socialist profits in the transactions which can be of material benefit to the individuals who achieve well. But let us make no mistake—it is a social system which differs greatly from the capitalist and social democratic environments in which Western European managements operate. The interest of the socialist marketeer is in the methodology of demand estimation, in the methodology of marketing logistics and the panoply of promotional techniques that can diffuse information about products within legitimate social bounds. No invisible hand from 1776 is envisaged to guide the destiny of socialist societies.

THE CONTEMPORARY SOCIALIST MARKETING TASK

Our fieldwork in Eastern Europe was undertaken during the period 1969–70 and involved visits to and interviews with marketing executives, marketing educators and marketing researchers in the USSR, Poland, Czechoslovakia, Hungary, Rumania and Bulgaria. We have explored the nature of the contemporary marketing task in these socialist societies, all of which have taken their philosophical orientation from the thinking we have elucidated above. Each country is at a different stage on the path to achieving Universal Abundance but each seems to be treading in a broadly similar direction. Yugoslavia is a well-known example of a socialist society which made an early break with Stalinist marketing; Czechoslovakia recently suffered a severe setback as it moved ahead; Hungary, after a similar setback in 1956, has embraced much of the Yugoslav thinking and its own style of economic reforms under Janos Kadar with great success in recent years, as has Rumania. Poland and Bulgaria have been slower despite early reforms in Poland, under Gomulka in 1956. The Poles have, of course, suffered a substantial setback in very recent times.

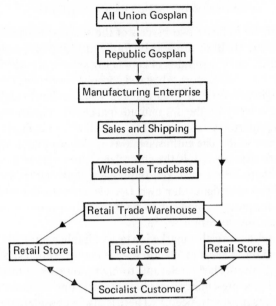

FIG. 7.2 *The Krushchevian marketing system* (1960).

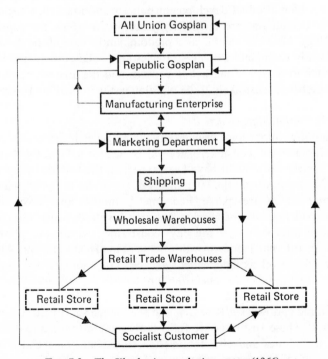

FIG. 7.3 *The Kharkovian marketing system* (1966).

Figs. 7.2 and 7.3 indicate two models of the socialist marketing process as we have identified it. Both are still operational today in Eastern European socialist societies, but the trend is of course toward the Kharkovian model in most of the economically more advanced socialist countries. The Krushchevian model originated around 1960 and the Kharkovian model about 1966. Certainly, the advent of the formalized marketing department within the manufacturing enterprise was one of the most talked-about facets of marketing at the time of our visits. The enthusiasm was analogous to that which Western Europe at large experienced at the end of the fifties and in the early sixties. However, let there be no mistaken impression that marketing departments have materialized overnight. Our own UK evidence on the rate of diffusion of marketing technology shows it to be a long-drawn-out process likely to take several decades to complete.[19]

The contemporary socialist marketing task of implementing the Kharkovian approach based on socialist profit criteria has made certain aspects of marketing technology particularly relevant to marketing executives in Eastern Europe. There is a pre-eminent interest in marketing research in which the Poles are perhaps most advanced.[20] There is also a considerable but cautious interest in above-the-line media of promotion and in packaging and merchandising. New product development policies and marketing logistics trail some way behind but are undoubtedly sectors in which the sophisticated methodology of social democratic predominantly capitalistic businessmen will be keenly examined. Pricing strategies and policies remain perhaps the most contentious area of marketing concern and the area where our professional expertise is least likely to be of value in the immediate future.[21]

The marketing intelligence activity

The paramount importance of marketing intelligence information, especially the development of consumer surveys, is acknowledged throughout the socialist societies. As might have been expected, the traditional background of demand analysis from the later stages of the Stalin era predominates and behavioural studies are sparse. Econometric models and forecasting techniques are widely used. The Market Research Institutes which were, until the Kharkovian approach won the day, constrained within the Ministries of Domestic or Internal Trade, or within some of the Heavy Industry Ministries, have been hived off as independent agencies. In Hungary, for example, at least two such units are operating on behalf of individual enterprises, including foreign enterprises trading within Hungary. We visited the Institute for Economic and Market Research and the Hungarian Institute for Market Research.[22] These Institutes are fully conversant with advanced marketing research techniques and also commission studies in non-socialist countries since 15% of all Hungarian output goes for export to the West.

Individual manufacturing enterprises now have the opportunity in Hungary of establishing direct marketing contacts of their own, for exports. Before the recent economic reforms all such contacts had perforce to be made through the Ministry of Foreign Trade. Now, in the quest for socialist profits, the Hungarian marketing manager may look beyond his own domestic market.

The Hungarian Institute for Market Research has a staff of over 100 and a field-force of 300 interviewers. It manages six information panels, each of 3,000 families, stratified by region, income, occupation and family composition. They started this panel work as early as 1960. Each panel member can expect to receive a questionnaire (they are postal panels with a percentage visit check) every two or three months. The response rate is phenomenal to the Western observer at 90 %; this is explained largely in terms of the enthusiasm aroused by such an opportunity to help improve the quality of market offering. Paralleling this is a low rate of panel fatigue.

Continuous research, although a major part of the research activity, is not of course the only facet. *Ad hoc* studies recently conducted have examined the potential for motor cars (Hungary imports cars, particularly the Polski Fiat) and for colour television. This latter was essentially a forecasting study and the researchers looked at eighteen socialist and non-socialist economies in their evaluation. Recent research into buying motives has quite clearly shown that price is of less overriding importance in Hungary now than quality and styling. They have used ordinal ranking methods so far but expect to deploy more sophisticated approaches shortly.

Distribution research, which would form an important research segment in the West, is of little concern. The government and cooperative-owned retail outlets and the wholesale enterprises both provide hard data on stock and distribution levels—sterling and percentage—without the 'spurious' device of retail auditing. Monthly retail sales data are, of course, readily available.

The situation in Poland in 1970 was less independent of the Ministries; this was also the case in the USSR. In Warsaw, the work of the Research Institute of the Ministry of Home Trade, which operates under the direction of a university professor, is outstanding. One other large marketing research activity exists in the Ministry of Foreign Trade and a marketing research unit has recently been established by PROMEX in the Ministry of Engineering Industries. Such operations have become increasingly independent as recent economic reforms began to take effect since 1971. (Some delay is now likely since the recent major changes in political leadership.) Formalized marketing education, emphasizing in particular the techniques of marketing research, has recently begun at the post-experience level. The Polish Management Development Centre ran its first four-week Senior Marketing Course in the autumn of 1970; it is also making intensive efforts to train a hard core of consultants to operate throughout Polish industry. (This particular decision was catalysed by some unsuccessful trans-cultural work by a British firm of consultants.)

We have commented particularly on the marketing research work at the Polish Ministry of Home Trade. It operates in three main departments concerned with the organization and techniques of trade, the economics of trade, and market and consumer research. Research has been conducted on marketing channels and on the sociological problems of trade which is more advanced than any undertaken in the UK to date. The Institute is well established and maintains strong links with the Hungarian Institute for Market Research already described above. A panel of some 3,500 families is maintained, as well as a capability for *ad hoc* studies of all types. A recent study examined the teenage market.

The marketing intelligence which Polish research units collate is currently deployed within ministries but not at the State Planning level; 1970 was, in fact, the year in which the economic debate concerning the Kharkovian approach reached its apogee in Poland. The precise way in which marketing research can be incorporated both into long-term and short-term planning tasks was still under active consideration.[23] Research into marketing as an operational system was also in progress even though the term marketing was often replaced by 'active selling' for philosophical reasons.[24]

Within the PROMEX marketing research unit in Warsaw we found our only evidence of the proposed development of a total marketing intelligence system in the socialist countries. Data banks are being established within PROMEX and within major factories using desk research data and an increasing volume of field data. The problematic areas are seen as consumer durables rather than industrial machinery at home, but in export markets the latter category requires careful forecasting. Technological forecasting was also incorporated in the general forecasting framework. Present pilot studies were exploring the demand for combustion engines and the most appropriate marketing channels to use. The resolution of the problem of centralization/decentralization for PROMEX marketing research activity, however, has yet to be made. The trend to allow individual enterprises to deal with direct retailers and customers, at home as well as in foreign trade, seems to argue for decentralized research within each major enterprise. One major problem of market research was continually emphasized—the hazards of forecasting the way the major economic decisions would affect demand and the pattern of activity of any enterprise. These decisions had to be forecast alongside market demand but they were not, of course, always reflective of demand patterns—the social desirability, as interpreted by the planning organization, of any demand trend must continually be superimposed.

Marketing research within the USSR is apparently considerably less sophisticated than it is in Hungary and Poland. NIKI, the Soviet Institute for Research within the Ministry of Foreign Trade, has provided the greatest impetus to marketing research to date. Its involvement and interest has been the outcome of its search for suitable foreign markets for the output of manufacturing enterprises. It is worth emphasizing that under the pre-Kharkovian systems, the individual enterprise had no responsibility at all for seeking out either domestic or export markets; it just made what was required by the plan. The Ministry of Foreign Trade was solely responsible for seeking out export business.

NIKI monitors some fifty product markets worldwide, for example, chemicals, minerals, machinery, agricultural produce, and issues a *Bulletin* three times a week. It is mainly a desk research activity. It has been in existence since 1947 and today has over 200 staff. Domestic markets are researched now by a recently established All-Union Market Research Institute although the debate as to how consumer-derived data can be incorporated into the planning process is as strong in the USSR today as in Poland.[25] Much argument still centres around the role which retail and wholesale levels of distribution should play as interpreters of demand for input to the plan and the extent to which macro-demand data should be treated statistically. The latter approach naturally has strong supporters amongst the planning hierarchy since it has its roots firmly in econometrics with its long-standing traditions. There seems little doubt, however, that the manufacturing enterprise level will itself demand an important part in the marketing research activity if it is to be held responsible for socialist profitability.

Promotional activity

Whilst the act of collecting and collating consumer data and marketing intelligence raises few philosophical problems in a socialist society, the same cannot be said for advertising and promotion. Socialist theory has been as consistent in its condemnation of the waste implicit in advertising as have senior corporate executives in Western societies. Socialist societies have boldly set their aim as identifying Lord Heyworth's famous 50% of advertising activity which is wasteful and more besides which is socially undesirable. The approach has accordingly been cautious, with incremental advances carefully evaluated. Most noticeably, the promotional mix is distinctly different from the British one. Below-the-line promotions, such a common feature of Western societies in the past decade or more, are almost totally absent. Packaging and point-of-sale display is noticeably less emphasized. Exhibitions and special display/design centres are more widespread. Trade and technical media hold a relatively more important share of total above-the-line promotion than in Western societies but all the above-the-line promotion is vastly less prolific than in our society. Statistics which can indicate how much in total is spent on promotion above the two-thirds line are not available, but what scant information exists indicates that it is well below 1% of the level of activity in the USA at retail, and an infinitesimal proportion at enterprise level.

The promotional philosophy implicit in socialist marketing is that media should be used for informative and educational purposes. Hence, particular emphasis is placed on the diffusion of information about new products.[26] Special newspaper supplements are issued in the USSR and television provides, inter alia, advertising magazine programmes of the type banned in the UK by the IBA several years ago. Television advertising normally takes the form, not of our commercials, but of discussions about the pros and cons of products—a sort of *Which?* This is not to suggest that advertising and promotion does not seek to dispose of surpluses of goods from time to time; it has generally been found to be less effective at this than price-cuts! One has only to visit what a Sears-Roebuck director recently described as the finest department store in the world, GUM on Red Square, or one of the fine supermarkets on the Kalinsky Prospect, to realize how little is the part which below-the-line, point-of-sale, promotion or packaging as yet play in marketing in the USSR. With such a relatively limited use of promotional media, it is perhaps not surprising that media research is an unknown phenomenon although factual data on specialized magazine readership profiles are available from the advertising agencies.[27]

Within the USSR two major advertising agencies operate—Vneshtorgreklama to handle foreign trade advertising both in terms of exports and imports, and Soyuztorgreklama to handle domestic trade promotion. Vneshtorgreklama operates in other countries via local agencies. In London it often uses Saward-Baker, who recommend on media and copy layouts, although copy is frequently prepared in the USSR. The total billings handled by Vneshtorgreklama in 1969 were estimated at approximately £5m—some 11m roubles. The agency employs a staff of about 180 with all the traditional departments plus a direct mail activity. Staff are partially specialized by country and by product field. Not all USSR enterprises have to work through Vneshtorgreklama, but many do. Notable exceptions are Aeroflot and Intourist.

Exhibitions and industrial trade fairs play an important part in both domestic and foreign trade. The USSR advertising agencies are fully capable of preparing promotional materials and displays for these media.

Particular emphasis was given in our discussions in Hungary and Poland to the use of posters as a medium for promotion. The fine traditions of European posters lives on in these countries. In Hungary, a new journal, *International Quarterly of Graphic Design*, was launched in 1970,[28] incorporating contributions from East and West. The major Hungarian advertising agency is Magyar Hirdeto. Its income is a percentage of billings from state enterprises whose accounts it wins and it competes with two or three smaller agencies. This competitive pattern for advertising agencies has so far emerged only in Czechoslovakia, Yugoslavia and Hungary. It has led Magyar Hirdeto to concentrate more on media research than Vneshtorgreklama or Soyuztorgreklama in the USSR. A special research unit conducts studies to measure the effectiveness of advertising and promotion, and television viewing habits were studied in 1961 and 1966. A special unit deals with exhibitions and a press-cutting service is maintained. Recently a packaging development group has been established, and work in a new promotional medium—factory gramophone records with advertising messages—has been pioneered. These records carry both cultural and commercial advertising. There is also an equivalent of *Exchange and Mart* produced in Hungary, *Intercare*, an illustrated monthly, which helps to clear surpluses between enterprises. Reader/membership qualifies the enterprise for advertising space.

Promotional research is not the monopoly of its creators, however. Other institutes also undertake detailed investigations, including advertising recall studies and the identification of target group media habits.

The Polish scene is dominated by two advertising agencies, each with its defined clientele. Agpol handles import/export advertising and Reklama domestic goods. Reklama employs over 1,500 staff and in 1966 had billings of some 200m zlotys (at least £5m). Markiewicz-Lagneau[29] has written one of the most effective descriptions of socialist advertising from the Polish context. Advertising is 'news' or 'education' to the Polish reader or viewer, rather than an attempt at persuasion; the competitive clamour which gives rise to so much potential confusion in Western societies is absent. It postulates a concept of harmonious advertising in contradistinction to conflicting advertising; it seeks to bring into harmony the purchasing patterns of consumers with the social rationality of the planner.

Product improvement and development

Little evidence exists of marketing responsibility or concern for product improvement or development. The initiative within the manufacturing enterprises seems to lie clearly with the technical staffs. Nonetheless, signs of concern about the quality of products available, most noticeably in Hungary but widely throughout Eastern Europe, have led to the introduction of product test procedures, consumer clinics and new product display centres. Most major cities have such showcases for new products. In Budapest we saw as professionally organized a consumer clinic for fashion goods as any in Western Europe which was operated by a marketing research agency for testing out new designs and new market offerings.

There is little doubt in any of the three major societies in which we spent a considerable period of time, that the impact of imported merchandise and machinery is very substantial on the standards sought after from domestic production. The extreme popularity of Western goods is everywhere apparent. There are many more Western goods in the shops in Hungary than in either Poland or the USSR, but the increase in trade has meant a particularly important growth in general availability. Hence, the competitive stimulus of foreign goods and their quality is acting as a vitally important catalyst in the improvement of product quality simultaneously with the increasing use of socialist profit centre approaches in the enterprise.

The adverse side of the product improvement argument for home markets is the need to match imports with exports. The influence which the search for profitable export markets in Western societies, to pay for imports, has had on management is already substantial. As more and more enterprises are actively permitted to pursue markets directly, the contact and spin-off in expertise must grow. Selling and marketing Russian watches, Hungarian textiles or Polish vodka in western societies required marketing expertise at the Western level of sophistication. Price policies become feasible, all forms of advertising are relevant for examination, distributors must be screened and carefully selected, product presentation must be most carefully attended to, and so forth. It can be a traumatic experience as the success story of Russian watches on the UK market over the past six years has shown. Global Watches handle the Russian merchandise in the UK and have built sales to over a quarter of a million. Total Russian exports at 9m in 1969 are second only to Switzerland and have recently overtaken the Japanese. In the UK, Russian watches are sold only after re-casing and adding new dials under the brand name Sekonda, and hold a 7% share of the market.

Global Watches received no Russian capital when it began but the Russians gave good credit to set it on its path. This is a new form of venture for the USSR and compares well with the generally preferred method of joint ventures or completely Russian-owned enterprises. In the field of scientific and photographic equipment, the Technical and Optical Equipment Co. Ltd is entirely Russian-owned now, having been bought out from two British entrepreneurs who started it in 1963. UMO Plant Ltd is a totally Russian-owned enterprise initiated in the last year to rent construction equipment to British contractors, and is succeeding well, as is its counterpart in France. In France Actif-Auto sells Russian tractors at 10–15% below their main competitors, and has two-thirds of its capital from the Russian export agency Traktorexport.

These companies, and many more besides, are being used as a training ground for Soviet executives in the techniques of modern Western business. The posts of USSR commercial attachés in Western societies are also now being deliberately used in this way. The trained marketing executives then return to posts within enterprises in the USSR concerned both with domestic and foreign trading activities.

Marketing logistics and physical distribution
One of the most paradoxical aspects of contemporary socialist marketing has been its lack of attention to marketing logistics. This is not to suggest that Western societies have been any more attentive to this major cost area, of course, but the awakening present in the West was not apparent in our discussions, nor is it in the nascent marketing literature.[30] The centralized structures of socialist marketing would seem to provide an ideal basis for the search for total cost minimization approaches with its allied profit criteria. Perhaps it has been the absence of any real concern hitherto in basically a seller's market which has led to little manifest interest levels and hence PDM approaches. If this is the case, we can confidently expect the so far discrete examination of stockholding, transportation and depot location to blossom in the coming decade and for major improvements in distributive efficiency to be realizable because of the structure of socialist marketing channels.

THE COMPARATIVE PERSPECTIVE FROM THE WEST

It is relatively simple and indubitably naïve to cast socialist marketing as just an adolescent specimen of social democratic or predominantly capitalistic approaches. Such adolescence is limited almost exclusively to the technology of marketing rather than to the socialist philosophy thereof. Philosophically it is different, and there seems to be within it a number of issues which are particularly germane to the problems which marketing faces in Western societies.

One of the major relevant considerations is that of the interdependent nature of the economies and marketing systems of the socialist countries considered here. In the same way that Britain and its Western European neighbours have been required to be involved with each other and with the economy of the USA, socialist countries in Eastern Europe are inevitably considering their interaction with each other, with developing countries and with social democratic and capitalist trading partners.

As far as relationships between socialist states are concerned, this review has highlighted the relative rates of development towards a society that is affluent in terms of consumer goods. The relatively advanced status of Hungary and Yugoslavia in this respect has made it necessary for them to come to terms with trading realities—such as the acquisition of management skills and even some development capital from the USA and the German Federal Republic—at an earlier date than their ideologically richer partners. However, the diffusion of the new practices of international cooperation has advanced to the stage where Western Europe is playing a major role in the establishment of private-car ownership in the USSR. As Hungary has found, such changes do not merely result in extensions of the consumer's purchasing possibilities. The entrance of Hilton and Inter-continental hotels, and filling stations displaying Shell and Agip logos, implies also an innovation to the total society which is aware of their implications for the future. It is likely, therefore, that in the future we shall witness not merely a transfer of marketing technology but an extension of the philosophical debates, both theirs and ours, that are at present so critically reviewing the nature of Western consumer societies.

Fundamental interdependence is clearly awaiting changes in the nature of financial transactions. The advance towards a rouble that is transferable between the members of COMECON will, it is privately hinted, be followed by the major step of making the rouble totally transferable—probably within the next fifteen years. When this occurs, we may increasingly expect the mutual transfer not only of marketing technology but also of the philosophical consideration of the role of marketing within our societies.

We can perhaps confidently expect to receive relevant theoretical fuel for our debates at the present time. Most socialist countries, whilst fully concerned with the development of their economies and marketing systems to a level close to that of social democratic countries, are not doing so without posing the necessary fundamental questions about the wisdom of Western approaches to, for example, product quality and the proliferation of goods which are differentiated mainly by their symbolic appeals. In particular, we can expect to observe the emergence of a carefully thought out approach to the inter-societal transfer of Coca-Colonialism. Although one can sip such an international beverage on the pavement restaurants of Buda and Pest today, the extent of its promotional activity is not that to which we are accustomed; what is more, no real need for such escalation is perceived. Rather, other Western-derived products, deemed more socially desirable, such as the Polski Fiat, are pressed forward as worthy of those additional florints which could have been consumed in the build-up of additional Coca-Cola sales.

The reassertion of an albeit more flexible planning concept, to take care of the allocation of social priorities, is the next logical step in the USSR and many Central and Eastern European societies.

Such philosophical strands may well afford us an opportunity to benefit considerably once the initial excitement provoked by exposure to goods and services on our own comparatively lavish levels dies down. The necessary and probably sufficient prerequisites for such an East–West transfer exist. The volatility of doctrine and theory, the profoundly academic approaches of the leading academic institutes, and the very existence of an experimental test-bed, may well enable us to borrow fruitfully and to conduct research of exceptional value. For example, research conducted by the Polish Instytutu Handlu Wewnetrznego,[20] on 'The effectiveness of advertising and consumer behaviour' in selected fields, provides a valid benchmark by which we can trace, over the next decade, the effectiveness of the promotional activity and patterns of innovation which will logically result from the Polish economic reforms recently instituted. These could have early significance for activities in societies which have moved much further along the roads to consumer affluence in the West.

Even if these developments do not result, the inevitable changes will provide substantial opportunities for the transfer of marketing technology. Manufacturers who are able to provide, for example, not merely petroleum products but advice on desired demand and on problems which result from marked increases in the private-car population, will have a very great appeal to socialist planners. Advertising agencies and research agencies which are prepared to invest at the present time may quickly find a substantial demand for their skills during this coming decade. We should also note the growth in academic institutions which offer courses and conduct research in marketing subjects. The possibilities for exchange and cooperation already exist and the socialist countries of Europe are continually extending the invitation to take part in their advance.

Our conclusion is therefore optimistic, if the precise timescale is uncertain. Whilst increasing international contact (especially via tourism, but also as an act of political rapprochement) is creating a spontaneous level of domestic demand for Western standards of life, socialist societies are determined to evolve an adequate philosophy based on the belief that social desirability is often something quite other than that which the vicissitudes of the market will occasion. In seeking this socialist definition and interpretation of the phenomenon we term marketing, they are likely to make a significant contribution to the further evolution of thinking in Western societies. This does not constitute a naïve movement towards the Western view of the market process.

There is undeniably greater concern in socialist societies today for the problems of what we term the post-industrial society than we can find in many Western societies. This intellectual searching and concern is likely to be particularly focused on promotional activity and advertising as well as the use of the price mechanism as a device for helping to secure goals perceived as socially desirable.

Our final comment is on the uncontroversial ground of marketing technology. We formed a very clear impression that in the field of marketing logistics and PDM the planned socialist marketing system is likely to be making substantial contributions in the coming decade. After the USSR computer industry has overcome its lag in commercial applications, we firmly anticipate major developments in logistics theory and practice. Socialist marketing systems place high value on minimizing total distribution costs and can hence be expected to tackle the challenge with great vigour and a reasonable chance of substantial success in the contextual structure they possess.

REFERENCES

1. Marx, K., *Das Kapital*, vol. 3. 'The process of capitalist production as a whole'. Foreign Languages Publishing House, Moscow, 1957.
2. Second Party Programme, 1919, Item 13, *Distribution*. Executive Committee of the Communist International, Moscow, 1920.
3. Lenin, V. I., *Collected works*, vol. 3. Foreign Language Publishing House, Moscow, 1964.
4. Lenin, V. I., *Selected works*, vol. 33. Lawrence & Wishart, London, pp. 35–9.
5. Lenin, V. I., 'State and revolution', in *Collected works*, vol. 25. Foreign Language Publishing House, Moscow, 1964, pp. 385 ff.
6. *See* especially, B. Southall, *The new economic policy*. Harcourt, Brace & World Inc., 1961.
7. Felker, J. L., *Soviet economic controversies*. M.I.T. Press, 1966.
8. Krushchev, N. S., *Report on the programme of CPSU to 22nd Party Congress*. Foreign Language Publishing House, Moscow, 1961.
9. Anchishkin, *Voprosy ekonomiki*, no. 1, 1963; cited in Felker, *op. cit.*
10. Kosygin, A., 'On improving the management of industry, perfecting planning and strengthening economic incentives in industrial production', *Izvestia*, September 28th, 1965, translated in *Current digest of the Soviet Press*, October 13th, 1965, pp. 3–16.
11. Liberman, E. G., 'The role of profits in the industrial incentive system of the USSR', *International Labour Review*, **97**(1), 1968, pp. 1–14.
12. An excellent analysis of the theoretical issues which the Kharkovian approach poses, and of the alternative solutions (particularly the NVP or normative value of processing approach) which were discussed prior to 1965, is given in Felker, *op. cit.*, chs. 3–6.
13. Skobe, M., 'Marketing and advertising in Yugoslavia', in *Marketing and economic development*, P. D. Bennett (ed.). American Marketing Association, 1965, pp. 96–101.
14. Bartels, R., *Comparative marketing: wholesaling in fifteen countries*. Irwin, 1963. This book contains chapters on the USSR, China and Yugoslavia.
15. Goldman, M. I., *Soviet marketing*. Free Press of Glencoe, 1963.
16. Miller, M., *The rise of the Russian consumer*. Institute of Economic Affairs, London, 1965.
17. Walters, J. H., Jnr. 'Retailing in Poland', *Journal of Marketing*, April 28th, 1964, pp. 16–21.
18. Richman, B. R., 'A firsthand study of marketing in Communist China', *Journal of Retailing*, **46**(2), 1970, pp. 27–47.
19. Our own studies of 'Marketing organization structures in British industry' have been reported in *BIM Occasional Paper No. 148*, 1970, and *Organisational Design for Marketing Futures*. Allen & Unwin, 1972.

20. The Polish Instyutu Handlu Wewnetrznego publishes two excellent marketing research journals, *Handel Wewnetrzny* and *Roczniki*, both with English abstracts. Recent issues included articles on: 'Trends in shaping the profile of assortment in retail outlets', 'Consumers' views on the degree of adaptation of offer to customers' needs on the clothing market', 'Opinions of students toward life aims in the field of material needs', 'Investigation of the teenager market', 'The morphology of product movements', 'Research on the efficiency of publicity'.

21. These areas, and the balance of contemporary concern, are evidenced in the syllabus of the Senior Marketing Course at the Hungarian Management Centre, introduced in 1970 at Budapest. Hungary's marketing system is as 'Kharkovian' as any; it is some three years since their economic reforms were implemented.

22. Szabo, L., 'Advertising and marketing in Hungary', *The Advertising Quarterly,* **25**, Autumn 1970, pp. 50–6.

23. Markiewicz-Lagneau, 'Advertising and politics in Poland', *17th Congress of International Advertising Quarterly,* **5**, Autumn 1965, pp. 39–47.

24. Professor Stutler of the Institute has published a major text, *An outline of an active selling system.* The concept contrasts neatly with the passive role of enterprise selling under Stalinist and Krushchevian approaches.

25. Hanson, P., *The consumer in the Soviet economy.* Macmillan, 1968, chap. 8, especially pp. 203–6.

26. Argunov, A., 'What advertising does: a Russian view', *Sovetskaya Torgovlya,* **2**, February 1966; reprinted in *Journal of Advertising Research,* **6**(4), 1966.

27. V/O Vneshtorgreklama, *Specialized magazines in the USSR* (Moscow M-461, Kakhovka 31). The magazine *Litejnoe Proizvodstvo*, for example, reaches 12,700 scientific research personnel, engineers, technicians, students and master foundrymen; monthly; 200 rbls. ($220) for a full page. We have no idea of the extent of reading or noting or multiple readership. Precisely the same page rate applies to *Kartofelj i Ovoshchi*, which reaches 48,500 farm workers.

28. In three languages, including English, from Interpress/Budapest, XII, Szarvas Gabor utca 20.

29. *Business week,* 'Soviets take a joint venture road West', June 6th, 1970, pp. 73–4.

30. Few Western marketing executives have given it the attention it undoubtedly merits, but it seems already set to become a significant area of activity in the seventies for the West. At Bradford University, for instance, we initiated post-graduate and senior management training in this field; launched the *International Journal of Physical Distribution;* and edited *Marketing logistics and distribution planning,* M. Christopher and G. Wills. George Allen & Unwin, 1971.

CHAPTER 8

Pragmatism in Advertising Research

There is no scarcity of elegant conceptual models of the advertising activity, no dearth of methodologies for checking out its efficacy for a company. Despite this there is a general feeling of unease at the usefulness of what has so far been proposed. Companies try first this technique for pre-testing, then another; they argue a need for standardization and then realize its great drawbacks; they seek to conduct post-tests but find the other environmental variables too diverse to grapple with meaningfully within budget constraints. Meantime, academics and intellectual research executives in advertising agencies continue to search for unique solutions in the face of these problems. This impasse led to the initiation of our research effort by twenty major UK companies late in 1971 to examine, in depth, exactly what their companies are currently doing and critically to appraise their efforts. We did not believe then, nor do we believe now, that we would make any dramatic advances. We simply wished to help the companies concerned to understand better what patterns were present in their behaviour and particularly the extent to which their behaviour in this context was congruent with any marketing communications goals they might have set.

The research plan adopted involved a series of reconnaissance visits at which the structure of each company's total advertising activity was assessed.[1] This evidence was then matched up against the normative models in the body of knowledge concerning pre- and post-display measurement. Over 1,100 contributions to the literature were examined as a basis for the comparisons we made, and their content distilled into two reports.[2,3] This chapter specifically reports on the matching-up of advertising research activities. Further studies have been completed that explore normative theories as to 'How advertising works'[4] and that critically evaluate the evidence available on a series of specific techniques, for example handbooks on *Pressure testing* and on *Advertising pretesting*.

EXTANT PATTERNS OF RESEARCH ACTIVITIES

Two essential patterns emerged from our analysis of how the twenty companies were structuring their advertising research. The first group had had a substantial market/marketing/commercial research function for many years. The second was, until relatively recently, serviced only by advertising agency research facilities. Consequently some research functions were an established part of the fabric of a company, whereas in others the function was relatively alien. In the newer departments, which were still growing, topics for research tend to be those of most immediate managerial concern. The portfolio of research undertaken would seem to be based mainly on two factors; length of time the research function has existed and how marketing-oriented top management is or has been.

The role of advertising research within different types of companies can perhaps be summarized generally as follows:

	High marketing orientation in company	Low marketing orientation in company
Well-established research activity	Strategy and tactics	Long-term strategy
Recently introduced research activity	Tactics	Tactics of very high importance ($N = 20$)

All twenty companies were actively interested in and involved with advertising research. As one looks across the spectrum from fast-moving consumer goods companies to service industries, it can be clearly seen that research involvement with top management decreases. It is also valid to comment that as the marketing function emerges in the latter industries so the perceived need for advertising research increases. The volume of research resource available in each company tended to vary with the size of profits of the company.

Most research departments were instrumental in providing data on market situations either via regular reports bought from survey organizations, or *ad hoc* studies specially commissioned from research agencies. Most acted as the company clearing-house for all research, advising on its use and monitoring its provision. Some had no substantial budget of their own, with the function requisitioning the research having to pay. In others it was the research department who paid the bills. None of the departments had a large staff and most had little manpower to engage in long-term research. Innovations in research were reportedly left to professional agencies or individual effort in personal time.

The provision of data or information for marketing decisions by research functions was undertaken either by acquiring information commercially available or by setting up a special facility to provide it (regularly or *ad hoc*).

The major problems encountered in this were that the commercially available data were seldom exactly what was required, and special surveys are often perceived as very expensive. Mainly because of expense, and the under-researched hazards of putting a value on information,[5] many companies opt for using existing data services. Further difficulties arise where several sets of data are acquired by this method, the sum of which is not quite sufficient for the purpose; which leads to an incomplete total picture. Decisions are normally made against such a background.

Not all the problems involved lie outside the company. Internally provided information for marketing purposes was often found unsatisfactory, for example delivered sales could not be provided by television area, or 'deal' expenditure analysed by outlet type. Selling via national account operations usually further complicates analysis. In an attempt to extract the most out of regularly bought and syndicated survey data, several companies have set up data analysis departments to collate, interpret and diffuse vital marketing data.

Only three out of twenty companies were engaged on what might be termed comprehensive studies of advertising effectiveness. All were using a model-building-and-testing route, two examining econometric methods and one developing a micro-simulation. Two were in what might be termed relatively simple markets where there were only one or two major brands; and the third was in what we have termed a 'neocommodity' market where there tends to be an own-label threat. Evidence of the beginning of a fourth such attempt was also collected.

The reasons why few companies seem to be engaged on such studies are mainly that budgets do not allow long-term research either in staffing or research expense items. Furthermore it is generally felt that since earlier findings have often been inconclusive, there is no sure pay-off. The same can be said of the model-building and experimental approach, which is not thought to have fulfilled its initial promise. As a result, because of a lack of interest and research resources, most personnel in marketing research departments have no experience of model-building and experimental approaches.

A few companies have even adopted the attitude that 'because their market is ever changing and difficult to understand it is not possible to build operational models'. They see their best policy as to set up information systems that can swiftly detect changes in the market and to ensure that a suitable reaction is rapidly effected. These tend to be highly marketing oriented companies with long-established marketing research departments. The information systems tend to be of their own provision. Two companies who had persevered with marketing models (which included an assessment of media advertising on sales) were presented with the apparent conclusion that media advertising was a poor investment. Interestingly, one company was sufficiently influenced by this and other circumstances to reduce its advertising weight; the other, after a change of management, concluded that 'product review' was the first course of action. The markets in which both these companies operated, although different, have many similarities and both could be viewed as being of the neocommodity type.

In general, it was observed that small-scale qualitative research was a very commonly used tool for diverse problems. Among the advantages quoted were speed and the modest expense. From the point of view of longer-term research, this is likely to be a far from satisfactory stance since changes over time in market variables probably cannot be monitored in this way. (Economic research units also existed in about half of the companies visited, but all these units were involved with corporate planning and/or monitoring the progress of the national or international economic scene and its implications. No visible impact on market, marketing or advertising research was observable, nor was it contemplated as a relevant possible area of involvement.)

The main purpose of the marketing research activity in all companies was to help describe the state of the company relative to its customers and competitors. The degree of knowledge existing within a company was generally greater with multi-product companies. In many of these, sophisticated and usually expensive research methods were being deployed to examine customer attitudes and behaviour and to categorize these. Such research was usually conducted by research agencies. No one 'technique' could be said to be universally useful for providing such information or to be universally accepted as valid or meaningful. Those companies committing themselves to these rigorous exercises seem to have benefited as much through the management discipline imposed and the team effort involved, as through any statistical or behavioural findings that emerged.

ADVERTISING RESEARCH BEHAVIOUR

Our company discussions enabled us to make a series of general observations which illustrate the current state of knowledge about, and behaviour in relation to, advertising research.

Sales analyses for examining advertising or promotional effectiveness, broken out for target market segments rather than the population as a whole, were almost universally practised. *Media research* was largely bequeathed to advertising agencies, although most companies bought extensive data on competitive activity. *Computers* are not greatly used operationally either in the marketing or advertising function. No-one analysed or interrogated surveys via *computer terminals* for immediate feedback. Only one company has a *planning model* accessible via a terminal that would enable marketing management to assess financial implications of different courses of action. This company could be described as being in a less complex, but nevertheless very competitive, market. No company knows anything fundamental about the *'wearout'* of its advertisements. Many examples were identified of coupon response *exercises*; but very few systematic exercises had been conducted to understand the relative quantitative effects of the different factors known to influence response. This seemed a disappointing state of affairs. Some examples of *'split run'* exercises were observed but these were for limited purposes.

Much research work undertaken for a specific purpose elsewhere in the marketing activity, which *could* augment the examination of the effect of advertising, was available in companies, for example repeat purchase analyses in brand loyalty studies, price sensitivity, the effects of seasonality. Little evidence was present of the development of systematic programmes to research all marketing mix factors for a product.

The management use of research sometimes suggested the potentially dangerous assumption that successive survey findings, for example, of awareness and attitudes, could be related back to individual behaviour. The fact that the *average* value of the measure of an attribute could remain constant by some people in the sample improving their rating whilst others declined, seemed sometimes to be missed. The nature of changes in segments was not always examined where it might well be extremely important. Time and expense to perform further analyses were the reasons given for these omissions.

Not all companies or organizations regularly conducted any *pre-test* of their advertisements. Those that do not test formally cited expense and mistrust of methods as the main reasons (five out of twenty). Some examples of advertisements were seen where no formal pre-testing had been carried out but where they were the subject of later scrutiny. The companies concerned examined these past advertisements by essentially pre-testing methods (group discussions) to determine if the advertisements could be used again. It was *then* found that some of these advertisements contained what were judged to be considerable negative aspects.

Those companies which regularly pre-tested did so for various combinations of the following main reasons:

(a) on principle, to stimulate the agency;
(b) to reassure company personnel;
(c) to check communication/copy point achievement;
(d) to screen out negatives.

No one method of testing was accepted as being satisfactory for all circumstances, within a single medium. Everyone using a particular method regularly, freely admitted that it was by no means perfect. Much has been written about the possible fallacies of methods of pre-testing and all companies were well aware of these. No satisfactory alternative was perceived to exist in the UK at the time. Most pre-testing undertaken by the companies was of a qualitative nature; quantitative methods involving 'scoring' of attributes/communication points seem largely out of favour. Recall studies were used by only one company.

The need for satisfactory *concept tests*, or pre-production testing, was strongly expressed. It was felt that this would ease the load on post-production testing and allow a wider spectrum of ideas to be tested. Some companies did use concept testing but doubt was expressed by others on the viability of the procedures. The mechanics of the methods would appear to require improvement for them to be more acceptable.

It was observed that different parts of the same company used different pre-testing methods. Rarely did a company policy exist on which method should be used. Where it did, the research department still exercised discretion to employ what was felt the most appropriate method. Pre-testing was usually used to see if advertisements were usable, not to select the best of several. Time was often not available to alter or remake advertisements found to be suspect—only if 'serious negatives' were thought to exist would an advertisement be withdrawn. Pre-testing methods were not used to check the validity of an advertising strategy. One-quarter of the companies assumed that it was the advertising agency's responsibility to pre-test all advertisements. A vast number of records of advertising pre-testing exercises do, however, exist.

No company or organization was found that formally analysed competitors' advertisements, either as routine or selectively; although this is contrary to what one might have expected. Nevertheless, in many markets companies do pay great attention to the volume and extent of competitive advertising. When such advertising is deemed very good creatively, it is believed that it can alter the market. Great effort is often expended creating advertising which reflects the total marketing strategy adopted by a company. (For these reasons it would have seemed worthwhile to analyse, or test, competitive advertising to determine what its objectives are and whether it will be very effective, so that defensive measures can be taken. By not adopting this practice companies force the conclusion they really regard *weight* of advertising as of paramount importance.) Competitive 'product' testing was commonplace.

Few companies used *sales measures as post campaign criteria*. The difficulties with data provision and problems of contribution of other factors have been discussed earlier. Nevertheless, several 'case studies' were observed where the apparently obvious effect of media advertising effort could be seen. These instances were related to special market circumstances where one major brand predominated in a relatively small market.

No *experimentation* was found within the companies. By experimentation we mean the formal conduct of an exercise to examine the validity of a proposed theory or hypothesis. The main difficulties in the use of experiments by companies to examine advertising effectiveness in particular were cited as:

(a) the lack of adequate data gathering facilities;
(b) the lack of suitable staff or staff time;
(c) the belief among research people that the likely outcome of any such effort is uncertain, except that the exercise will be expensive;
(d) the reluctance, or inability, of operational management to sacrifice short-term performance for some uncertain pay-off;
(e) the lack of incontrovertible evidence to support the case for experimentation;
(f) the insufficiency of experimental designs to cover changing environments.

One form of experiment is the building of models and their testing in the field. We have already noted the model-building activities of the companies. The initial work on these was always done by specialist consultants or academics. Only one company uses a marketing model operationally, while another company's model is still being developed.

'Pressure tests' or media weight experiments were a form of experiment upon which much information was available, but virtually all these exercises had yielded inconclusive findings. Invariably, the reason for this failure was confessedly inadequate planning, design and management. Information requirements and provision were not thoroughly thought out prior to the experiment and conceptual errors occurred, *e.g.* using as control or comparison areas those areas not worth upweighting because they contained the poorest outlets. The difficulty of translating any findings from these experiments into actionable decisions is yet another problem. Consequently it would seem that, as a means of gaining substantial insight into the quantitative effect of weight of advertising on sales, 'simple' pressure tests are not deemed a worthwhile activity. The frequency of occurrence of these exercises can only be explained if their real purpose was to achieve some other goal, *e.g.* a tactical move to combat some competitive measure.

Few *exercises*, as opposed to experiments, examining the effect of advertising on sales performance were found which would stand careful scrutiny. More examples were found where the metric of effectiveness was some attitudinal or communication quantity.

THE PRAGMATIC RATIONALE

It will be readily apparent to readers that the companies we have met fall a considerable way short in their behaviour and their structure of the norms which theoretical knowledge would suggest should operate. It would be easy simply to criticize the company as 'backward' in their research practices and

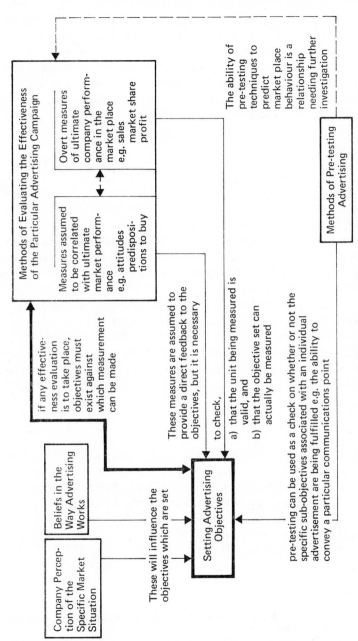

FIG. 8.1 *A pragmatic approach to advertising research.*

Methods of Evaluating the Effectiveness of the Particular Advertising Campaign

Overt measures of ultimate company performance in the market place
e.g. sales
market share
profit

Measures assumed to be correlated with ultimate market performance
e.g. attitudes
predispositions to buy

The ability of pre-testing techniques to predict market place behaviour is a relationship needing further investigation

Methods of Pre-testing Advertising

if any effectiveness evaluation is to take place, objectives must exist against which measurement can be made

These measures are assumed to provide a direct feedback to the objectives, but it is necessary

to check,
a) that the unit being measured is valid, and
b) that the objective set can actually be measured

Beliefs in the Way Advertising Works

These will influence the objectives which are set

Company Perception of the Specific Market Situation

Setting Advertising Objectives

pre-testing can be used as a check on whether or not the specific sub-objectives associated with an individual advertisement are being fulfilled e.g. the ability to convey a particular communications point

N.B. The dotted lines indicate an assumed, but little substantiated relationship, and also areas in which it is desirable to study, but which will seldom form the main emphasis of the research to suggest that they employ 'more competent' research staffs. That, however, would be to miss the point. The behaviour reported here is perceived as 'reasonably satisfactory' in the companies concerned, bearing in mind the resource constraints in operation. Those constraints can be clearly seen to be relative to the nature of the market in which the company operates and the consequent nature of top management attitudes. Whilst 'textbook norms' constitute a professional point of reference for the advertising researcher in the companies concerned (and many of the individuals concerned are leading experts in their subject areas), company realities dictate a quite different pattern of executive activity.

It is accordingly our belief that any constructive attempt to improve the effectiveness of advertising, by ensuring that adequate measurement of all activity is undertaken, must begin with a determined effort to create a company environment in which factors other than competitive pressure bring about the will to be more effective. In simple terms, we believe the innate professionalism of the practitioners can be released within many more companies provided a realistic and pragmatic framework for understanding what is involved is available to management, both within and without the marketing communication group.

It is against this background that Fig. 8.1 was prepared. It has already acted as a most effective catalyst to discussions between our research team and the companies concerned in the studies here. By clearly and firmly identifying the relationships we are assuming in the process of advertising management and control, we have found that sympathetic appreciation is enhanced with companies.

CONCLUSION

We have tried to indicate an emergent view, after looking in great depth at company practice in twenty major UK enterprises, that a pragmatic approach to the improvement of professional operations is likely to be more effective than a 'textbook deficiency' reaction. A scheme of relationships which were found to be present in the empirical studies conducted has been presented as a basis for improved environmental acceptance of the need for information to enhance marketing communications effectiveness.

REFERENCES

1. Corkindale, D. and Kennedy, S., 'The identification of current company advertising practices', MCRU Report No. 1, 1972.
2. Corkindale, D. and Kennedy, S., 'Pre-display analysis of advertising effectiveness: a literature review', MCRU Report No. 2A, January 1973.

3. Corkindale, D. and Kennedy, S., 'Post-display analysis of advertising effectiveness: a literature review', *MCRU Report No. 2B*, January 1973.
4. Corkindale, D. and Kennedy, S., 'How advertising works: a literature review of the process of advertising', *MCRU Report No. 3*, May 1973.
5. Christopher, M. G. and Wills, G. S. C., 'Cost–benefit analysis of external information', *UNESCO Bulletin Library*, January, 1970.

CHAPTER 9

The Value of Information

Few academic teachers of marketing and logistics would either describe or consider themselves to be economic theorists, although there can be not the slightest room for doubt that marketing knowledge seeks to explain certain facets of economic behaviour in any society. Perhaps the most important reason why marketing and logistics folk do not perceive themselves as economists is simply because they reject the proposition that monetary rationality can on its own offer an adequate explanation of economic activity at the level either of individual customer or firm. Such a statement is not intended to suggest that all economists refuse to countenance any other formative influences on economic behaviour. The overwhelming impression given by theoretical economics is, however, of that ilk.

Whereas an economist may not be unduly taken aback by such a statement (he may indeed accept it as a realistic reflection of how he intends to be perceived), to a marketing practitioner it is a considerable indictment. Marketing seeks to understand economic activity in order to influence it in a technological or engineering sense, against time and other constraints. It has inevitably been forced to examine the totality of influences at work in shaping any particular act of purchase or company initiative. Whereas an economist can simply regard sociological influences on economic behaviour as something assumed to be constant, in order that he may concentrate the more on economic factors, the marketing man has no such discretion. Rather he must seek out the 'salient' features in the situation, whatever origins they might have. He is accordingly an empiricist first and often a second-rate theorist.

Conversely, many economists are first-rate theorists working at so remote a level of abstraction and so remote from the realities of the economic activity under examination, that their elegant theories describe and/or predict nothing of real value. Such men also often regard marketing practice as a scurrilous manipulation of quasi-divine economic laws which we are *supposed* to believe will allocate resources in some optimum social manner.

Marketing is not about selling products which an entrepreneur has willed to exist. It is the study of how to match production to the desires and wishes

160

of customers, and of the problems and issues involved in so doing. How a company can most effectively share in such a social process is a complex field of study where success and effectiveness will seldom be the crowns worn by those who worship simply at the shrines of economic rationality. To take but an instance—the economics of advertising. Advertising, we are told, shifts the demand curve. Sometimes, is the truth; but even if we concede the proposition, we are no wiser about how to advertise. What really matters is *where* to advertise, *how* to advertise and, once those decisions are made, how to measure how well we have done. To perform econometric feats with sales and promotional expenditure data tells us little if anything at all by way of explanation of economic activity.

In general, therefore, marketing eschews the grand design. It *seeks to explain* through micro-analysis of market situations such small facets of economic activity as brand-switching or purchase-source loyalties. As soon as it does, marketing analysts find themselves looking broadly across the behavioural sciences for theoretical propositions which might be of assistance. There is no pride which limits that search for explanations of customer behaviour; there cannot be since the consequences of true error or excessive abstraction are often dire in commercial terms. Such self-discipline is seldom visited upon economists although I gather several monetary economists do have a similar experience when they advise governments and international institutions.

Marketing's lack of concern with, or will to reform, economic theory, its unwillingness to wean it away from its dominant mode of approach to attempting to describe economic activity, is one of the great disappointments of the past twenty-five years. It is scarcely surprising since marketing has been struggling in many countries to assert itself as a worthwhile branch of applied economics as economic engineering against the implacable opposition of the pure economist. Economics has also failed at other interfaces such as those with operational research and financial management. Such has been the scope of that failure that today men who wish to understand how the economic world operates are more likely to study at a business school than in a school of economics. I do not believe that such a state of affairs is desirable, but I find that it is virtually inevitable. In general terms, the effective understanding of, and teaching *about*, micro-economics has shifted away from the theoretical propositions of economics to the synthetic disciplines with their empirical focus. A state of apartheid exists in micro-economics between theory and practice which leads to sterile theory and poorly learnt lessons of experience. The challenge of the next twenty-five years must be to destroy the fences which separate us. We must readily admit the truth of the location of micro-economic knowledge—in the management structures and boardrooms of our most successful companies. The true professors and leaders via an understanding of micro-economics will normally be found with the title of Marketing or Finance Director, or Manager. A few of them can be found in business schools. Far too few ever grace the corridors of the economics schools.

BUYER BEHAVIOUR AS A FOCUS FOR STUDY

Despite these biting criticisms of pure micro-economics, there is a welcome body of knowledge which the *brotherhood* of economists can claim to have developed over the past score of years which demonstrates the complex nature of the influences at work on a single customer. With the aid of statistics this knowledge can often be aggregated to furnish a valuable set of information and afford an empirical basis for theorizing to some effect.

'Buyer behaviour', as the area is dubbed, is a focus for truly multi-disciplinary study. We examine from anthropological and sociological standpoints how we are culturally constrained in our economic activity of buying goods and services; we explore the psychological aspects which influence our decisions; we examine the impact which geographical distance and topography might have; the influence of demography; we identify how technology makes available new modes of consumption behaviour. Marketing's early attempts at integrating these various influences—and more besides—are best demonstrated to date by Amstutz[1] and by Howard and Sheth[2] but there are now some five or six treatments in this field and countless papers and sets of readings which adopt this synthesis.

Admittedly, the predominant thrust of these analyses has been in the area of consumer markets. Yet momentum has been building up very rapidly during the past five years for a closer examination of industrial buying behaviour. It has many similarities with familial decision-making in consumer goods in that the purchaser is often reflecting group pressures and decisions rather than simply his own. (Webster and Wind[3] have perhaps done most in the industrial purchasing area.)

Marketing men examine purchasing behaviour in this total contextual manner because they wish to understand as exactly as possible the dynamics of that behaviour. How, other influences being removed, will the purchaser behave? How can he be influenced to behave in any given way that is worthwhile encouraging from the point of view of a specific company, and which is also compatible with the social context in which business is undertaken? The answer which we find is seldom if ever that price taken alone can elicit a required pattern of behaviour. Gabor and Granger,[4] Katona,[5] Adam[6] and many more besides have demonstrated quite clearly that there are far more Giffen goods about than that distinguished economist ever imagined. Price is, on more occasions than not, taken as indicative of quality—and almost always in the absence of branding. Furthermore, assumptions of price knowledge and awareness in a market are likely to be highly misleading. Many of the basic assumptions on which economics has sought to explain buyer behaviour cannot be made if a worthwhile usable theory is to result. The level of abstraction is ludicrous. Usable theories of buyer behaviour are the only category that marketing academics can or will accept. Their students in colleges and in industry demand nothing less.

I realize I am continually discussing the relative degrees of abstraction involved. I have no hesitation as a political economist by training in identifying the marketing academics' approach as considerably more worthwhile simply because it is more likely to give rise to the understanding of fundamental issues which is surely the purpose of all theory construction. The integration of the empirical basis of most marketing analysis of buyer behaviour with the more conventional but intellectually more rigorous approaches of economists must accordingly be one of our major goals over the next decade. If marketing scientists have been careful to avoid making sweeping assumptions about market conditions, and have overlaid economic theories with a range of more realistic propositions about economic behaviour, they have also conspicuously failed in most cases to develop an adequate theoretical consolidation which can supersede the economist's naïve teachings about economic behaviour. For this very reason, a teachable body of marketing knowledge has been slow to emerge and a very considerable emphasis on pragmatism can be seen in its stead. The case method is perhaps the exemplar of pragmatism in management teaching.

RESOURCE ALLOCATION AS A FOCUS

I indicated at the outset that the discipline of marketing can readily be seen as having two predominant foci for analysis. The first, the behaviour of a customer, I have now briefly discussed. The second is concerned with the allocation of resources within the operational marketing activity of an enterprise. Economic theory has offered a wide range of analytical approaches, most particularly perhaps the concept of marginalism. The importance of that *concept* is not in doubt in terms of profitability analysis; what we know, however, is that it is seldom an effective operational tool. So many factors other than marginal costs (assuming we can and do measure them) affect corporate economic behaviour, for example brand/market share or product line strategies, critical strategies in promotional activity to gain distribution or defend a position, or social pressures of a national or regional nature, consumerism or environmentalism.

Once more, a total behavioural approach is demanded for the marketing situation if any understanding of an organization is to emerge. If pricing strategy is to be understood, it must take cognizance of a wide range of non-price factors—such as competitors' wholesale and retail propensity to stock, or the psychological perception of prices by customers, or the level of expectation of after-sales service in market segments. Marginal cost analysis alone within the producing enterprise cannot suffice. It is nowhere near rich enough in its scope.

Now economists can reasonably answer that little of what I have said invalidates the theoretical postulates of marginalism, and by their own terms of reference they can be exonerated. The problem remains that marginalist theory does not explain the behaviour we observe in markets. Time and time again highly knowledgeable and intelligent managers take quite contrary allocation decisions. One of the clearest attempts to explain this behaviour is to be found in Cyert and March's classic work.[7] My colleagues and I have been engaged since 1965 in a wide-ranging series of research studies in marketing which continually identify such patterns of behaviour in relation to individual marketing activities such as test marketing,[8] below-the-line promotion,[9] selection of channels of distribution,[10] selection of overseas markets to penetrate,[11] assessment of advertising effectiveness,[12] the choice of logistics mode,[13] and also in studies of the overall planning of marketing organization structures.[14] In each and every situation we have examined, economic rationality as an explanation of behaviour had to be rejected because of the intervention of social psychological influences, because of unwillingness to change arising from the social dynamics of proposed change, because of unwillingness to allocate resources to achieve demonstrably economically rational goals. Such consistently deviant behaviour nullifies the validity of economic theories which purport to explain such marketing behaviour. It also nullifies the validity of such propositions (as are contained in a rational economic point of view) as catalysts for normative goals towards which we should strive. Surely the reality for management is that most of us strive simply to perform satisfactorily in the organizational context wherein we are employed. Effective and successful management is concerned with trade-offs between competing sets of goals within any enterprise, of which rational economic goals are but one. The best-managed and most effective enterprise can be expected to be that which so organizes its activities to balance those competing claims.

The theoretical proposition that the goal of our corporate behaviour is to maximize financial gains is so obviously invalid in most contemporary institutions that I can perhaps turn without further comment to a theoretical prospect which has captivated my imagination for some six years now. The prospect to which I refer is an empirically based assault on the problem of assessing the value of information to an organization. I hope, through this particular prospect, to demonstrate some of the opportunities which I sincerely believe a judicious combination of marketing empirics and economic rigour can afford.

THE VALUE OF INFORMATION

My interest in this issue was triggered in 1967 when the UK Market Research Society asked me to cull and edit all the published *Sources of UK Marketing Information*[15] I could into a single volume. I located over 1,000 and in his Foreword, the Chairman of the Society observed that in his view it was unforgivable for any marketing executive to be ignorant of the existence of such information. The publication of the volume, he felt, would do much to fill a very real need to make known the existence of such sources. My immediate and enduring thought was 'how much benefit did all the sweat and tears, involved in getting that volume together, bring to its users?'

I was readily able to identify the sales statistics for the book. They were not particularly good, but that I concluded was a separate issue of awareness of the book's existence rather than awareness of existence of the sources listed in the book by any marketing executive, whether or not he had purchased the book. On asking further, however, I found to my consternation that most information services measure their value in sales terms, in terms of the number of people who use their facilities. If enquiries/usage rates/loans go up, that is considered indicative of increased value which has been derived from the system. Whilst I would not query the proposition that use is likely to be a *necessary* condition of deriving value from any information system, it can hardly be deemed sufficient. Many titles are misleading; much information has a value which is time-constrained (this is of course especially so for commerce).

In any event, although most systems employ 'usage rates' as a surrogate for value, they implicitly admit by their stocking policies that they do not endorse it. Any public library could readily increase its 'value' by simply stocking multiple copies of all the best-selling novels. Whilst this is normally done up to a particular service level, a point is frequently reached where the officer concerned will call a halt in the interests of 'breadth' of stock. *He will exercise a value judgement which, as I understand it, he is unable to quantify.* I believe that the sort of task we should set ourselves over the next decade or so is finding out how to quantify such values in a generally acceptable manner. I do not know how, any more than social economists yet really know how to assess and aggregate the benefits of arriving home fifteen minutes earlier from work. Whilst I do not expect us to be able to produce simple quantified assessments of value, I see no reason why we should not be able to pose an array of alternative choices and perhaps by the use of non-metric scaling methods derive measures of value which can be actionable in management terms.

If such an approach is to be feasible, it will indubitably demand a wealth of empirical evidence to facilitate the formulation of meaningful choices in the face of particular sets of missions open to any enterprise. Indeed, it rapidly becomes apparent that any examination of the value of information can only be commenced in the context of defined missions and then the derived information goals. Yet information systems seldom have meaningfully defined goals against which value can be assessed.

Such thoughts have led my colleagues and I over the past five years to look with considerable care at the obviously tantalizing possibility of applying cost/benefit analyses to the problem. We have explored both company test marketing/new product launch decisions[16] and library planning/budgetary models.[17] The economic rationality of Bayesian approaches will be familiar to economists. An expected value of perfect information can be derived using prior probabilities, provided by managers, of the occurrence of various outcomes. If we then make realistic assumptions as to how far short of perfect our information will be, that is, we derive conditional probabilities, we can determine via posterior and pre-posterior analyses whether or not the information improved discriminately in the situation under consideration. Accordingly, we would appear to have a simple decision rule based on economic rationality. Yet despite the fact that all the inputs have been made by a given manager, he will almost invariably refuse to follow the economic logic which emerges. He will refuse to invest on acquiring information, an expenditure equivalent to the benefits which he has indicated will emerge. In many cases, the divergence is vast. Tests and experiments in markets are not done which ought to be done; library budgets are not allocated in directions in which they should be allocated in economically rational terms.

You might wonder why I am dwelling on the economics of information at such length, especially in the context of the prospects for economic theory in the eighties. My concern is to emphasize how marketing empirics approach problems and, in particular, how deeply concerned effective marketing is and must be with the quality and availability of information for decision-making. Perfect knowledge in any market is a nonsense assumption; imperfection rules, but not only because information cannot be made available to all. Some members of a market-place steadfastly refuse to collect it. They perceive other corporate goals as of greater importance. Equally often, limitations of executive time prevent the quest from being effectively conducted. My plea is for the examination of micro-economics in a framework of corporate politics; it is a plea for the reassertion of the correctness of the study of politics and economics in tandem. Two realistic foci for the next decade are, therefore, the political economy of the firm and the political economy of the customer.

COST/BENEFIT OF INFORMATION SERVICES

It may well be useful if I devote the final section of this chapter to looking at how the new political economy might relate to the planning of information systems in libraries. The key to success will lie, I believe, in identifying an operationally viable methodology whereby the value derived from library services can be meaningfully quantified and compared with the costs incurred in the provision of such services. If we can achieve it in a meaningful managerial sense, guidelines can be developed on the assessment of value and benefit to library users from the services offered, in terms other than sheer quantitative levels of utilization. The reckoning of books issued, or reading desk occupancy, ignore the value derived from a 'title' or 'seated hour'. Through a continuous dialogue with those who have borrowed books, sat in the library and so forth, we can perhaps seek to identify and then quantify the value or benefit which is being derived from such activities.

Equally, sheer use of a bibliographic system or a card index is no indication of value. Both may prove not to have the information required by the reader. Provision of multiple copies of titles or journals, in order to furnish 95% or 67% service levels (whilst simple enough in operational research terms) is once again not necessarily a measure of the value actually derived.

To attempt to develop a measure of effective value or benefit is a hazardous undertaking. The costing of library services is a similarly difficult task. It is for this reason that I initially propose a modest framework for thought. Let us explore certain limited facets of the library service in order to develop a set of experimental tools for measurement which we can refine and hope to see more widely applied. We have at our disposal the intellectual skills from the areas of attitude scaling, social costing and output budgeting, which are the logical fields of knowledge on which to draw. We can be confident that by taking the value analytic rather than the more directly operational research approach, we can make a unique and considerably overdue contribution. It is a contribution that is indispensable if the discussion of library appropriations, for example, is to advance beyond its present relatively primitive state to a position where some better estimates of the real values derived can be perceived in the context of their costs, and more effective budget allocation made accordingly.

I have conducted an exhaustive review of the background to this strategy to discover what previous attempts have been made to tackle this problem, but although there is a considerable amount of writing on output budgeting (PPBS) in library systems, there is very little on actual installations.

Mrs Maybury[18] covers the problems of programme determination and costing. However, the setting of objectives and evaluation of cost-effectiveness are not examined. Neither does her procedure consider alternative methods and their evaluation.

The PPBS for Libraries Seminar held at Wayne State University in Spring 1968, produced a number of useful conceptual papers. C. G. Burness discussed 'Defining library objectives', which covered the full procedure for establishing objectives, together with an extensive list of questions that should be considered. F. Mlynarczyk Jr, in 'Measuring library costs', considered the problems involved in total system costing. He suggests that conventional business costing procedures be employed. Mlynarczyk, sad to say, relates sales to circulation; inventory to a catalogue department; materials to books and periodicals; and production departments to subject classifications, for example physics or economics. David Palmer in his paper on 'Measuring library output' pointed to the need for libraries to provide meaningful unit cost information. He perceived a basic need for librarians to know what data required measurement and why. Data sets might then be exposed. His recommendations included:

(i) statistics should compare the library last year with the library this year, and five years hence;
(ii) the data gathered should be meaningful to the library;
(iii) sampling techniques and experts should be contacted to deal with problems.

The problem of costing information/library services was given a completely different perspective by Harvey Marron, Chief, Educational Resources Information Center, US Office of Education, in 'On costing information services'. He identifies problems peculiar to library installations:

(i) a library cannot categorize its output with such precision or certainty as a manufacturing concern;
(ii) information services have special problems in measuring product and service levels;
(iii) depreciation as it is understood in business does not pertain to many information centres. Many assets appreciate. In order to be useful, a document collection must reach a critical size from which it becomes more useful as accessions are made. For reasons of this sort, Marron concludes that business accounting methods are not applicable and directs readers to other contributions by authors looking at the problem from other approaches.

One attempt at measuring cost-effectiveness is suggested by J. E. Martyn.[19] Martyn deals with bulletins produced by specialized information centres which are made up of titles and citations to documents considered relevant to the subject-interests of users of the centres. 'Comprehensive effectiveness' is measured by the service coverage of bulletins with whatever material the user finds from sources outside the service. The method determines relative proportions of interest/non-interest by the user ticking off items of interest to him. 'Currency effectiveness' is compared by checking notification dates with availability dates of material. The objectives he identifies are saving user time, money or effort. To measure whether these are met, a sample of users is asked to indicate items of whose existence they were glad to know. Then, by careful study of the information environment of each sample member, it is suggested that it may be possible to discover the cheapest way each could have found references he marked, had the bulletin not existed. Ratios may then be produced of bulletin cost against the notional cost for getting the same volume of information by the cheapest alternative means.

King and Lancaster[20] suggest a conceptual framework for a cost/performance/benefit approach to information system evaluation. 'Cost' refers to the input of resources in terms of monetary units. 'Performance' relates to attributes directly controlled by the system, such as recall, precision and speed of response. 'Benefit' is the consequence of system performance in terms of value, ROI, effect on behaviour of the user, direct effect on other systems, and residual non-quantifiable consequences. Flow charts are used to illustrate examples. The problem of cost/effectiveness measurement is not adequately dealt with, however. Lancaster's article[21] suggests a number of measurement devices but none are detailed, although he does suggest potential areas for trade-offs within information systems.

Although there is an extensive literature available, and a considerable body of conceptual approaches are proposed therein, few attempts are reported that grapple with the basic problems of determining clear and specific library objectives, costing the services provided to meet them, and assessing the pattern of values derived. It is therefore considered that a wider view of cost/benefit be adopted as our starting point. Hence contributions such as E. S. Quade's[22] and the work of like-minded authors will, we believe, provide the best basis in our search for an apposite methodology and our attempt to implement the output-budgeting approach in library management.

Let us therefore take a longitudinal view of the actual and potential use of library services by selected users throughout the full length of a programme of work. Certain parts of our examination can involve a census of all concerned, but the continuous assessment of derived value from library services can perhaps be undertaken with a sample of those involved. A possible fall-out of up to 20–25% should be allowed for initial samples participating, in order to avoid undermining our purposes. These numerical estimates are, however, left open at this juncture for further consideration once the nature of the measurement instruments has been clarified. Any investigation should be conducted in at least four broad stages. They can be separately described in the following terms, although stages II and III will be conducted simultaneously.

STAGE I: *The identification in specific terms of the objectives for library services to meet the selected needs*

These would be elicited from three groups of informants—leaders, library staff and users. *All* users would be interviewed. One would anticipate that there will be dissonance between the perceived objectives of each group. We should seek to expose and so far as is possible reconcile this as a prelude to the further development of our investigation. This reconciled objective, or library services mission, is what we can describe as the 'initial normative requirement'.

We should anticipate that perceptions of the actual requirement of library services will change as time progresses, most particularly in the view of the users concerned. We should seek to measure this movement in perception at intervals throughout, continuing to interview all users concerned. The contrasting opinions of those who do or do not make extensive use of library services will be noted in particular. We could perhaps commence work on Stage I from the basis provided by C. G. Burness, as described earlier.

STAGE II: *The identification in specific terms of the costs implicit in providing the levels of library service deemed to meet the 'initial normative requirement'*

This part of the investigation, which will involve library staff in particular, will examine all costs attributable to mission fulfilment in output-budget terms. Where economies of scale accrue they will be identified and notional allocations made at both discrete and actual operational levels, and their implications explored.

It will be appreciated that the output budget approach cuts across conventional budgeting lines which normally allocate costs to accessions, issues, etc. In identifying the most appropriate approach to employ, we can take as our starting point the contrasting views of Mlynarczyk and Marron, described earlier.

STAGE III: *The identification, on an on-going basis throughout the courses selected, of the perceived value of each library service received and the perceived loss of value for each library service not received when required*

The development of specific research instruments here presents perhaps the major challenge. We should attempt to assess each library service deployed in scale terms on at least two dimensions: relative value to the whole span of services provided, and specific value for the need at hand. Through the continuous compilation of weekly diaries by all sample members, supplemented by three or four personal interviews during the time period, as well as formal briefing and debriefing sessions at the commencement and end of the period, general data can be elicited.

Such detailed scrutiny of the use of library services is almost certain to influence the 'typicality' of any sample. To gain some insight into the nature of such biases, non-sample members of the groups concerned should be consulted on occasion to assess their reactions to certain situations also experienced by sample members.

STAGE IV: *The reconciliation of cost and benefit data to improve the management of library resources*

From the data derived in Stages I and III we shall have obtained an overall perspective on the normative requirement and the relative values placed on specific services available at various points in time. We should also have, from Stage II, a reasonably clear impression of how costs have been incurred, in providing services. The matching of these two sets of data to compare the reported benefits against costs—when reconciled with maximum cost constraints—should indicate to what extent the pattern of services can be modified.

It is such a process of reconciliation which exemplifies economic engineering, or marketing technology. We have described how user information can be collected as a basis for understanding behaviour and of then acting to affect or improve the circumstances. At the risk of excessive repetition, it is in foci such as these that marketing empirics and economic theoretical rigour can come together. I believe that they soon will.

CONCLUSION

Marketing practitioners found very little of immediate value in economic theory when they began to develop their own body of knowledge in the fifties and sixties. The attempt to explain behaviour solely in terms of economic man, and the levels of abstraction adopted, meant that marketing had to develop its own range of basic propositions. Without the benefit of an intellectually rigorous tradition, however, marketing's contribution has been predominantly piecemeal. Economics, for its part, has tended to scorn the empirically based pragmatism of marketing, failing often to recognize that it constitutes a rich source for developing a viable, useful theory of economic behaviour, albeit without exclusive reliance on economic rationality.

The paramount lesson to be learnt from marketing at this juncture is that economic behaviour can normally only be explained in multi-disciplinary terms. I have taken this lesson and explored its meaning in terms of the behaviour of buyers and of operational marketing executives.

By way of a prospect on the next decade, a critique of economic rationality in the field of information buying was developed and a framework for a multi-disciplinary approach suggested. The problem of valuing information in multi-disciplinary terms is explored. The imperfect quality of the information used in micro-economic decision-making, and the lack of enthusiasm on the part of executives to buy on economically rational terms are, it is suggested, fundamentally important phenomena to understand if organizational goals—be they simple economic, behavioural or a combination of both—are to be attained. Intellectual rigour is required in the face of such problems which a synthesis of the traditions of economic theory and the empirical pragmatism of marketing can provide; the challenge to let this happen lies before us over the next decade.

REFERENCES

1. Amstutz, A., *Computer simulation of competitive market response*, MIT Press, 1967.
2. Howard, J. and Sheth, J., *Theory of buyer behaviour*. John Wiley, 1971.
3. Webster, F. and Wind, Y., *Organisation buying behaviour:* Prentice-Hall, 1972.
4. Gabor, A. and Granger, C. J., 'Price as an indication of quality', *Economica*, 1966.
5. Katona, G., *Psychological analysis of economic behaviour*. McGraw-Hill, 1963.
6. Adam, D., *Les réactions du consommateur devant le prix*. Sèdes, Paris, 1968.
7. Cyert, R. M. and March, J. G., *Behavioural theory of the firm*. Prentice-Hall, 1963.
8. Hayhurst, R., *Test marketing in practice*. BIM, Occasional Paper No. 74, September 1968.
9. Christopher, M. G., *Marketing below-the-line*. George Allen & Unwin, 1972.
10. Saddik, S. M., 'Manufacturer toleration of channels of distribution', chap. 7 in Wills, G. S. C., *Exploration in marketing thought*. Crosby Lockwood, 1971.
11. Purnell, M., *Identifying European marketing opportunities*. Cranfield Research Papers in Marketing and Logistics, 1973/4 session.
12. Wills, G. S. C., 'Pragmatism in advertising research', *Journal of Advertising*, **2**, 1973.
13. Christopher, M. G., *Total distribution*. Gower Press, 1971.
14. Hayhurst, R. and Wills, G. S. C. *Organisational design for marketing futures*. George Allen & Unwin, 1972.
15. Wills, G. S. C. *Sources of UK marketing information*, 1967 (2nd edition, 1974). Ernest Benn.
16. Wills, G. S. C. 'Cost benefit of a test market', in Wills, G. S. C. & Seibert, J. (eds.), *Marketing Research*. Penguin Books, 1970.
17. Christopher, M. G. and Wills, G. S. C., 'Cost benefit of external information', *UNESCO Library Bulletin*, January 1970.

18. Maybury, G., 'Performance budgeting for the library', *ALA Bulletin,* 1961.
19. Martyn, J. E., Report in *ASLIB Electronics Group Newsletter,* No. 70, October 1969.
20. King, M. and Lancaster, J., 'Cost performance and benefits of information systems', *Proceeding of the 32nd annual meeting of the American Society for Information Science,* Vol. 6 (1969), pp. 501–5.
21. Lancaster, J., 'The cost/effectiveness analysis of information retrieval and dissemination systems', *Journal of the American Society for Information Science,* January–February, 1971.
22. Quade, E. S., *Cost-effectiveness: an introduction and overview,* Wiley, 1967.

CHAPTER 10

Product/Market Strategies Reconsidered

Marketing studies have continually manifest a tendency towards normative conceptual statements about areas of vital concern to business.[1] The price paid is a decreasing technological validity of much that is written in textbooks on the subject. Perhaps the most recidivistic area has been 'product strategy and management' which undeniably lies at the heart of marketing's claim to a major voice in corporate planning activity. The product is normally the company's sole revenue generator and attention to its health can readily be seen as fundamental to successful operations.[2]

Such recidivism is scarcely alleviated by the continual repetition of 'current best practice' in marketing which almost invariably means the way a few of the more public-relations conscious, untypically large businesses, in fast-moving consumer goods industries, set about developing product strategies and undertaking their management. Such firms undergo a process of continuous innovation, and have evolved techniques of venture analysis,[3] relying on new enterprise divisions or task forces to sidestep the present/future management dichotomy which is ever present in large/medium and small concerns. Bayesian decision theory, even d.c.f., are unheard of and certainly unused in such organizations.[4] The product strategy and management problem is seldom faced because managements are absorbed with problems of their present operations.

Blakey and McGuire,[5] in a pilot study of innovation and organization structures in the wool textile industry, found there a striking lack of innovation of any form, and new product introduction the exception rather than the rule. Most product changes introduced were classifiable as 'alterations to existing lines'. Rainie[6] has suggested that the pattern, or as he termed it

> the basic handicap, is an inability to shake off the attitudes of a craft-based family business, and to develop or acquire the management organization and technique of a progressive industrial organization.

Within the engineering industries as a whole (we shall be concerned here solely with textile engineering) Hammouda[7] has reported that

> in the application of the concept of product planning, the personalities of management (its philosophies and attitudes) and the environmental circumstances within which the firms operate, are the major factors which affect the

174

evaluation and development of product planning. The former factor (the personalities of management) appears to be the more important of the two.

He continues: 'biased attention to the technical activity at the expense of marketing activities is a common phenomenon'. Liander[8] has reported in a similar vein concerning the dominance of technical consideration over marketing in the EEC at large.

Only when we switch to big company evidence, as in Udell's examination[9] of key elements in competitive strategies amongst the leading 200 firms in the USA, does 'product research and development' rise to anything like the normative status we give it textually. Udell found 79% of his top 200 perceiving 'product research and development as one of the five most vital sectors for corporate marketing success'. (There can be little doubt that 'product research and development' is not synonymous with 'product strategy and management'. It seems a reasonable assumption to make, however, that most firms with the former will have the latter even if only by implication in their R & D strategies.)

The challenge to normative thinking about the formalized way in which product strategy and management should be undertaken, which this fragmentary medium and small firm evidence presented, led to an empirical examination of this area of marketing activity within three sectors of the textile industries. As we expected, and as we and other colleagues had found earlier in respect to the total marketing mix concept,[10] all was not normative. In this chapter we deal with what does in fact take place in terms of product strategy and planning within the textile machinery, wool textile and clothing industries, together with their explanation as to why capable, competent and in many cases apparently very successful organizations within their own industrial environments, deviate from textbook norms. We suggest that this is the unavoidable preliminary analysis which must be undertaken before we can presume to give advice to these industrial sectors on how to do things 'better' or in any 'optimal' manner. As such, our research study is intended to act as a modifying influence in the codification of marketing technology for all save the very large enterprise, and as a caution even to them when they become technique-bound and inflexible in their approach to product strategy and management.

THE SAMPLE AND RESEARCH METHOD

This chapter reports evidence from a wide-ranging examination of all aspects of marketing practice within three selected sectors of the British textile industries—those covering textile engineering, wool textiles and clothing.[11,12] The investigation involved two stages; thirty-six in-depth company interviews ranging from one day to two weeks duration each, and

322 completed postal questionnaires constituting a 53% response rate from the sample contacted. The postal universe was all companies in the three sectors listed in the current edition of *Kompass Directory* and which had over twenty-five employees. Questionnaires were answered by chief executives within the companies, and all responses were received during summer 1968.

The thirty-six in-depth interviews were made with those companies who agreed to collaborate on the basis of a judgemental sample of seventy-two (a 50% response rate). Judgement was used to select a cross-section of firm

Industrial sector	Positive response		Negative response		No response		Total approached	Universe
	N=	%	N=	%	N=	%	N%	N=
Textile machinery	73	65	4	4	33	30	110	110
Wool textiles								
Textiles	134	54	12	5	104	41	250	748
Clothing	101	40	10	4	139	56	250	763
TOTALS	308	50	26	4	276	75	610	1,621

FIG. 10.1   *Textile sector response patterns for quantification study.*

sizes and structures within each of the three sectors. The purpose of this initial stage was to generate worthwhile hypotheses for quantification and qualitative information to afford some explanations of the emerging statistics. The statistical significance of the qualitative data is hence of a lower order than the postal study.

Sector postal survey sample factors and response patterns are given in Fig. 10.1. The samples contacted within wool textile and clothing sectors were selected by an interval sampling procedure from an alphabetical listing within regional strata. A census was undertaken within the textile engineering sector.

Whilst response rates of 50% and 53% in the two stages of this investigation are undoubtedly good by normal criteria for this type of study, we took special steps to check so far as possible on the representativeness of those who had replied. In Stage 1, all non-respondent firms had been contacted by telephone initially to request permission for an interview following a letter announcing the conduct and nature of the study. Refusals were in four main groupings—lack of time to collaborate; engagement of late in similar studies; undergoing reorganization; felt the study to be irrelevant. The first category accounted for 60% of all refusals.

A similar pattern of reasoning was given by the sample of twenty non-responding postal survey companies who were contacted by telephone. A new category appeared, however: those who declined as a matter of corporate policy. On further discussion, fourteen of these twenty companies completed the questionnaire and returned it. Analysis did not indicate any particularly unusual characteristic inherent in the non-respondent companies which would lead us to doubt that our sample of firms was representative of the universe in the study's key dimensions.

In this study company size was defined as: small >24 but <200; medium >199 but <500; large >499 employees.

PREVALENT PRODUCT POLICIES

We have seen that the need for a product policy has been consistently emphasized in the literature; it specifies a company's product objectives, the types of product and/or service it should offer, and the market(s) at which the business should aim. Such a strategy can orient effort and set criteria for the selection of product avenues to corporate success. It should stem from the normalized, careful and skilful process of matching the capabilities of a company to the opportunities of the markets it identifies as its area.

One of the most significant facts which emerged from our research was the lack of any acceptance or appreciation in most companies of any specific need to develop formal product policies. Only one of the thirty-six companies visited in-depth had a written-down product policy, and fully one-quarter of them reported that they had no general view of a corporate product policy of any kind.

Such lack of formal clarity and attention manifests itself further in that most companies visited take their extant field of business for granted. The identification of 'which market a business is in' has normally been viewed as perhaps the most fundamental of all decisions. It must of necessity be made at least once, and the philosophy of a dynamic marketing concept requires that it be revised continually thereafter. This need for revision is dictated by constant change in the environment external to the company, and in germane technology as well as by shifts in the pattern of internal weaknesses and strengths which can themselves be partially or wholly caused by external factors.

The absence of any pattern of review of the field decision is particularly demonstrated in the reluctance of managements to consider diversification seriously. Very few companies report any readiness to diversify even in face of potential profit opportunities. The majority reject diversification in principle without any attempt to support their attitudes in terms of the existence of

sufficient opportunities in their existing product fields. Most advance explanations usually amount to field inertia; an attitude of resistance to change. The
postal survey revealed that one-third of companies had never given any
consideration to the possibility of diversification. We do not wish to propose
that diversification is necessarily the right answer to achieve business growth
and health. What we do question is the validity of the attitude which refuses
even to consider the possibility of change. It is epitomized by such comments
as: 'It never occurred to us'; 'We have enough trouble on our hands'; or
'We'd better concentrate on what we know, which is always better than what
we do not know'. All three comments were made by chief executives of
companies which have been experiencing a decline in their turnover and
profitability in recent years. Resistance to change also seems to account for
the marked reluctance of most companies to search for opportunities in sub-
sectors of their existing industries which they have not so far tackled. The
focus of operations in particular sub-sectors seems to be a matter of heritage
rather than deliberation.

All concepts of the product line seemed to rest on manufacturing rather than
on market or marketing considerations. One company's managing director
commented: 'Our policy is simply to produce goods that are suited to our
machines'.

All companies did not reject normative concepts so vigorously. Textile
machinery companies generally had a wider concept of product line than
companies in the two other sectors. A number of wool textile companies had
in fact developed appropriate strategies to enter new fields of business,
strategies stemming from their conviction that old markets are either saturated,
declining, or involve too much competition. Whilst many companies were
unaware of market segmentation analysis and attempted to be all things to all
people within their industrial sector, others were making effective use of
segmentation, especially clothing companies. Interrelationships of demand on
the other hand received markedly less attention and that largely within the
clothing industry.

INNOVATION POLICY

Little effort was directed by the majority of companies towards the development and introduction of new products. Many companies reported that the
only innovation they undertook was the improvement of their existing
products. Several reasons were advanced to explain this behaviour. Some
companies indicated that their small size limited their ability to invest in
research and development. They behave as they do because they cannot do
otherwise, and some argued that even if they did succeed in developing a
new product at a cost which they could bear, they would not be in a position

to take full advantage of it because of the strength of competitors who could produce substitutes in no time. Other companies followed this course because it was thought to be safer and easier. Still others postulated that there was nothing new under the sun, and hence very little room for innovation. One managing director observed:

> we are producing and selling virtually the same lines which we started with forty years ago. What enabled us to survive for forty years is able to carry us through for any period of time to come.

Nevertheless, some companies reported that their innovation effort was directed both to improvements of existing products and to development of new products and new processes. One wool textile company reported:

> Because we have got to keep our lines up to date in terms of fashion we have to fill any gaps in our line; we have to look for growth opportunities by introducing new cloths which we can profitably make and sell; we have to look for new applications for our products; and we have to investigate our processes continually to increase efficiency. We also watch for opportunities outside the clothing industry, outside the wool textile industry, and outside the textile industry as a whole.

Generally, three patterns of orientation in the innovation process were identified:

1. *Production-facilities orientation;* under which the company regards innovation as a process of developing improved versions of the same products or less frequently new products which are suited to its production facilities. 'You have got to take advantage of the facilities you have and confine yourself to what they can do. Then you have to convince customers that this is what they should buy. We do not think of something which our machines cannot do' [managing director, wool textiles]. Thus, the starting point is not what the market wants but what the existing machines can produce. Half the companies in these textile sectors conform to this pattern, and not just the smaller enterprises.
2. *Product orientation;* under which the policy is to press for a technically superior product. Technical superiority is the main asset and hence research and development is a much more important function than under other patterns. Less than a quarter of the sample companies, mostly from textile machinery, adopt this approach. These companies tend more than others to introduce novel products.
3. *Marketing orientation;* under which the company endeavours to make products which are wanted by the market. The comment made by a clothing managing director illustrates this approach: 'Satisfaction of customers is what we are here for; they are the only road to success and the only guarantee against the future. Hence, our product policy is to

introduce whatever styles, designs, weights or materials our customers want'.

Almost all textile machinery companies report, not surprisingly, that fashion considerations seldom affect their process of innovation. Companies in wool textiles and clothing pay considerable attention to the fashion element.[13] Their behaviour can be classified under three patterns.

1. *Fashion creation;* very few companies in the study indicate that their policy is to set new trends in fashion. Where they do, however, their image is built around being leaders in fashion.
2. *Fashion following;* the majority of companies report that they do not attempt to create fashion, or to influence a change in consumer tastes from a fashion point of view. They are content to follow it.
3. *Fashion antagonism;* a very small number of companies pay no attention to fashion either because the users of their products are thought to be far from fashion-conscious, or because they believe that mass production of standard lines pays better dividends.

DIFFERENTIATION AND VARIETY POLICY

Most companies in wool textiles and clothing report a policy of wide variety, which is considered to be most essential. In designing products to meet needs they attempt to achieve extensive rather than selective coverage. The product range is not designed to solve selected consumer problems but to embrace all or most needs which could exist. A basic reason for this behaviour is the uncertainty of the manufacturer as to what the customer wants, as this comment demonstrates:

> Since we are not sure about the market, we introduce forty to fifty items and hope that three or four of them will hit the target. Other people can be more certain and shoot only one or two bullets which, they know, will hit the target. As for us, we cater for a big variety of tastes, qualities, etc., to cover all possibilities, and expect a few to achieve the object [managing director, wool textiles].

This policy of wide ranges, it may be argued, is the extreme marketing orientation case, of attempting to satisfy all customers. However, trying to be all things to all people is normally reckoned as poor corporate strategy. Effective segmentation requires a company to concentrate on carefully selected groups of needs which it can serve best. The argument that companies are aiming at all groups of customers' needs, and can serve them all best, is superficial. The much more likely reason for adopting such a policy, far from the desire to satisfy known wants, is to hedge in the face of uncertainty. Large proportions of R & D can be wasted on the development of items that stand little chance of selling. The company knows it is a wasted effort, but does not know how to determine which part to cut. This situation focuses on a lack of knowledge about demand and an inability to improve that knowledge due to lack of resources. In such circumstances many companies feel they have no choice but to follow such a course. *Whilst they feel they can afford to introduce products which never sell, the irony is that they feel they cannot afford to find out what will sell in advance.*

USE OF NEW PRODUCTS AS A COMPETITIVE WEAPON

The majority of companies do not regard new products as a major element in their competitive strategies. Prevalent attitudes in wool textile companies suggest that development of new products is not their business; it is a task which should be accomplished by the machinery makers. Conversely, machinery and clothing manufacturers tend to criticize the wool textile industry for its lack of appreciation of the need for development and for its reluctance to undertake any notable innovative activity. For their part, clothing companies tend to assume that there is very little scope for innovation at their end and hence new products cannot be relied upon in their competitive strategies. In contrast, the majority of machinery companies indicate their use of new products as a major competitive weapon. We found significant patterns of company behaviour by sector in these textile industries with machinery companies most concerned with new products as a source of competitive advantage, and clothing companies least concerned. Large companies tend to be marginally more frequent users of new products as a competitive weapon than small or medium-sized firms.

USE OF NEW PRODUCTS AS A GROWTH TOOL

Almost all companies report growth as a major objective. It can normally be expected to emerge by tackling the serious obstacles to growth that are encountered since they exert a significant influence on the choice of strategy. Managements emphasized the following obstacles, cited in order of frequency of mention:

1. *Decline in total market demand;* this factor was widely and predominantly mentioned in wool textiles and textile machinery companies.
2. *Severe competition from home and foreign manufacturers;* this factor was mentioned across all industries.
3. *Shortage of labour;* only wool textiles and clothing companies mentioned this factor.
4. *Lack of finance;* in all sectors and most frequently in smaller companies.
5. *Lack of managerial resources;* some companies find this the most insuperable obstacle of all.

The product/market combinations implicitly adopted as the basis for growth strategies in the thirty-six companies where in-depth interviews were made can be categorized in terms of the Ansoffian matrix[14] as follows:

Old products to old markets—33 companies
Old products to new markets— 3 companies
New products to old markets—12 companies
New products to new markets— 2 companies

Although some companies indicated more than one approach, nothing approaching a development portfolio was to be found along the classic lines we are led to anticipate in normative models.

Growth attempted	Textile machinery		Wool textiles		Clothing	
	No.	*%*	*No.*	*%*	*No.*	*%*
Mainly through existing products	43	57	92	68	84	76
Mainly through new products	30	39	36	26	19	17
Through both courses equally	3	4	7	5	6	5
Not indicated	—	—	1	1	1	1
TOTAL	76	100	136	100	110	99

FIG. 10.2 *Strategies for growth—analysis by sector.*

The obstacles already reported scarcely indicate much chance of success through the first combination as a path to growth; yet it predominates. Lack of virtually any propensity for the development of new markets is noteworthy; reliance on new products as a major growth tool is obviously very low.

In the postal study companies these indications of growth strategies were quantified. Companies were asked whether they relied *mainly* on existing products, *mainly* on new products, or on both equally. Their replies can be seen in Fig. 10.2.

The majority of companies do not regard new products as a major growth tool. More use is made of them in the growth strategies of textile machinery companies than among wool textile companies which are, in turn, more prone to use them than clothing companies. With such a low propensity to use new products as the basis for growth, it is perhaps not surprising that only a small minority report the use of test marketing. An oddly assorted set of reasons was advanced, as follows:

1. There is little production for stock, and many lines are merely dummies.
2. The cost/benefit of the situation rules out market testing.

3. Competition is feared or quick action is important.
4. The company does not believe in the efficacy of test marketing as an indicator of market performance, particularly in fashion sectors.

The majority of companies believe test marketing is useless, too costly, or unnecessary in the light of the product strategies they deem appropriate for their sector of the textile industries.

There is a wide divergence between textile machinery companies and the other two sectors in the extent of test marketing; while 45% of the former indicate use, only 20% of the latter do so. A similar gap exists between large and all other companies; while 46% of large companies report its use, only 20% of medium and small companies do so. Use of test-marketing was also significantly associated with whether the company had a formally trained chief marketing executive and whether its chief executive had a favourable attitude towards the marketing concept. (This may, of course, be no more than a measure of the professional influence of a single function in the firm.)

SYSTEMS OF PRODUCT PLANNING AND DEVELOPMENT

In order to gain further insight into the innovative behaviour of the textile sectors examined it was necessary to examine closely the process of product planning and development and the informational and philosophical environment of that process. Emphasis was placed on how decisions are made, by whom, and in what sequence. This type of examination does not lend itself to the format of a postal questionnaire, and it was consequently confined to the qualitative stage of the research with the thirty-six companies which were studied in depth.

As a result of this examination two basic systems of company product planning and development behaviour were identified. Although there is every possibility that these two patterns may overlap in practice, they are analysed separately because of the distinct characteristics of each.

Present-mix oriented model
The first pattern which we propose to describe as 'present-mix orientation' can be illustrated as the flow model, Fig. 10.3. This empirical model analyses the process of product planning and development in wool textile and clothing companies. Some of these companies supplement this pattern with the second pattern which is discussed later.

The product planning and development activity is a continuing process from one year to another, or from one season to another. The company starts the process with a list of extant products and not with a list of new product ideas. Last year's sales performance of all items on the present product range

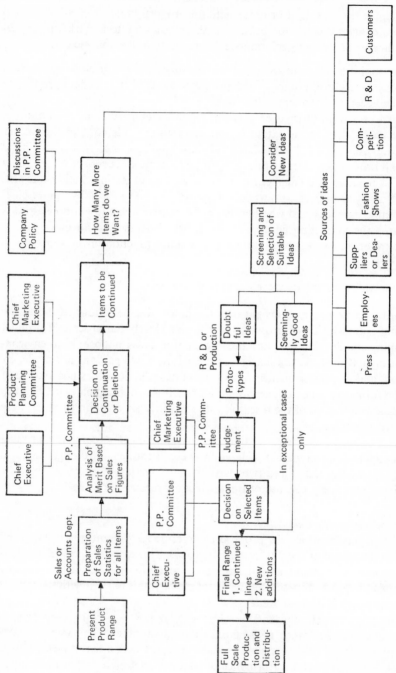

FIG. 10.3   *The first pattern of product planning and development—present-mix orientation.*

is assessed to sort out the items which did succeed (in terms of sales volume) from the items which did not. The Product Planning Committee (PPC) carries out this assessment. This is a process analogous to the popularly prescribed Product Range Audit.[15]

On the basis of this assessment a decision is taken on each item, either to continue or discontinue it, by the PPC chief executive/chief marketing executive, depending on who is assigned the authority to make such product decisions. As a result of this decision a number of items are identified from the present range which will continue to appear on the range during the next period.

The next task of the PPC is to decide how many more items should be added to the range to replace discontinued lines. This decision is an attempt to keep the breadth of the range in line with the company's variety and differentiation policy. At this stage there may be changes in policy stemming from discussions among PPC members. When the decision is reached on *the approximate number of new items* to be added to the range, movement can be made to the next stage.

New product ideas are assembled drawing on a number of sources which include press, employees, suppliers or dealers, fashion shows, competitors, research and development staff, and customers. The PPC assesses the merits of these ideas and selects a number of them to go through the prototype stage. In exceptional cases, for example when a competitive product is being copied, the final go-ahead decision may be taken at this stage, and the research and development staff will be instructed to prepare the product for full-scale production. Even if a prototype is developed in these exceptional cases, it will be a matter of production requirements rather than for the purpose of revising the go-ahead decision which has already been given at the screening stage.

Apart from these exceptional cases, the normal course of events is to develop a prototype within R & D or the production department for all provisionally accepted ideas. Having developed these prototypes the PPC meets again to evaluate all developed product alternatives. On the basis of these evaluations, a selection of new products gets the final go-ahead from the PPC chief executive/chief marketing executive, depending on who wields ultimate authority. This final selection of new products, together with those products continuing from the previous range, constitutes the new product range which will be offered next cycle round. At the end of the following season or year this new range will itself constitute the next starting point for the product planning process.

1. *Procedures.* The present-mix oriented model of product planning behaviour does not attempt to garner the information which we would normally consider vital to make almost any decisions at almost any stage.

Opinions of managers, albeit frequently successful, seem to be the most important basis for making choices. Only one piece of formally collated information is widely used, namely sales figures; but apart from this there are very few formalized sets of facts to guide product decisions.

Furthermore, the characteristic search for new products here is passive, rather than an active effort directed continuously towards the identification of new ideas. No procedures are employed to ensure a steady flow of new ideas in the model.

Giving the final 'go-ahead' to some ideas at the screening stage is normally viewed as dangerous practice. Furthermore, the approval of the final selection on the opinions of managers with very little, if any, direct information from the marketplace is normally regarded askance. Test-marketing is not employed by most such companies.

2. *Philosophy*. This model illustrates a *status quo* philosophy where management is so preoccupied with its present product mix that its product planning activity is in most cases a mere revision of that mix. The model does not provide a suitable environment for any constant effort to discover new ideas and to develop new products for old or completely new markets which are emerging to undermine present patterns of business. The model is therefore consistent with the attitude of management which is reluctant to change and is content to carry on as before. For example, if at the stage of evaluating the present range it was decided that all items were to be continued, the probability is very high that companies would skip all subsequent stages involving exploration for new ideas and new opportunities arising from new market needs, and continue to produce and distribute in the same way as for the previous period.

Despite these apparently fundamental weaknesses, the model provides a framework which successfully integrates most elements of product planning and development. With a refinement of some of its procedures, a reappraisal of the attitudes of those working it, and the addition of the elements of the product planning and development process which are missing from it, the model could perhaps be even more successful for such firms as employ it than it has already proved to be.

Innovation-oriented model

Fig. 10.4 presents a flow model which illustrates the second pattern of company behaviour with regard to product planning and development. It follows to a greater extent the normative textbook models of product planning and development.[16] Eight textile machinery companies follow this pattern exclusively, and four clothing and two wool textile companies adopt it to supplement their major product planning and development activity

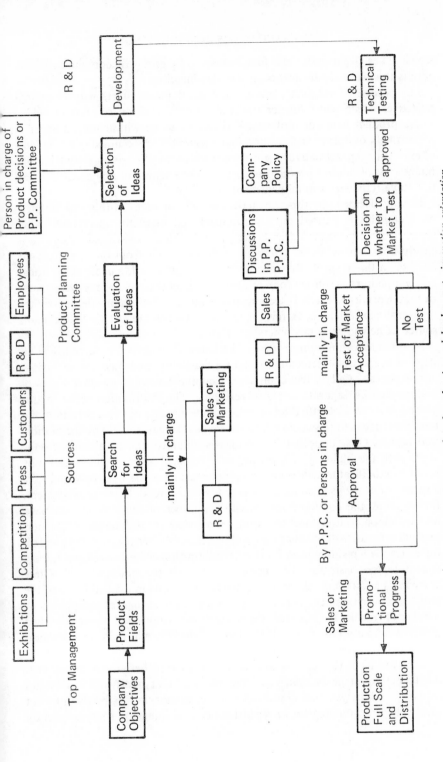

FIG. 10.4   *The second pattern of product planning and development—innovation orientation.*

which takes place under the first pattern. The group of companies which adopts this pattern cuts across all size classifications.

The process of product planning and development starts with company objectives which will influence the choice or the revision of product fields. These product fields do not necessarily have to be within the limits of a present field of operations. Rather, management is preoccupied with the idea of exploiting *any* attractive opportunities which may lie within or outside the boundaries of present product/market mix. The setting of any constraints at this stage rests with top management.

Having decided on this, an active search for ideas within the defined product fields is carried out by technical and marketing personnel. This search cannot be regarded as being generally highly organized to ensure a steady flow of new ideas. There are wide variations from one company to another in this respect. Reliance on research and development, exhibitions, and competitors as sources for new ideas is heavier than reliance on customers. In that sense, the search is technically-oriented or imitation-oriented rather than customer-oriented. A few companies, however, report that their main source of new ideas is customers' problems.

Next comes evaluation of ideas. The tendency observed is to combine all steps of evaluation—screening, technical feasibility, and business analysis—in one process. Only a few companies view these steps as separate stages of evaluation with separate terms of reference. The information input in this process is more adequate than practices under the first pattern. Selection of a number of ideas to pass through to subsequent stages is made by the authorized person. Once approval for an idea is obtained, the development stage starts with the building of a prototype. Technical testing follows and may result in modifications. Market acceptance testing is the next task and here a variety of methods to conduct these tests was recorded. In textile machinery, for example, the company may invite a number of selected customers to attend demonstrations and to express their view on the merits of the new product regardless of whether they will buy it or not. Whenever well-founded, these views will result in modifications. These customers' reactions also largely constitute the basis for the decision to launch the new product. Three companies in clothing, all large, conduct market tests in the full sense of the term. Many companies do not carry out any tests of market acceptance. A number of reasons are reported which were synonymous with those described earlier. Company policy and discussions at the PPC will indicate whether a test of market acceptance is advised.

If the results of the tests indicate a go-ahead, or if there is no market test, the launching stage is reached. Here we find that nearly all companies adopting this pattern undertake some form of impersonal promotion but with widely varying degrees of sophistication and intensity. Market reaction to the new product is then fed back to management and may effect new changes, new courses of action, or even a reconsideration of company objectives.

Whilst the present-mix oriented company approaches its product planning and development activity with a narrow outlook, the innovation-oriented company starts more appropriately with a statement of its objectives—profits, growth, etc. From there it defines those product fields it can legitimately enter, whether they fall within or without the boundaries of the present field of operations. The focus in this second pattern is on making and/or identifying new opportunities and discovering new ideas which are capable of achieving company objectives. This is what we normally view as the more appropriate environment for innovation. This innovation-oriented pattern of behaviour conforms broadly with the pattern implied in the marketing concept. There are, however, wide variations among companies adopting this pattern in the extent of their customer orientation.

CONCLUSION

There is no doubt that practices in the textile industries sectors examined diverge from the predominant normative approaches. New product strategy and management in these sectors is not what the textbooks lead us to suppose it ought to be. Are these firms just backward or are our models deficient? Ultimately, the answer will depend on a comparison of the assumed objectives behind the textbook models and the operationally effective objective of the business studied.

To take a prime example, almost all companies agreed that growth was a major objective, but few were manifestly prepared to pay the full price of securing the maximum theoretical potential available to them. Personality and environmental constraints hold business back from the total pursuit of the sort of goals which normative marketing models posit. The lesson should be salutary for our teaching efforts and for our research. It focuses attention on the need for a much closer examination of the true goals of business and the function of marketing in meeting them.

The marketing textbooks are making an arrogant value judgement, the sort economists are continually criticized for, when it is suggested that reluctance to change is a wrong attitude to adopt. Company goals are formulated through a process of trade-offs between such a legitimate reluctance and possible greater reward in terms of net cash flow.

Nonetheless, there seems to be ample evidence that sheer ignorance is at times leading to misallocation of effort and resource. Here, sensibly moderate views of the role of product strategy and management can surely be of considerable benefit to the firms engaged in these industries. The most obvious area is perhaps to be found in the proliferation of market offerings in the face of uncertainty rather than making a bold attempt to eliminate some of that uncertainty.

We have also, however, been made particularly aware of the constrained pattern of options available to a small resource business, to the business which is virtually unable to influence the general course of product development in its sector of operations. Much product policy is of necessity limited to applications-engineering or direct imitation, rather than the grander alternatives of first-to-market and follow-the-leader so often mentioned in product strategy models.[17,18]

Finally, we have discussed an empirically viable pattern of product strategy and management for businesses operating in a seasonal market, in itself a facet of product planning.

REFERENCES

1. Borden, Neil, 'The concept of the marketing mix', in Schwartz, G. (ed.), *Science in marketing*. John Wiley & Sons, 1965.
2. Drucker, P., *Managing for results*. Heinemann, 1964.
3. The major contributions here include: Hanan, M., 'Corporate growth through venture management', *Harvard Business Review*, 47(1), 1969; O'Meara, J. T., 'Selecting profitable products for development', *Harvard Business Review*, 39(1), 1961; Pessemier, E. A., *New product decisions*. New York: McGraw-Hill, 1966.
4. NEDO, *Investment appraisal*. HMSO, 1963.
5. Blakey, N. and McGuire, A., *Innovation in the woollen and worsted industry*. University of Bradford Management Centre Project Report, 1967.
6. Rainie, G. F., *The woollen and worsted industry*, pp. 86-7. Clarendon Press, 1965.
7. Hammouda, M. A. A., 'The concept of product planning and the contribution of marketing to the planning activities in the engineering industry', unpublished Ph.D. thesis, University of Manchester, 1968, pp. 504-5.
8. Liander, B., *Marketing development in the EEC*. McGraw-Hill, 1964.
9. Udell, J. G., 'How important is pricing in competitive strategy?', *Journal of Marketing*, 28(1), 1964, pp. 44-8, reprinted in Taylor, B. and Wills, G. (eds.), *Pricing strategy*, pp. 317-25. Staples Press, 1969.
10. Mann, J., *The nominal and effective status of chief marketing executives in Yorkshire industry*. Proceedings of 2nd Conference of Teachers of Marketing, University of Bradford Management Centre, 1967.
11. The full results of the investigation are given in Saddik, S. M. A., *Marketing in the wool textile, textile machinery and clothing industries*. University of Bradford Management Centre, April 1969.
12. Saddik, S. M. A., 'Marketing orientation and organizational design', *British Journal of Marketing*, 2(4), 1968.
13. Wills, G. and Christopher, M. G. review this facet more fully in 'What do we know about fashion marketing?', *Marketing World*, 1(1), 1969, pp. 1-15,

reprinted in Wills, G. and Midgley, D., *Fashion marketing*. Allen & Unwin, 1973, Chap. 1.

14. Ansoff, H. I., *Corporate strategy*. McGraw-Hill, 1965.
15. Drucker, P., *Managing for results*. Heinemann, 1964.
16. Ashton, D., Gotham, P. and Wills, G., 'Conditions favourable to product innovation', *Scientific Business,* 3(1), 1965, pp. 24–39, reprinted in Taylor, B. and Wills, G., (eds.), *Long range planning for marketing and diversification.* Crosby Lockwood for University of Bradford Press, 1970.
17. Ansoff, H. I. and Stewart, J. M., 'Strategies for a Technology-Based Business', *Harvard Business Review,* 45(6), 1967.
18. Wills, G. and Ridgley, D., (eds.) *Creating and Marketing New Products,* Staples Press, 1973.

CHAPTER 11

Marketing of Services

The application of marketing lines of thought to the offer of services to customers is still comparatively recent. Problems abound. By way of a focus on this vitally important field of activity over the next decade, two recent cases with which my colleagues and I have been concerned are recorded. The first is an unusual study for the City of Bradford; the second a somewhat more straightforward examination of the market for the services of Wira—originally the Wool Industries Research Association.

THE CITY OF BRADFORD

The application of market analysis procedures to problems of regional economic development has long been neglected. This study presents a framework for regional economic analysis and then proceeds to a detailed examination of the City of Bradford in Yorkshire within that framework. We worked for a period of four years on behalf of the Bradford Area Development Association (BADA) to identify ways in which economic growth within the city could be stimulated. Eight major studies were undertaken which explored both the extant structure of Bradford's industry and resources and its external economies, and the most viable directions for growth.

The studies led BADA to the conclusion that, although new employers could be attracted to the area, the greatest effort should be applied to accommodate, facilitate and encourage the growth of indigenous companies. The strategy which was evolved within the city led to the establishment of an Industrial Officer within the City Hall; to the founding of a regional Merchant Bank; to a determined series of political lobbies to get the city's problems aired within the Planning Region and at Ministry level in London and much more besides.

By late 1973, when the City of Bradford was absorbed into a Metropolitan District within the Metropolitan County of West Yorkshire, and BADA formally wound up, a considerable record of success could be reported. These achievements must be seen against the background of sluggish economic growth within the UK economy over the period.

INTRODUCTION

Bradford grew from a series of small villages at the start of the nineteenth century to become the world centre of the woollen industry by its close. Its growth in population was dramatic, moving from 13,000 in 1801 to 280,000 in 1901. In 1850, 45% of all woollen textile workers in the country were employed there. The Wool Exchange still stands today (although seldom used) and the city depends on wool for the jobs of over a quarter of its working population. Some new industries have grown up alongside wool, most successfully perhaps, mail order and heavy engineering—but the city's livelihood is still uncomfortably dependent on wool during times when that industry has been undergoing metamorphosis. If wool is not an industry in decline, those parts of it with which Bradford is particularly associated (for example wool tops and worsteds) have not seen any spectacular growth. The continuing development of synthetic fibres, and the location of such industries away from the original homes of natural fibre-based industries, must always leave a question mark over the city's prosperity and well-being.

Since the turn of the twentieth century, Bradford's population has remained static in absolute terms, but even this position has only been achieved by successive waves of immigration to replace indigenous young people moving away from the city. Some 20,000 Irishmen and 20,000 Germans had come to the city in the late nineteenth century. They were followed in the twentieth by more than 10,000 Eastern Europeans after World War II and by 15,000 or more Pakistanis in the sixties.

Against this background of emigration and immigration, and the static position overall, it was not surprising that the city's resources and assets became obsolete from housing to the industrial workplace, most of which had been built in the heyday of prosperity some century ago. The city centre and the urban environment were, to put it gently, uninviting if not a positive deterrent; buildings were blackened with industrial grime. Yet Bradford is a proud city. Its natural response was to do something dramatic to ensure that it did participate in the newfound prosperity in England, and that it did shake off the undesirable consequences of its nineteenth-century success.

The Bradford Area Development Association (BADA) was a grass roots movement from the Junior Chamber of Commerce in the city which rapidly won civic and university support as well as the backing of a wide range of private individuals. Launched in the mid-sixties, it was determined not simply to join the general clamour from other development areas in the country, pleading for new industry to come to town. Rather it was determined to undertake a deep and thorough assessment of where the city really stood and what the alternative paths forward might be. In particular, what was the total nature of the 'process' which made movement forward possible at all.

The industrial growth strategy which the city has pursued for several years now arose from a series of studies undertaken by the University of Bradford for BADA. Alongside that strategy, however, has been a deliberate policy of environmental improvement most obviously seen in the new city centre development, the motorway and trunk road building programme, the fight to improve the city airport facilities and the mass cleaning of buildings— once all of the city was zoned for clean air. Of equal importance has been the stimulation of social activities and civic pride. Support for the theatre, for a series of Bradford Festivals and for the International Print Biennial, and a new Industrial Museum, all demonstrate the city's determination to improve the quality of life in parallel with, or even ahead of, major industrial/economic regeneration.

A FRAMEWORK FOR REGIONAL ECONOMIC ANALYSIS

Regional economics has become a subject in itself in recent years. Innumerable papers and books have appeared describing theoretical models of economic behaviour within regions. Regional geography, too, has become increasingly concerned with the problems of the economic structure of regions and the dynamics of relationships between regions. Unfortunately, however, the majority of the work in this area has been theoretical and ex-post; that is it has attempted to describe regional phenomena in terms of economic theory. Empirical analysis has been hindered, at least in the UK, by the lack of necessary data—particularly income data which in Britain are limited to five-yearly statistics on income tax, with a considerable number of shortcomings.

Action-oriented approaches to regional analysis, as opposed to theoretical studies, have been rare. Standard research techniques, employed by individual companies for many years, have only recently begun to be utilized by those bodies concerned with regional development.

The study described in this chapter, therefore, had to start with a minimum base of prior methodological experience. The model that eventually emerged was, in fact, based almost as much on an analogy with corporate growth processes as on straight economic theory. Nevertheless, certain acknowledgements must be made to some important tenets of regional economic theory which were utilized in the eventual model that formed the basis for the methodology of this study.

Two key facets of economic theory which have a central importance in regional analysis are the concepts of the propensity to consume and the capital/output ratio. The marginal propensity to consume is a measure of the extent to which additional income within an area is spent as against saved.

Obviously the magnitude of this propensity will affect the total recycling of income over time—a multiplier relationship which will be explored in more detail later. The capital/output ratio is an expression of the extent to which a given injection of capital will be reflected in additional output—the 'accelerator' effect. In the marginal sense the capital/output ratio is given by the incremental expenditure of capital divided by the increment in output that it produces. Clearly there will be linkages between the two variables—propensity to consume and the capital output ratio—which will have a considerable effect on the extent to which self-sustained growth can be generated within a region.

In economic theory, a direct analogy can be drawn between a region and a complete economy. Thus the effect of imports and exports and the movement of capital are of some importance in the creation of regional wealth. In fact the regional analyst can make use of the basic formulation of national income:

$$Y = C + I + G + X - M$$

where Y = regional income
C = regional consumption expenditure
I = gross regional investment
G = current regional government (local and central) expenditure
X = exports from the region
M = imports into the region.

C (regional consumption expenditure) is determined by regional disposable income—affected by regional taxation and the marginal propensity to consume.
Thus:

$$C = a + bYd$$

where a = autonomous regional consumption unrelated to income
b = regional marginal propensity to consume
Yd = regional disposable income.

These basic variables will affect the level of regional wealth. The research problem is essentially to determine their value.

In addition to these structural relationships, the regional analyst must explore the extent to which linkages exist within the regional economy. The types of linkage that are implied are the extent to which there is interregional trade between companies, linkages between institutions in the channels of distribution, and indeed linkages between labour catchment areas and employment within the region.

Parallel with the concern for linkages is the need to identify the existence of regional 'external economies'. In other words the extent to which the agglomeration of firms in the same industry in a given region can exploit joint economies such as specialist services, transport availability, labour skilled in particular operations and so on.

All these features taken together will determine the extent to which growth can be sustained and wealth created within a region. Richardson[1] has succinctly summarized the economist's point of view:

> The main factor in regional expansion is interaction between key industries ('propulsive' industries) which form the nucleus of the development pole. These industries have certain characteristics: a high degree of concentration, high income, elasticity of demand for their products which are usually sold to national markets, marked local multiplier and polarization effects (for example, they probably draw most of their inputs from within the region), an advanced level of technology and managerial expertise which by force of example are diffused to other sections in the region.

The aim of the study reported here was to research these aspects in a given region—the city region covered by the Bradford Area Development Association. Clearly a total systems approach was necessary if all the interconnections were to be thoroughly explored and suggestions for action made. To this end, therefore, a conceptual framework was established, within which the research would take place. This framework is shown in Fig. 11.1.

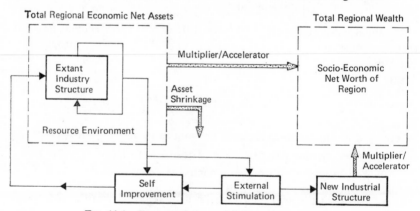

FIG. 11.1   *Framework for regional economic analysis.*

The extent to which this framework would be appropriate to circumstances other than an existing region was considered—for example, could the same approaches be applied in an expanding town such as Northampton (where it is planned to increase the population from 130,000 to 230,000 in twenty years), or a completely new town such as Milton Keynes (where a population of 250,000 is planned for 1990 compared with a 1970 population of 45,000)? It was felt in fact that the structural determinants of regional wealth would be the same no matter what the nature of the development. Clearly, though, the scope of the problem would be of a different magnitude. Following the Bradford study described in this paper, a brief comparative study was made of Northampton and Milton Keynes to check out the applicability of our approach. Our opinion was that with only minor adaptations it would have been equally suitable for use in these different circumstances.

THE BRADFORD STUDY—RESEARCH STRATEGY

The research strategy adopted for the Bradford study followed a logical sequence:

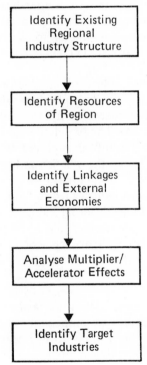

Thus the essential approach was to identify the potential 'growth points' within the region with a view to stimulating them by the addition of further resources and new enterprises and/or industries. A summary of the major stages now follows.

The structure of existing industry in the Bradford region

Bradford developed as a major industrial and commercial centre from approximately 1750 to 1870. In 1700 the area possessed limited agricultural and industrial resources and was isolated in terms of the pre-steam technological developments of England. The scattered hamlets surrounding the nuclear zone were engaged in wool manufacture under the domestic system. This system proved to be of vast importance in later years, in that it provided a skilled labour force on which rapid industrial development could be based.

During the period 1690 to 1826 there occurred an expansion of the town due to canal construction. A local man, Hustler, played a large part in the building of the Leeds–Liverpool canal, and in 1774 the Leeds and Bradford canals were connected with York, Hull and the Midlands by means of improved river navigation from Leeds. Bradford then stood on a trans-Pennine route, and the value of the city as an industrial site was transformed. The area also possessed numerous natural advantages as the city lies where the middle coal measures outcrop onto the surface, and these coals include steam, domestic and coking coal. Ironstone containing iron ore is also present in these coal measures.

Yet it was to the woollen industry that Bradford owed its early growth. The growth of the industry was itself phenomenal; in 1742 the first steam-driven mill was built; by 1805 there were five steam-driven mills; by 1834 some thirty-four; by 1877 over 200. The population grew from 13,000 in 1801 to 67,000 in 1841, and by 1850 Bradford employed 45% of the woollen workers of England and Wales. Today the woollen industry employs some 40,000 workers in the city or 27·8% of the total working population.

The growth of the woollen industry led to the parallel growth of a textile machinery manufacturing and repairing industry, which itself provided the basis for a much wider engineering industry, whose products today range over a large field. Some 24,000 people are engaged in the engineering industry, representing almost 10% of the total working population.

(a) *The wool textile industry.* The wool textile industry in Bradford has undergone some traumatic changes in the years since 1945. The industry has suffered something of a decline from its former peak of profitability and only recently has there been anything approaching rationalization within the industry. Traditionally the industry has comprised a vertical chain of processes with numerous companies concentrating on all of these processes—integration in the vertical sense is rare. More recently a number of amalgamations and takeovers have been made horizontally, thus reducing the number of units competing at each stage in the process.

The market for wool textiles has also undergone a decline since 1945 as other fibres and processes have made inroads into traditional wool markets. Foreign competition has also kept the UK industry's export level down.

The decline in the demand for the product has led to a decline in the numbers employed. The capital employed has also declined, but not by such a magnitude as labour; consequently on balance the industry has become marginally more capital intensive, for example the number of looms running declined by 34% in the last twenty years while the number of personnel employed has fallen by 42% in weaving in the same period. Productivity has increased as a side effect, as the industry made better use of its remaining capacity.

The fragmented nature of the industry has tended to mean that many companies in the process chain are remote from the final customer. There is still in many companies a refusal to recognize the derived nature of their demand.

(b) *The engineering industry.* As the second largest industrial sector in Bradford, engineering was also studied in some detail. Its early growth was largely based upon textile machinery and related products. Now the industry covers the whole range of heavy and light engineering from piston rings to electrical switchgear. Unlike the woollen industry, engineering in the Bradford area has achieved a steady growth in the post-war years.

The industry is similar to the woollen textile industry in that it has a number of linkages within the region—other companies from whom it buys materials or to whom it sells its output. This high structural linkage works in favour of the region when the industry is growing, but against it when it is not—as in the case of the woollen industry. A major problem with the engineering industry is that it has suffered from a shortage of skilled labour, a shortage that has probably held expansion back.

Electronics is a new feature of light engineering in the Bradford region. A major manufacturer of television sets is located in the city and a number of smaller companies specialize in electronic control equipment for automatic looms. Here again shortage of skilled labour (mainly female) has held the industry back.

(c) *The mail-order industry.* One of the most remarkable industries in Bradford is the mail-order industry. Established in the city for over a century, it has sustained a dramatic growth since the war. Its original establishment was due solely to historical reasons and if anything its present location poses problems in terms of labour availability and, importantly, the less-than-perfect facilities for postal and package delivery. It is an industry with very little linkage within the region.

(*d*) *Miscellaneous Industries.* Of the remaining industries in the Bradford region, the major employers are chemicals, printing and building. Chemicals are of some note because of the strong linkage with the woollen industry. Many of the firms engaged in chemical manufacture in Bradford started life as suppliers to the wool industry for various processes in textile manufacture as well as the dyeing process. From this base they have tended to develop more broadly and now offer a wide range of products.

Resource analysis of region

The second stage of the Bradford study was to analyse in detail the morphology of the region's resources. It was argued that only by an examination of the strengths and weaknesses of the region could a case be made for the injection of additional resources. It would also provide evidence to would-be promoters of new industries.

The resource analysis examined three categories: Land, Human and Capital, whilst a further study was concerned with external economies.

The Land study showed that a major problem was the shortage of land for industrial and residential expansion, although ambitious programmes for clearance of existing property were getting under way in the late 1960s. Even so the shortage appeared to be a major stumbling block to real expansion within the city boundaries if not within the region.

The location of the city, however, when taken into consideration with the growth of the motorway system, was a major advantage from the communications point of view. As a national distribution centre, few cities in the UK are better placed.

The Human resources study painted a picture of an age-heavy population with a constant emigration of younger people, evenly balanced by an immigration from overseas. The city was also 'down-market' in the sense that the socio-economic profile was weighted to the lower end. Earnings too were below the national average, considerably so in some sections such as wool textiles. Whilst the city had a major technological university, only 10% of its students came from the region and far fewer actually stayed behind when qualified. The labour market was characterized by too few unskilled women and too many unskilled men.

On the Capital side, the study was concerned with the general back-up available for industrial activity. Mention has already been made of the region's motoring links; additionally the region is served by a major domestic airport. Rail communications are poor and provide a severe discouragement to companies considering the use of rail freight. With the exception of motorways, roads within the region are generally poor, although major programmes are currently in action to remedy this. The city has always been a major commercial centre and so it can provide the complete range of financial and professional services required by any company. The study has revealed the all too obvious fact that the 'social capital' of the region was severely under par; years of neglect to the non-profit side of life had taken its toll. Many companies believed that this was a major reason why new companies and indeed individuals were loath to come to Bradford. On the positive side, housing was considerably cheaper than the national average.

As might be expected, a number of external economies were found to exist surrounding the wool textile industry. For example: companies providing machines, tools, repairs and other services; chemical firms providing scouring agents and dyes; a special sewage disposal system; the Wool Industries Research Association; the Wool Exchange; a conditioning house; and various trade associations.

Outside the wool textile area, however, very few external economies were apparent. The financial and commercial services were perhaps an exception to this, particularly in the field of exporting. For instance, Bradford has more shipping and forwarding agents than any other non-port area in the world. Facilities also exist for container groupage.

One further area of study in the search for external economies was an examination of the basis for possible synergy between the university and the industry within the region. The concept here was that there might be scope for external economies in the joint utilization of university facilities, including personnel, particularly for the encouragement of R & D activities by local industry, but also in the provision of management expertise. The model for the concept was the development in the United States of 'research parks' where autonomous and semi-autonomous research institutes clustered around the university with a backwards and forwards movement of personnel and ideas.

MULTIPLIER/ACCELERATOR EFFECTS

Mention was made earlier of the importance of the multiplier and accelerator effects in determining the growth of regional net worth. A central part of the Bradford study was an attempt to determine the magnitude of the Bradford regional multiplier.

The multiplier process can be illustrated by a simple example. Suppose there is an increase in expenditure on new machinery being produced locally. The income of the company concerned in producing it is increased, and this in turn increases the expenditure of those who benefit from the increase in income. Just as in the first case, so here again the increased expenditure is income to someone else. And so the process will go on, but at each stage the amount of expenditure will get less if the marginal propensity to spend is less than 1; that is, if less than the whole of the increase in income is spent on consumption. This is very likely to be the case because marginal increases in income will be taxed; part of the increase in income will be saved and disappear from the 'flow' of income; and, from the point of view of the local community, part will be spent on imported goods and, therefore, represent income to people outside the locality. In order to derive the marginal propensity to spend locally, we must deduct from the marginal propensity to consume the marginal propensity to import.

The immediate problem encountered in attempting to ascertain these values is lack of data and in particular income data. Inland Revenue data relating to the West Yorkshire conurbation had to be used, combined with Family Expenditure Survey data on spending. The final estimate based on this imperfect data was a figure of between 1·10 and 1·23. In other words, an input of additional income of £100 would in total generate between £110 and £123 of consumption expenditure in the region. Nationally the multiplier at the time of the study was estimated at 1·46. (Calculations were made for us by colleagues John Sparkes and Marion Taylor.)

The implications of this are that for a given input of any of the components of demand in Bradford—whether it be in the form of industrial expansion, public expenditure, or whatever—it will only have a minimal spillover effect in the region. To a much larger extent it will imply higher imports from outside Bradford, with the consequent stimulus to production and income there and not in Bradford; except in so far as Bradford benefits through an increase in demand for its exports, the effect of which is likely to be minimal.

Perhaps the policy indicator here is that the propensity to import (which was high at about 0·8) should be reduced by encouraging import substitution. In other words the industries to be encouraged should be of an appropriate type. This assumes that the Bradford region is in fact large enough to meet more of its own consumption requirements from within its boundaries.

TARGET INDUSTRY IDENTIFICATION

The final stage in the Bradford study was the identification of growth industries to be screened against the criterion that emerged from the previous stages of the study. The criterion of a growth industry that was used was any section of manufacturing industry having a production output trend which showed a sustained level of growth greater than the national average. The unit of analysis was the Standard Industrial Classification and the leading sectors were:

Plastics, mouldings and fabricating
Radio and other electronic apparatus
Toilet preparations
Linoleum, leathercloths, etc.

Contractors' plant and quarrying machinery
Domestic electrical appliances
Mineral oil refining

From the point of view of compatibility with the regional resource profile then the key areas were thought to be plastics, mouldings and fabricating; radio and other electronic apparatus; contractors' plant and quarrying machinery, and domestic electrical appliances. Whilst not amongst the leaders, printing and chemicals, two established Bradford industries, had experienced considerable growth over the period of the study. This evidence was not eventually used to form the basis for a campaign to attract new green-fields industry, however. Rather, it gave the city's officers a clear understanding of the extant situation in the area and an effective base for determined action.

STRATEGY FORMULATION

The process within local government, by which the market analysis we have described was converted into strategy, was directly influenced by the authority which BADA commanded within the city. BADA had always enjoyed the support of both political parties in the area, and had been subsidized in its work by the city. It was readily apparent to BADA, however, that the formulation of strategy had ultimately to be accomplished by the local government in whose hands lay the power to permit development to take place, most especially via planning 'permissions'. But the national government was also involved. IDC's (Industrial Development Certificates) are necessary before any significant developments can take place and these were issued from the national Department of Trade and Industry. So long as Bradford was not a designated 'development area', but was surrounded by them, it was exceedingly difficult to afford opportunities for locally based business to expand, let alone attract new firms.

The strategic decision was therefore taken that the city must press for *either* the removal of the anomalies which prevented strong local industry from developing, *or* the designation of the Bradford area as a full 'development area'. The outcome, eventually was that the city gained full 'development area' status in 1971. Such an outcome provides the opportunity both to develop existing strengths in the area, and compete for foot-loose industry on realistic terms with other areas of the country which are facing similar, or often worse, economic conditions.

STRATEGIC IMPLEMENTATION

The overwhelming evidence of the studies undertaken showed a need to plan to improve the environment of the city and its industrial infrastructure. The first stage, as we have already indicated, is most obviously apparent in the 'clean-up' campaign which has been under way for a decade. It received a particular fillip in the late sixties when the national government gave grants for clearing dereliction. Environmental improvement has also encompassed development of the arts and theatre, assistance to the Bradford Festival, neighbourhood improvement schemes to introduce greenery, pedestrian shopping precincts and much more besides. The housing stock of the city has been improved noticeably by council building, but also by a vigorous campaign to get citizens to take advantage of those improvement grants available from central government sources.

The city's particular concern can, however, be seen in its determination to put Bradford at a focal point in the national motorway network. Its enthusiasm for its spur motorway (M606) connecting with the Lancashire–Yorkshire M62, was so great that it was ready well before the other roads were completed. Its urgent concern for the Aire Valley Motorway which will connect the M62 and M1 to the M6 at Kendal, following the line of the now almost extinct railway across the Pennines, is equally significant. As and when that motorway is complete, Bradford will no longer be a branch line of the railway system from Leeds, but a focal point in its own terms astride an east/west axis from Hull to Liverpool and with easy access to Scotland, the Midlands and the South. Already the promise of this transformation of the city's logistics problems is bringing in new freighting activities, depots and the like. Furthermore, the new trading estates set up within easy access of the motorway are attracting light industries as well.

Finally, a major £10m transport interchange between car/rail/bus is under construction in the city centre. The most ambitious project of its kind in the country, it qualifies for substantial national government assistance.

Financial and managerial services

Perhaps one of the most important infrastructure decisions, which was translated into actuality in December 1971, was the establishment of a regional merchant bank—the West Yorkshire Finance and Management Company. It was established to mobilize local capital in support of local industrial growth. It set out in particular to identify sectors where diversification of the area's industrial base could be accomplished and it is already playing a role in this way—even attracting new firms into the area. Equally important with the provision of funds for growth was the bank's intention to offer managerial advice as and when appropriate to applicant companies and to place nominee directors where investments are made to offer similar skills. This facet was seen as vitally important in an area where the predominant size of company is small or medium and where growth inevitably carries managements away and beyond the dimensions of management activity with which they have been familiar and at which they have been successful. In particular, the bank drew in its early days on help and advice from the city's own University Business School where very extensive knowledge of management skills and techniques was available.

The city's determination to make development happen was reflected in its decision in 1970 to appoint an Industrial Officer. He acts as a unique contact point for all industrial development enquiries, and is able to find his way through the maze of necessary official requirements for the potentially expanding business of the newcomer. His appointment was shortly followed by the designation of the local office of an international advertising agency as publicity advisers to the city. The coherence which these two acts have brought to the city's efforts at industrial development has been frequently noted and commented upon in the past.

GENERAL CONCLUSIONS FOR MARKET ANALYSIS

The approach we have reported for the city of Bradford is certainly unusual for market analysts. We have not eschewed forms of analysis which might more often be found in the hands of regional economic analysts. We have chosen to present our study in the context of market analysis and marketing strategy formulation, because we believe that these are the fundamental principles we have applied. In determining the strategies which Bradford would adopt to attract industries ('customers' for her work-force and for her assets of land and capital and the like) we chose to examine life-cycle patterns of industries in the city; how they might be extended; how they might be diversified. We sought to identify how economic growth (or revenue flows), could be stimulated. We also arrived at a not-too-uncommon solution—that the city was probably better advised to concentrate on its indigenous strengths as the main basis for its growth or development, rather than to place its faith in diversification. Where synergy could be identified, let it flourish. But we believe we unearthed no mean body of indigenous growth potential and as with so many marketing analyses, called upon management to act to release that pent-up potential.

The application of marketing minds and marketing analytical approaches to services such as we have reported are as yet scarcely attempted. Meta-marketing, as the issue has been described, is indubitably an area for future concern where our skills and knowledge can be further deployed for the social good.

THE SERVICES OF WIRA

Wira (originally the Wool Industries' Research Association) was established as a joint industry activity to undertake research, materials and machinery testing, and to assist in any other appropriate ways in ensuring that the wool industries were maintained on a fully competitive basis. Apart from fee income, Wira traditionally recovered a levy from industry members which the central government matched pound for pound. The new Heath government in 1970, amongst many of its new measures, required that Wira and other similar associations, in different industries, should work towards a totally self-financing basis, and government support was to be progressively withdrawn.

These proposals catapulted Wira into a totally new budgetary, and hence managerial environment. Its most obvious outward manifestation was the appointment of a marketing director and the initiation of a rigorous assessment of the market worth of Wira services currently on offer. We were asked to undertake a study of Wira members to collect marketing data which would assist management in the difficult transitional period.

The four main objectives of the investigation were as follows:

(i) To assess the current state of awareness of the activities of Wira amongst the wool textile industry and to establish what opinions are held regarding its present range of products and services.

(ii) To assess the present requirements of the industry (both fulfilled and unfulfilled) for research services of this nature.

(iii) To evaluate any changes in present requirements, or any new requirements which are perceived by members of the industry as likely to occur in the next five to seven years.

(iv) To suggest possible marketing strategies that would enable Wira to fulfil these future requirements in the most effective manner, subject to the overall objectives of Wira.

It was decided that the most efficient way to obtain information to tackle the objectives was to conduct in-depth interviews with executives throughout the wool textile industry and analyse these interviews on a qualitative basis. The investigation was carried out by the Wira Research Fellow, John Cantlay. These comments are the responsibility of the investigators alone, and the confidentiality of information supplied by respondents is protected, *i.e.* Wira is not aware of who said what. (The study was conducted in complete accord with the Code of Practice of the Market Research Society of which the investigators are members.)

SURVEY METHOD

It became clear at an early stage in the project that obtaining a statistically correct sample of firms within the wool textile industry, to give certain confidence limits concerning the results, was not feasible because of a number of factors, the most important being a time constraint. Indeed, since the information was to be analysed qualitatively rather than quantitatively it was felt to be far more important to obtain a representative sample of Wira members whose attitudes would largely reflect those of Wira members as a whole.

An initial examination of the complexity of the end-products and manufacturing sectors encompassed by the common phrase 'the wool textile industry' eventually led to an acceptance of the divisions laid down by the Wool Industries Bureau of Statistics which defines eleven distinct groupings.

Once again, using WIBS figures, the number of companies to visit in each manufacturing sector was determined. It was originally intended to visit fifty firms out of approximately 900 Wira full-levy-paying members. Using a ratio of 18:1, therefore, each manufacturing sector was reduced to the appropriate number of firms required to make up the total to be visited. For instance eighty members are involved in 'woollen spinning only' and on an 18:1 basis this means that four or five firms were to be visited in the 'woollen spinning only' manufacturing sector.

The geographical location of the firms to visit was determined by splitting the country into three main areas—Scotland; Yorkshire and Humberside; and the West of England. Using a percentage membership/area basis the number of firms/area out of a total of fifty was calculated.

Finally, the size of firm to visit, in terms of number of full-time employees, was decided. It was clear that the majority of firms in the wool textile industry were in the medium to small grouping and a table of priority ratings for inclusion in the area sample was drawn up.

One other factor was allowed for: the geographical location of certain manufacturing sectors of the industry. It would have been a pointless exercise deciding to visit a large vertical worsted plant in Wales, since none exist.

The sample is not random, therefore. A determined attempt was made to stratify the population and thereby to take a representative cross-section of the wool textile industry in terms of size, geographical location and significance of manufacturing sector. Most importantly, it was not known at the time of selection if those firms included in the survey were 'pro' or 'anti' Wira; if they used Wira for their problem-solving or not; whether they had Wira equipment or not. Since the data to be obtained were essentially qualitative this 'randomness of attitude' was the most important factor we wished to preserve.

The method of investigation used was simple. We constructed a questionnaire. Next, using standard reference books, firms corresponding as nearly as possible in size, manufacturing sector and geographical location were selected as possible interviewees. These firms were contacted, first by a joint letter from the Chairman of Wira, Mr Whitworth, and the Project Leader, then by telephone to confirm their willingness to take part in the investigation and to arrange a suitable time for the interview to take place. The interviews lasted about thirty to forty-five minutes and where feasible involved not only the senior executive of the firm concerned but also the Quality Control Manager or Production Manager. Fieldwork took place between January and July 1973.

THE CONCLUSIONS AND RECOMMENDATIONS

After discussions with Wira, it was decided that the most useful way of presenting the findings might well be in the form of 'answers' to the four objectives in the original research brief.

(*i*)   *Awareness and opinions of Wira*

All respondents were aware of Wira. Fig. 11.2 indicates what 'first comes to mind' when Wira is mentioned. It will be seen that there is no single view. Wira means different things to different people. 35 out of 40 respondents had a positive view of Wira, 5 out of 40 thought it to be 'little or nothing'. Amongst the 40, 8 thought of it as a 'pool of knowledge' and a further 8 as a 'pure research establishment'. In essence, however, Wira's image was largely based on its members' view of the services they *used* rather than the range that Wira offered.

The concern with which Wira met the existing needs of members is perhaps perceived by study of Fig. 11.3. Only 6 out of 40 companies saw little or no benefit from Wira. All the rest perceived real benefits as flowing and could enumerate them for their own industry.

(*ii*)   *Present requirements of the industry*

Figs. 11.4 and 11.5 indicate what Wira services were used and how they performed. There is no room for doubt that the information/education services were the most widely employed. This correlates with earlier comments on the image of Wira as a 'pool of knowledge' etc. Nonetheless, Wira equipment was widely used by members.

The question deliberately included in the study to identify the extent to which other 'competitive' services were being used, where Wira could have helped, proved abortive. In such circumstances where two sources of assistance were available, companies tended to use both as and where necessary, perceiving them as complementary rather than competitive.

(*iii*)   *Necessary changes over the next five to seven years*

A bare majority of respondents felt that in the context of any changes which might be made the overall *balance* was correct at the present. The most important developments requested were clearly in terms of added 'direct personal contact' and an 'expanded machinery assessment programme'.

Question 1: (a) Could I begin by asking you what is the first thought that comes to mind when I mention Wira to you, personally?
(b) Probe: What else do you associate with Wira? (Continue probing.)

Functions of Wira	GEOGRAPHICAL AREA			INDUSTRY SECTOR					SIZE OF COMPANY		
	Yorkshire	West of England	Scotland	Worsted spinners	Combers	Woollen spinners	Spinners and weavers	Dyers and finishers	0–200	200+	Total
Neutral arbitrator	4	—	—	—	—	1	1	2	1	3	4
Testing establishment	1	—	3	1	—	—	3	—	2	2	4
Insurance	4	—	2	3	—	—	3	—	3	3	6
Pure research establishment	7	1	—	1	2	1	3	1	7	1	8
Pool of knowledge	3	2	3	3	—	—	5	—	4	4	8
Little or nothing	3	—	2	—	1	—	2	2	5	—	5
Problem-solver	3	—	—	—	—	3	—	—	1	2	3
Fault identification	1	1	—	—	—	—	1	1	1	1	2
	26	4	10	8	3	5	18	6	24	16	—
		40				40				40	40

FIG. 11.2 *First thought about Wira.*

Question 2: What benefits do you think a typical company in your sector of the wool textile industry gains from Wira?

Benefits of Wira	GEOGRAPHICAL AREA			INDUSTRY SECTOR					SIZE OF COMPANY		
	Yorkshire	West of England	Scotland	Worsted spinners	Combers	Woollen spinners	Spinners and weavers	Dyers and finishers	0–200	200+	Total
Long-term practical research	15	2	1	4	3	3	6	2	12	6	18
Filtering channel for information	2	—	—	—	1	—	1	—	1	1	2
Problem-solving	5	—	—	3	—	2	—	—	2	3	5
Neutral authority	3	—	6	1	—	—	7	1	4	5	9
Faults classification	2	—	—	2	—	—	—	—	—	2	2
Testing institution	1	—	2	1	—	—	2	—	2	1	3
Information source	2	4	6	1	—	—	10	1	6	6	12
Little or none	4	—	2	—	—	—	2	2	5	1	6
											57

FIG. 11.3   Benefits gained from Wira.

Secondary but by no means unimportant requirements were for further 'long-term yet *practical*' research and a continuation of the role of 'filtering channel for information'.

Full details of answers given are provided in Fig. 11.6.

(iv)   Possible marketing strategies for Wira over the next five to seven years
The evidence arising from the studies we have made, supplemented by the series of attitude scales presented (as reported in Fig. 11.7, lead to the following recommendations for marketing strategy:

(a) Where possible place more emphasis on direct personal calls on members, both to examine problems and to discuss affairs; communicate generally about recent developments.
(b) If possible, expand the machinery assessment programme.
(c) Continue to emphasize and, if and where possible, extend the information services.
(d) Seek to continue (but improve) the quality of training sources, and trade up in terms of content.
(e) Seek to 'forecast' those areas of technical competence that members will be needing in the coming decade, and then get on with the practical long-term research.
(f) Make Wira's services more accessible to non-Yorkshire members—can a regional officer/office be opened in the West of England for instance, and the service strengthened in Scotland?
(g) *Very importantly*, let the industry know that this study has been done, what its results are, what steps are being taken and invite comments on the proposed five-to-seven-year plan for Wira from members; that is involve them in the planning. In this way, the 'value-for-money' they are not too sure they get (*see* Fig. 11.7(b)) can be more clearly demonstrated, and the confidence they have in Wira (*see* Figs. 11.7(a), (c), (d), (e), (f), (g) and particularly (h)) is both justified and is seen to be justified.

FOLLOW-UP

Senior management at Wira accepted these findings. They were, not surprisingly, pleased to find that their stature as an industry research association was high and that the need for improvement not overwhelming. It was possible for budgetary adjustments to be made and for development activities to be undertaken which brought the services offered by Wira more into line with its market needs. It is, nonetheless, useful to realize that *without* market pressures Wira had been able to do a satisfactory job within the industry.

Question 3: (a) Which Wira products or services (if any) can you recall being used by your company since the beginning of 1972?
(b) Probe: Can you recall any others? (Continue probing.)
Show checklist 1. Have you omitted any? Here is a comprehensive listing.

Products and services used	GEOGRAPHICAL AREA (N = 40)			INDUSTRY SECTOR (N = 40)					SIZE OF COMPANY (N = 40)		
	Yorkshire N = 26	West of England N = 4	Scotland N = 10	Worsted spinners N = 8	Combers N = 3	Woollen spinners N = 5	Spinners and weavers N = 18	Dyers and finishers N = 6	0-200 N = 24	200+ N = 16	Total N = 40
Rapid oil extraction	9	—	4	—	3	2	6	2	5	8	13
Fibre fineness metre and calibration	6	1	1	3	2	—	1	1	2	5	7
Hygrometer and probe	5	1	—	1	2	2	1	—	4	2	6
Fibre diagram machine	4	—	—	2	1	—	—	1	1	3	4
Fibre length machine	2	—	—	—	1	—	1	—	1	1	2
Rapid regain tester	5	—	—	—	—	2	2	—	1	4	5
Autocount	3	—	2	—	—	3	2	—	1	4	5
Cop grinder	1	—	1	—	—	1	1	—	1	1	2
Fibre diameter machine	1	—	—	—	—	—	1	—	—	1	1
Dropper pinning machine	1	—	—	—	—	—	1	—	—	1	1
Beam stand	1	—	—	—	—	—	1	—	1	—	1
Full-width temple	1	—	1	—	—	—	2	—	1	1	2

Product / Service	1	2	3	4	5	6	7	8	9	10	Total
'Reaching-in' machine	1		4				5		3	2	5
Abrasion tester		1					1		1		1
Basic testing equipment		1	1				2			2	2
Variation across card			1				1			1	1
Graphing balance			1				1			1	1
Yarn tension meter			1				1			1	1
Skein gauge			1				1			1	1
Carpet abrasion tester			1				1			1	1
Carpet static leader			1				1			1	1
Carpet thickness gauge			1				1			1	1
Carpet dynamic loader			1				1			1	1
Tuft withdrawal tensometer											
Library services, publications	24	4	10	8	3	5	17	5	22	16	38
Lectures, forums, conferences	18	4	6	7	1	4	13	3	13	15	28
Machinery assessment	7	2	5	3	1	1	8	1	8	6	14
Testing and investigation	7	1	5	3	2	2	7		7	6	13
Training courses	9		3	2	2	3	5		2	10	12
Servicing equipment	5			1		1	1		2	3	5
											176

Fig. 11.4 *Wira products and services used.*

Question 4: How satisfied or dissatisfied were you with the Wira products or services used? (Show Card A for each service.) (NB: +, satisfied; −, dissatisfied.)

Products and services used	ALL COMPANIES ($N = 40$)					Average
	+2	+1	0	−1	−2	
Rapid oil extraction	3	5	4	1	—	+0·8
Fibre fineness meter and calibration	3	2	2	—	—	+1·1
Hygrometer and probe	2	1	3	—	—	+0·8
Fibre diagram machine	1	2	1	—	—	+1·0
Fibre length machine	1	1	—	—	—	+1·5
Rapid regain tester	1	3	1	—	—	+1·0
Autocount	—	3	—	2	—	+0·2
Cop grader	—	—	2	—	—	0
Fibre diameter machine	—	1	—	—	—	+1·0
Dropper pinning machine	—	—	1	—	—	0
Beam stand	1	—	—	—	—	+2·0
Full-width temple	1	—	1	—	—	+1·0
'Reaching-in' machine	1	—	4	—	—	+0·4
Abrasion tester	—	1	—	—	—	+1·0
Basic testing equipment	—	—	2	—	—	0
Variation across card	—	—	1	—	—	0
Graphing balance	—	—	1	—	—	0
Yarn tension meter	—	—	1	—	—	0
Skein gauge	—	—	1	—	—	0
Carpet abrasion tester	—	1	—	—	—	+1·0
Carpet static leader	—	1	—	—	—	+1·0
Carpet thickness gauge	—	1	—	—	—	+1·0
Carpet dynamic loader	—	1	—	—	—	+1·0
Tuft withdrawal tensometer	—	1	—	—	—	+1·0
Library services, publications	3	10	25	—	—	+0·4
Lectures, forums, conferences	2	8	16	2	—	+0·4
Machinery assessment	1	7	5	1	—	+0·6
Testing and investigation	—	8	4	1	—	+0·5
Training courses	—	5	4	3	—	+0·2
Servicing of equipment	1	3	—	1	—	+0·8
						+0·7

FIG. 11.5   Satisfaction with Wira products and services.

Question 7: Could we now turn to the future role of Wira within the wool textile industry. What new products and services would you like to see Wira offering over the next five years, either as extensions of present activity or in totally new fields? (Probe fully.)

Future role envisaged	GEOGRAPHICAL AREA			INDUSTRY SECTOR					SIZE OF COMPANY		
	Yorkshire N = 26	West of England N = 4	Scotland N = 10	Worsted spinners N = 8	Combers N = 3	Woollen spinners N = 5	Spinners and weavers N = 18	Dyers and finishers N = 6	0-200 N = 24	200+ N = 16	Total N = 40
Overall balance OK	11	3	7	4	2	3	11	1	14	7	21
Long-term practical research	4	1	2	—	1	3	3	—	4	3	7
Filtering channel for information	3	—	1	—	1	—	3	—	2	2	4
Expand pollution programme	2	—	2	1	1	—	2	—	3	1	4
Expand machinery assessment programme	6	1	3	5	—	—	5	—	5	5	10
Direct contact by Wira personnel	5	3	2	2	—	—	7	1	7	3	10
Yarn/tops fault classification	1	—	—	1	—	—	—	—	1	—	1
Amalgamation with other associations	3	1	—	1	—	1	2	—	1	3	4
Long staple OE spinning	1	—	—	—	—	1	1	—	—	1	1
Non-woven fabric development	1	—	—	—	—	—	—	1	1	—	1
Continue RF drying programme	1	—	—	—	—	—	—	1	—	1	1
Research into wool/blends	1	—	—	—	—	—	1	—	—	1	1
Standardization of units throughout EEC	—	—	1	—	—	—	1	—	—	1	1
											66

FIG. 11.6 *Future role of Wira.*

Question 9: What are your views on the following.　(N.B. +, agree; −, disagree.)

Statement presented	GEOGRAPHICAL AREA			INDUSTRY SECTOR					SIZE OF COMPANY		
	Yorkshire	West of England	Scotland	Worsted spinners	Combers	Woollen spinners	Spinners and weavers	Dyers and finishers	0-200	200+	Total
(a) Wira's technical competence is a match for any company's R & D	+0·7	+1·0	+1·0	+1·0	+0·7	+1·2	+0·8	+0·3	+0·7	+1·0	+0·8
(b) Wira offers good value for my levy money	−0·1	−0·3	+0·1	−0·1	−1·0	0	+0·2	−0·2	−0·3	+0·4	−0·1
(c) Wira's information services do not do justice to its strength	−0·8	−1·0	−0·9	−0·5	−1·3	−1·0	−0·9	−0·7	−0·8	−0·9	−0·8
(d) Wira's role in the industry can be potentially greater over the next five years than hitherto	+0·5	+1·0	+0·7	+0·5	0	0	+0·9	+0·7	+0·5	+0·8	+0·6
(e) Companies are better advised to develop their own R & D competence than to rely on Wira's if they wish to stay profitably in business	−1·2	−1·5	−1·3	−1·1	−0·7	−1·6	−1·4	−0·7	−1·2	−1·4	−1·3

(f) Wira's information services keep all my company's key personnel abreast of important developments in the industry	+0·8	+1·3	+0·9	+0·9	+1·3	+1·2	+0·8	+0·3	+0·8	+0·9	+0·9
(g) My Wira levy money could be better spent elsewhere within the company	0	−0·5	−0·2	+0·3	+1·0	−0·2	−0·5	+0·2	+0·2	−0·5	−0·1
(h) Wira's main contributions to the wool textile industry have already been made	−0·8	−1·0	−0·7	−1·1	+0·3	−1·0	−0·9	−0·3	−0·5	−1·2	−0·8
(i) Wira's services are more accessible to some companies than to others	−0·2	+1·0	+0·1	−0·5	+1·0	−0·4	+0·1	+0·2	+0·3	−0·4	0
(j) The current balance of Wira's activities is right for the industry for the next five years	0	+1·0	+0·8	0	+0·3	+0·2	+0·6	0	+0·2	+0·4	+0·3

FIG. 11.7 Image of Wira.

CONCLUSION

Whilst in a very real sense, both these applications of the marketing way of thinking to service industries might be considered primitive in comparison with some of the more rapidly moving consumer goods industries, it is our belief that in both cases very considerable benefits accrued in terms of managerial attitudes towards the use of the research approach from a marketing viewpoint. At very little expense—neither assignment had a budget in excess of £1,750—both organizations were able to orientate their resource allocations with very considerable increased effectiveness. The meta-marketing approach had shown its worth.

REFERENCE

1. Richardson, H. W., *Elements of regional economics*. Penguin, 1969.

CHAPTER 12

Adaptive Patterns of Marketing Education

European university-level education for marketing was essentially born during the mid-sixties, although limited Scandinavian activity began prior to World War II. By mid-1972, more than 200 universities/advanced education institutions were offering long courses for degrees and similar qualifications across Europe—including at least a dozen or more institutions in Eastern Europe. Faculty members in these centres have been drawn mainly from three sources:

(a) Marketing practitioners, with a university level education but not in marketing (*N.B.* the most common origin of such faculty is marketing research).

(b) Marketing practitioners, with a university level education, who took themselves to North America to study at business schools there during the fifties and sixties, for example, the Director of the Polish Management Centre in Warsaw is a former MIT Fellow; the Cranfield School of Management in Britain was founded almost entirely by Harvard alumni, as was CEI in Geneva; the Centre des Etudes Supérieurs at Jouy-en-Josas, near Paris, has North Western University (Evanston, Illinois) trained faculty members.

(c) Academics, educated in economics, statistics, social psychology and the like, who moved over into marketing education. In general, such faculty members perceive marketing as a branch of their fundamental discipline, and teach it as such; for example, econometrics, consumer psychology, quantitative analysis of consumer survey data, etc. This group also includes the emerging output from European Doctoral Programmes in marketing.

In their first phase of development, most European Schools tended to fit neatly into one or other of these categories. The Department of Marketing Studies at Cranfield initially recruited all its staff from category (a). It has now become clear that no single pattern of faculty background can suffice to produce an adequate educational institution for the future generation of marketing executives. The predominantly emerging pattern of activity is to blend category (c) with either (a) or (b), that is, to include in each centre faculty members who are both discipline and applications based. In this way, such centres ensure that the necessary creative tension between training and education is enshrined within the faculty and the need for a proper and a necessarily adaptive balance is continually appraised. This is the way Cranfield is proceeding now.

In the mid-sixties, such creative tension simply produced a dichotomy between training for the acquisition of technical skills, and instruction in the basic disciplines in a generally unrelated manner. We can now perceive the opportunity for a much more constructive integration of marketing knowledge. It is this which we assert should form the basis for a necessarily adaptive pattern of marketing education.

The total professional framework

We have attempted to describe in Fig. 12.1, not a marketing system as such, but the total professional framework within which the marketing executive will increasingly be expected to work. We identify the marketing executive as the major focus of ethical and managerial responsibility in such a total framework. In the exercise of that responsibility at present he has little assistance from his professional body—in the UK that is the Institute of Marketing—although there is an emerging professional consensus in certain sectors of marketing activity, most noticeably research and advertising. But the tenor of advice remains in the negative: 'thou shalt not . . .', rather than

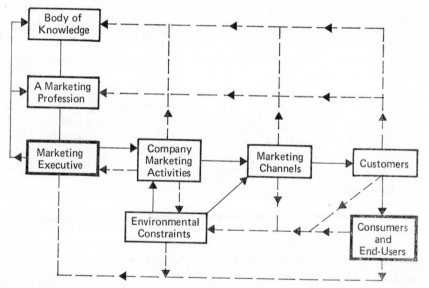

FIG. 12.1 *The total professional framework including marketing outflows and reverse communications.*

offering a lead. It is the authors' contention, nonetheless, that the current of affairs, most especially as demonstrated in the growth of consumer syndical-ism and anti-pollutionist lobbies, will change this stance. Amongst our educational goals must accordingly be the need to make marketing executives sensitive to the social necessity for a positive professional stance which will broadly delineate each individual executive's responsibility to all his customers (intermediate/trade and end-users alike) *as well as* to his employing organiza-tion, its shareholders and his colleagues.

If professional responsibility to customers involves a positive approach to his own and his company's marketing behaviour, his responsibility to his employer demands a continual updating of operational and developmental competence. Hence, the marketing executive's feedback loop with the body of knowledge is fundamental to his professionalism. This need for the continual updating of knowledge has to be recognized and provision must be made for it to occur.

We shall now proceed to examine some possible patterns of marketing education against such a professional background. We shall look first at the issues raised by the need for sensitivity to the social implications of marketing and then at the knowledge required for executive competence.

SOCIAL SENSITIVITY IN MARKETING

Marketing stands at the interface between society and the organization of products and services to satisfy its needs and wants. As such it has a thankless task. It is often open to criticism from established economic interests and from those who deprecate the concomitant march of materialism that market-ing frequently implies. Whilst marketing's tendency to exploit our latent materialism will long remain a subject for justified debate and disagreement, we shall not take up that issue here. More important at the present time is the divorce which so much mass-marketing brings about between the provider of goods and services and his *customers as individuals*. In this deficiency, marketing research stands indicted along with mass advertising and promo-tion. We need, in fact, to turn to industrial marketing and selling to see some partial solution to our dilemma for here the individual contact between supplier and customer normally remains a totally human relationship.

To those who reply that without mass marketing there could be no sufficient level of economic well-being, we would at once agree. Our point is that we must build upon the aggregation of customers and the hitherto implicit dehumanization of relationships, a new pattern of disaggregation and re-humanization. Only by such a process can the syndicalist tendencies of frustrated customers be turned back. Consumer syndicalism represents not an iconoclastic reaction to 'big business' or 'mass marketing', but a manifestation of the nascent social inadequacy of the way we have become used to trading with customers. To simplify the issue, we need a much greater emphasis on reverse communications in the marketing channel. In the final analysis, no customer is average—we are distributed normally (or not so normally) throughout a population and maximization of customer satisfaction will not occur until that is recognized.

Reverse communications

Most customers in sophisticated marketing systems have no really good way of talking directly to a manufacturer. Neither the process which has been adopted originally in generating the transaction, nor the process of physically distributing a product, is equipped for reverse communications. It has been estimated, for instance, that it costs *nine times as much* to return a defective product as it does to despatch it in the first place. Small wonder, therefore, that for low-value items many manufacturers instruct their agents to exchange without question and scrap the offending product. It can be cheaper and more economic, if less than totally satisfying psychologically. When it is not, a procedure must be provided which can operate efficiently. What we need to develop in our enterprises is the least-cost method of affording the right level of service in handling complaints.

Throwing the Managing Director's office into chaos is one of the high-cost alternatives. Ignoring all complaints is a deceptively low-cost way of coping in the short run. A slightly more expensive method is to employ a few complaints clerks. One more useful proposition involves the appointment of a senior executive as Customer Ombudsman. His or her office is responsible for developing a corporate strategy towards faults or complaints. It is responsible for finding out precisely who within the company is the right person to deal with a problem. It is responsible for control and follow-up procedures which ensure that customers' complaints are taken care of without the customer having to harry the delinquent enterprise. In other words, such a senior post involves acceptance by the company of a positive approach to reverse communications.

Why should it bother? Apart from the obvious socio-legal arguments one can advance, it is simply good business practice. Such a considerate and helpful approach can do much to ameliorate the adverse effects of the fault in the first instance. A company's helpfulness in this way can make an even greater and more favourable and lasting impact than a trouble-free transaction. Finally, an organization which has to drop what it is doing to cope with complaints will incur an opportunity cost to the business which an efficient approach can avoid, or at least minimize.

We believe the concept of a Customer Ombudsman, within each medium or large enterprise, to be preferable to any extension of the Weights and Measures Administration, as a sensible course of action for coordinated local enforcement of any Trades Descriptions, Foods and Drugs and the Weights and Measures legislation. The Ombudsman function must, however, go further than sitting at the receipt of complaints. In association with conventional marketing researchers, it must search out the unvoiced dissatisfactions of customers if its full contribution, both to society and to the enterprise, is to accrue.

Few companies today employ professional experts in customer relations as we have described them. Few men or women have been educated specifically to do such a task. Little or no coherent body of teachable knowledge exists which can be deployed immediately as a basis for education. However, its outline is discernible in two areas of expertise—personal communications and logistics. The professional has to be able to understand the issues implicit in service to customers and to deal as efficiently and effectively with colleagues within the enterprise as with the complainants from without. It requires a level of managerial competence normally associated with senior line functions in a business, plus personality characteristics most commonly seen in personal selling and/or public relations.

Back-up services

Closely paralleling customer need for a reverse communications mechanism in modern marketing to supplement conventional marketing research feedback, is the need for a carefully thought-out pattern of back-up service. Perhaps the most immediately critical aspect of back-up service is delivery-on-time and, in appropriate cases, efficient installation. Efficient operational activity in this field is generally dealt with under discrete headings such as stock control, distribution and transportation. The totally integrated view of marketing logistics where overall cost reduction of the distributive system is attempted is relatively new. It is a focus for scientific marketing attention in the coming decade which no company concerned with its customer relations will be able to overlook. The trade-offs between increased transportation costs, for instance, and reduced stockholding costs, must be explored. Most significantly of all, a consciously determined view of an appropriate service level for customers must be developed. Do we wish to offer a 95% level of service on all our product lines within forty-eight hours, or something more, or something less? Can we not segment our service level offer both *by* customer and *within* product range? Indeed, can we not offer a differential speed of delivery on a broad scale at a varying tariff to all our customers, and thereby allow truly for their often very different patterns of need? The naïvety of simple cost reduction exercises in all distribution departments must be exposed.

Nonetheless, efficient distribution with the right delivery schedules of the wrong product will never afford us an adequate profit. It behoves the business to ensure that all within its power is done to get the product right before it leaves the factory. It is also fundamental to any sustained success that a realistic view is taken of after-sales service during the design life of any product offered to customers. Sidney Weinberg, Chief Engineer with NCB,

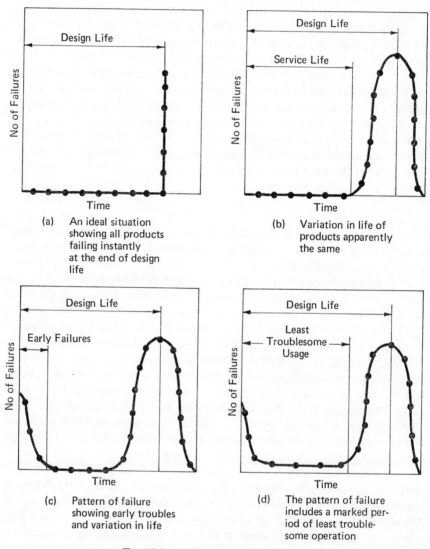

(a) An ideal situation showing all products failing instantly at the end of design life

(b) Variation in life of products apparently the same

(c) Pattern of failure showing early troubles and variation in life

(d) The pattern of failure includes a marked period of least troublesome operation

FIG. 12.2 *Product design failures.*

who was associated as Chairman with the work of National Quality and Reliability Year, has eloquently analysed these twin issues in the late Consumer Council's final publication.[1]

Few manufacturers are likely to be able to afford a product which is as fault-free as Fig. 12.2 (a); in value analysis terms they will normally settle for less and so will their customers. However, once a degree of fault has been engineered into a product in order to keep it in the right market price segment, the after-sales service necessary to alleviate the inevitable hardship which will occur must be engineered into the total marketing activity as well. Fig. 12.2 (d) shows the classic *bath tub curve* which after-sales service must normally expect and with which it must be able to cope at the requisite service level, that is, not necessarily six hours' notice, but over a reasonable time-scale related to the inconvenience which arises.

EXECUTIVE COMPETENCE IN MARKETING

We have chosen to discuss the need for social sensitivity as an educational goal in marketing in terms of reverse communications and back-up services. We can perhaps usefully focus on yet another contemporary social issue as we shift the discussion to executive competence. That issue is socio-technological forecasting which sprang to importance in the late sixties and is now beginning to be deployed in a limited number of European companies.[2]

Extended research in England and Wales, involving some 550 companies with over £¾ million gross sales revenue in 1967, showed quite clearly that far fewer marketing executives than we cared to believe were actively responsible for new product planning and development. Some were not even involved in it at all.[3] We were not, however, downcast at this evidence. Marketing's discerned lack of full responsibility for new product development perhaps represents a step forward beyond earlier marketing mix concepts, but it demands at the same time a distinctly broader level of competence from the marketing executive. The reconciliation of what is technologically feasible, what is socially desirable, and what the market will be prepared to purchase, is at any time a hazardous task. It is a process of reconciliation into which the marketing executive of the future will be increasingly drawn. Such a process of corporate reconciliation brings together the conventionally discrete business functions of finance, research and development and marketing. It also demands, in a rapidly changing environment, knowledge of organization theories and practices if the appropriate structures are to be in place to facilitate effective development in required directions. The need for such a broadly based marketing education has been discussed at length elsewhere.[3] Its impact on the separate consideration of operational marketing activity and marketing development, through a host of concepts such as brand and venture management, can be expected to be very considerable.

Yet further areas of reconceptualization are necessary to meet the tasks which lie ahead. Suffice it here to mention that a total approach to the marketing communications[4] of an enterprise must be painstakingly developed, integrating above- and below-the-line promotion and personal selling; as well as the total logistics concept to which we have already alluded.[5] Finally, that which is routine must be seriously routinized and that which demands creativity allowed to blossom.

The quantitative/behavioural spectrum

Where does all this comment leave marketing education on the quantitative/behavioural spectrum, that great all-purpose North American binary classification for a decade or more? Our answer is at once both 'nowhere and everywhere'. Marketing education must be *applications oriented*. All marketing executives must comprehend the nature of marketing data and the possibilities for its manipulation and analysis to provide action frames of reference; even solutions to problems. Yet this does not make statisticians of them. All our marketing executives must be aware of the social and psychological forces at work within their markets and their chosen channels of distribution, as well as within their own marketing organization. Yet this does not make them behavioural scientists. Marketing must accordingly be seen as a synthetic subject for study and marketing practice as an art.

In this context we can accordingly examine typical educational programmes in marketing at which we have developed since 1965 both the University of Bradford and at Cranfield School of Management.

(a) *Marketing theory* lays the basis of an understanding of how customers, trade channels and corporate marketing organizations work. It is heavily rooted in the behavioural sciences and draws upon industrial and consumer markets alike, as well as service industries. By way of an illustration of our approach, the nature of industrial buying processes is compared with familial decision-making. The Purchasing Officer is seen as surrogate for a complex pattern of company influence in the same way as a housewife buys for her family group. The theoretical examination is also handled on a comparative basis, exploring the transnational differences encountered in marketing analysis and drawing on themes from anthropology.

(b) *Marketing information, planning and control* explores the nature of the total market system of an enterprise paying especial attention to the institutions which are available and the quantification of alternative strategies for the satisfaction of customer needs once understood. Our total conceptualization is posited on a system of marketing information being available (to a greater or lesser degree, hopefully determined on cost/effectiveness criteria) as the basis for planning and decision-making as well as for control of on-going activities.

(c) Finally, and certainly to the astonishment of many commentators on our activities, we offer not a detailed programme in marketing research, but a full course in *Marketing logistics*. Since we have already touched upon this issue, here we would simply wish to reinforce our viewpoint that this sector of corporate affairs is greatly in need of marketing attention, almost totally unstaffed save by erstwhile transport managers, and offering substantial rewards to marketing executives who grapple with it.

A missions approach
Just as we anticipate less debate in future on the behavioural/quantitative dichotomy, so can we see an increasing emphasis in marketing companies on corporate mission analysis.

We have already commented on the need for marketing education to focus on the organizational structure with which a company faces its markets. It is necessary also for us to impart an understanding of the financial basis of cost and profit calculations within an enterprise. The accountancy profession is in turmoil at the present over the *missions approach* to financial analysis. This seeks to cut across the conventional pattern of functional budgets to relate company resources and profit centres to the achievement of corporate goals via product/market missions. Such an approach has considerable implications for the more familiar concepts of brand management and venture groups, and it places much marketing research activity as we know it into a company-wide information system context.[6]

It follows that information-gathering, like any other business activity, must be planned. Furthermore the information-gathering process must be viewed in total, not discretely. Commercial intelligence is the result of a continuous process which takes data of a commercial nature and creates intelligence which is directly useful to the manager in planning and operating the business. The specific concern of the marketing function is to deploy the information available to optimize its pursuit of corporate mission goals. The origins of such marketing information stretch from raw materials to post-consumption. The entire continuum of information requests, from *search* through *collation*, *presentation* and *assimilation*, is in fact a total information function.

Such an integrated concept of information gives rise to an information system whose essential features are:

—centralization of the information flow;
—separation of marketing research into developmental and operational;

—inclusion of the long-range planning information requirements;
—emphasis on greater use of internal information.

The system we have described proposes the inclusion of traditional marketing research activity within a larger organization which embraces information outputs from, and inputs to, all other functions within the firm.

Let us distinguish between three broad categories of customary marketing research:

(i) *Basic curiosity-oriented research:* wide-ranging examination in depth or breadth of areas of current interest to the researcher.
(ii) *Action research:* directed specifically at overcoming or illuminating a specific problem.
(iii) *Mission-oriented research:* more loosely structured programmes designed to produce data pertinent to the attainment of mission goals.

Marketing researchers will usually have had experience of all three forms at some stage in their career, but probably the most common experience is with action research. It is our general contention, however, that emphasis on solving problems rather than on the identification and exploitation of market opportunities has tended to constrict the full potential of marketing research and to ensure its virtual exclusion from the higher levels of decision-making in the corporate structure. This divorce of marketing research from the real business of marketing is a more widespread phenomenon than we usually care to concede. From this point of view, therefore, it is probably the latter category of research that is more likely to provide the effective basis for this integration we believe essential.

The definition of corporate missions logically leads to an identification of a series of related information activities. A recent activity example was as follows:

> A mission of the ABC company was to seek an established position in the UK frozen food market over the next ten years. The marketing research mission which followed from this statement was defined as: the provision of information upon which judgements could be made concerning possible technological and societal futures, relating to our activities in this market.

Here the operational activities of marketing research are clearly linked to the policy-making process. The requirements of the information activity will involve inputs from several distinct areas of the company—from the economic analysis group, from the personnel concerned with technological forecasting (perhaps the R & D group), from the marketing departments concerned, from the company library and from the marketing research department. Sources external to the company may also need to be utilized. Once the full requirements of such a programme of research are realized, and an attempt to cost them in company-wide terms is made, it becomes apparent that it will probably incur the company in greater total costs than were initially realized.

This is the first step in the output budgeting approach to marketing research expenditures—the exploration of the likely pattern of involvement of individual areas inside the company, and without, in such an information activity. The second stage is to consider how these stated information goals may be met by alternative means. For example, one alternative may be to subcontract the complete research activity to an outside agency. Another may be to bring together a group drawn from all the company areas involved, specifically charged to deal with the need. Whatever the number of feasible alternatives, evaluation takes the form of examining their capability to meet the specified goal and the impact on corporate resources that end would make, that is, a cost/benefit appraisal of the alternate research programmes. It must be a total costing.

Problems will arise because of the difficulties of assigning costs to each input to the research programme. Often costs will have to be forecast, thus adding further uncertainty to the situation; for example, the number of man-hours to be expended by the company librarian. In other cases it will be possible to make highly accurate estimates of costs; for example, the purchase of trade, panel or media data.

ENTREPRENEURIAL CONSUMMATION

No matter how extensive a knowledge base we build, and no matter how adaptive we make the individual executive we educate, the consummation of our work lies in executive action. Our final comments must accordingly focus not on gathering information, nor on bringing knowledge to bear on problems, but on the entrepreneurial act. How can we educate marketing executives to act, to choose to move forward. This remains the great unanswered question. Some of our more scurrilous critics even suppose that the net effect of our educational efforts is to dull the ability to act, rather than to temper it with due wisdom; rather than securing improved profitability from perhaps a given sales volume, we are arraigned for securing less of both for the most sophisticated reasons, and with an almost total understanding of the problems involved.

Our partial answer is that we seek throughout the educational experience we provide to emphasize the nature of market risks and of the decision-making process. Through case studies, simulations and business games, the future marketing executive has the opportunity to try his hand. Project work and industrial attachments all help. Yet we know the final answer lies with the experienced company managements with whom our educated executives begin to work. Only the true artist, locked in combat on his own battlefield, with tactical and strategic opportunities ranged before him, and the sound of gunfire in his ears, can finally make a competent marketing executive from our intellectual product.

As more and more educated marketing executives venture onto the battle-field, there is no doubt in our minds that they will also bring about a trans-formation of the orientation of those warriors already on the field. They will be even more demanding in their analysis. They will perceive the nature and purpose of marketing activity and of research in marketing more widely. They will raise the standard of total marketing activity to a more professional plane than marketing research alone has been able during the past twenty-five years.[7]

REFERENCES

1. Consumer Council, *Servicing: a symposium*. Forbes Publications, 1971.
2. Wills, G., *Technological forecasting*. Penguin Books, 1972.
3. Wills, G. and Hayhurst, R., *Organisational design for marketing futures*. George Allen & Unwin, 1972.
4. Christopher, M. G., *Marketing below-the-line*. George Allen & Unwin, 1972.
5. Christopher, M. G., *Total distribution*. Gower Press, 1971.
6. Wills, G., Christopher, M. G. and Walters, D., *Output budgeting in marketing*. Management Decision Monograph Series, No. 1, 1972.
7. Wills, G., *Exploration in marketing thought*. Crosby Lockwood for University of Bradford Press, 1971.

Appendix 1
Survey of UK Marketing Organizations

The universe was defined as all companies in the United Kingdom which, on the most recent figures available, had an annual turnover of £¾m or more. A list of all firms which met this criterion was obtained from the then Board of Trade and consisted of 2,400 companies.

It was decided that all firms in this list should be approached to provide information at some stage in the research.

Two hundred firms, selected by a random interval procedure, were asked to cooperate in the first stage of the research by trained interviewers. A great deal of information was obtained from the sixty-seven firms who consented to this, on the outcome of which we constructed the questionnaire which was administered on a postal basis. A copy of this questionnaire is available from the authors.

From the complete list of 2,400 companies we deleted the 200 which had been approached in the first stage of qualitative interviews. A further 310 firms had to be excluded from the mailing list either because no reliable address could be found or they had ceased trading.

Questionnaires were therefore sent to the remaining 1,890 firms on the Board of Trade list; thus we were aiming to carry out a census of all appropriate firms. A covering letter, routed to the chief executive, explained the purpose of the survey and contained an assurance that the information provided would be treated as confidential. Subsequently, two reminders were sent to non-respondents; on both occasions a further questionnaire was enclosed.

BROAD INDUSTRIAL GROUPING

	Number	%
Manufacturers of industrial goods	28	49
Manufacturers of consumer goods	11	20
Distributive trades	6	10
Advertising agencies	12	21
	57	100

DETAILED INDUSTRIAL GROUPING

	Number of firms	Employees (in '000s)	Percentage of total employed in the industry
Food, drink and tobacco	6	111·8	13·8
Chemical and allied industries	9	54·2	17·0
Metal manufacturers	1	11·0	1·9
Engineering and electrical goods	16	255·2	11·1
Vehicles	3	20·4	2·5
Metal goods (not elsewhere classified)	3	46·8	8·2
Textiles	1	0·2	0·03
Brick, pottery, glass, cement, etc.	1	25·0	7·2
Paper, printing and publishing	2	10·5	1·7
Other manufacturing industries	2	101·2	28·6
Advertising agencies	10	1·4	85·0
Unclassified	3	0·2	NA
	57	637·9	

A total of 1,063 (56%) of the companies approached replied to our letters. Of these, 553 completed and returned questionnaires which were usable. A further 312 firms explained that they had not completed the questionnaire because it was not applicable to their situation. The major reasons given for this were that they were reorganizing their activities internally, were merging with another company or that they were holding-companies where the marketing function was carried out by subsidiaries.

The final reason was that they judged the questionnaire to be irrelevant to their business activity; responses in this area normally indicated that marketing had not been established formally within the firm.

Letters were received from 198 firms who, although not finding the questionnaire irrelevant to their business activity, refused to complete the questionnaire. The principal reasons for refusal were concerned with the time and effort involved, and very few replies indicated a lack of sympathy or hostility to the objectives of the survey.

A 5% telephone check was made on the firms who did not reply at all; these firms explained their non-response in the same terms as the reasons stated above for inapplicability or refusal.

Fieldwork took place during the spring and summer of 1969. Full sample details of the replication survey are given in the two reports listed as references 3 and 4 in Chapter 3.

Appendix 2
Delphi Study of Distribution Trends

Retailing Futures

1. Weekly food expenditure, as a percentage of total consumer expenditure, will:
   (1970=21.3%)

   By 1980 represent
   By 1990 represent

2. Of total grocery sales convenience foods will:
   (1970=27.8%)

   By 1980 represent
   By 1990 represent

3. Convenience food sales development for the following categories of convenience foods:
   (1970=100)

   By 1980:
   Frozen foods
   A.F.D.
   Remainder

   By 1990:
   Frozen foods
   A.F.D.
   Remainder

4. a) The Multiples' share of grocery sales:
   (1970=42%)

   By 1980 will be
   By 1990 will be

   b) The Co-ops' share of grocery sales:
   (1970=15%)

   By 1980 will be
   By 1990 will be

   c) The Symbol Independents share of grocery sales:
   (1970=23%)

   By 1980 will be
   By 1990 will be

   d) The Independents share of grocery sales:
   (1970=20%)

   By 1980 will be
   By 1990 will be

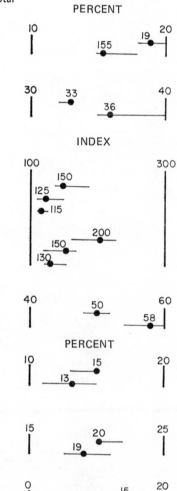

234

5. The variety chains food sales will increase relative
   to 1970 levels:
   (1970=100)

   By 1980 to
   By 1990 to

6. The non-food items proportion of total turnover
   of the following outlets will represent:

   By 1980 for:
   •Multiples
   Co-ops
   Symbol Independents
   Independents

   By 1990 for:
   Multiples
   Co-ops
   Symbol Independents
   Independents

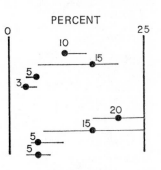

7. Grocery product sales developments for:
   (1970=100)

   Supermarkets in central shopping areas will be:
   In 1980
   In 1990

   Superettes in central shopping areas will be:
   In 1980
   In 1990

   Supermarkets in out of town locations will be:
   In 1980
   In 1990

   Superstores in out of town locations will be:
   In 1980
   In 1990

   Supermarkets in suburban areas will be:
   In 1980
   In 1990

   Superettes in suburban areas will be:
   In 1980
   In 1990

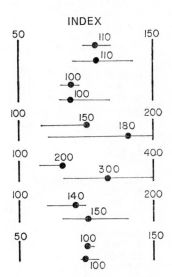

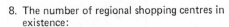

8. The number of regional shopping centres in
   existence:

   By 1980 will be
   By 1990 will be

9. The number of hypermarkets in existence:

   By 1980 will be
   By 1990 will be

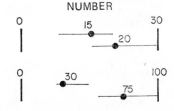

10. Housewives shopping trip frequencies will be:

% FOR EACH FREQUENCY

Everyday
By 1980
By 1990
(1970=23%)

Every 2/3 days/week
By 1980
By 1990
(1970=38%)

Every 4/5 days/week
By 1980
By 1990
(1970=11%)

Once a week
By 1980
By 1990
(1970=25%)

Less often
By 1980
By 1990
(1970=3%)

11. Percentage ownership rates of consumer durables
will be:

% OF HOUSEHOLDS
OWNING ITEM

Washing machines
By 1980
By 1990
(1970=64%)

Refrigerators
By 1980
By 1990
(1970=63%)

Food and drink mixers
By 1980
By 1990
(1970=24%)

Dishwashers
By 1980
By 1990
(1970=1%)

Two cars
By 1980
By 1990
(1970=6%)

One car
By 1980
By 1990
(1970=45%)

Telephone
By 1980
By 1990
(1970=35%)

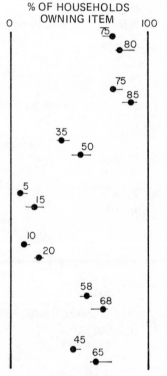

12. The proportion of total sales represented by own
    brand products will be:

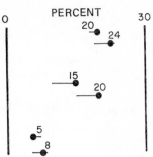

For Multiples
In 1980
In 1990
(1970=12/14%)

For Co-ops
In 1980
In 1990
(1970=9/11%)

For Symbol Independents
In 1980
In 1990
(1970=2/3%)

13. The cash and carry share of total grocery sales
    will be:

In 1980
In 1990
(1970=13/14%)

14. Cash and carry sales will be shared by:

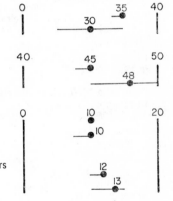

Grocers and General Stores
In 1980
In 1990
(1970=40%)

Caterers
In 1980
In 1990
(1970=40%)

Confectioners, Tobacconists and Newsagents
In 1980
In 1990
(1970=10%)

Greengrocers, Butchers and Non-food Retailers
In 1980
In 1990
(1970=10%)

15. Product group shares through cash and carry
    outlets will be:

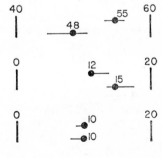

Groceries
In 1980
In 1990
(1970=63%)

Wines
In 1980
In 1990
(1970=10%)

Confectionery
In 1980
In 1990
(1970=10%)

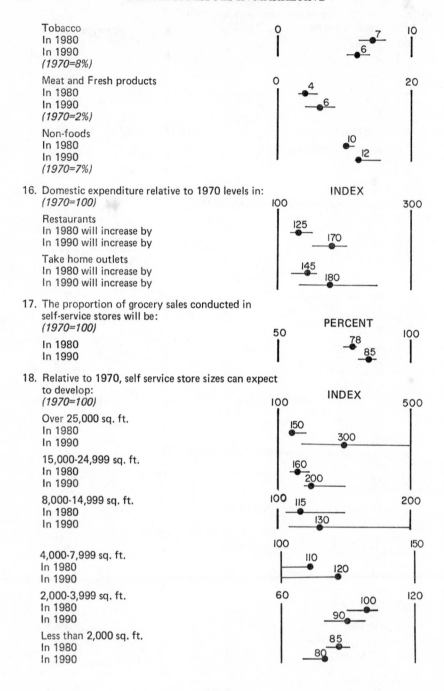

Tobacco
In 1980
In 1990
(1970=8%)

Meat and Fresh products
In 1980
In 1990
(1970=2%)

Non-foods
In 1980
In 1990
(1970=7%)

16. Domestic expenditure relative to 1970 levels in:
    (1970=100)   INDEX

    Restaurants
    In 1980 will increase by
    In 1990 will increase by

    Take home outlets
    In 1980 will increase by
    In 1990 will increase by

17. The proportion of grocery sales conducted in
    self-service stores will be:
    (1970=100)   PERCENT

    In 1980
    In 1990

18. Relative to 1970, self service store sizes can expect
    to develop:
    (1970=100)   INDEX

    Over 25,000 sq. ft.
    In 1980
    In 1990

    15,000-24,999 sq. ft.
    In 1980
    In 1990

    8,000-14,999 sq. ft.
    In 1980
    In 1990

    4,000-7,999 sq. ft.
    In 1980
    In 1990

    2,000-3,999 sq. ft.
    In 1980
    In 1990

    Less than 2,000 sq. ft.
    In 1980
    In 1990

19. Sales of grocery products manufactured by fellow
    E.E.C. member countries can expect to develop
    relative to 1970 levels, for:
    (1970=100)

    1980 by
    1990 by

```
100                                    300
 |  ●120                                |
 |    ●————                             |
 |        ●170                          |
```